ADVANCES
IN
ENVIRONMENTAL
PSYCHOLOGY
Volume 5
Methods and Environmental Psychology

ADVANCES IN ENVIRONMENTAL PSYCHOLOGY

Volume 5
Methods and Environmental Psychology

Edited by **ANDREW BAUM**
JEROME E. SINGER
Uniformed Services University
of the Health Sciences

LAWRENCE ERLBAUM, ASSOCIATES, PUBLISHERS
1985   Hillsdale, New Jersey   London

Copyright © 1985 by Lawrence Erlbaum Associates, Inc.
All rights reserved. No part of this book may be reproduced in
any form, by photostat, microform, retrieval system, or any other
means, without the prior written permission of the publisher.

Lawrence Erlbaum Associates, Inc., Publishers
365 Broadway
Hillsdale, New Jersey 07642

LC Card Number 85-15941

ISBN 0-89859-680-7

Printed in the United States of America
10 9 8 7 6 5 4 3 2 1

Contents

List of Contributors

Andrew Baum, *Uniformed Services University of the Health Sciences*
Raymond Fleming, *Uniformed Services University of the Health Sciences*
Ronnie Janoff-Bulman, *University of Massachusetts*
Stanislav V. Kasl, *Yale University*
Rosemary Lichtman, *University of California, Los Angeles*
Jerome E. Singer, *Uniformed Services University of the Health Sciences*
Siegfried Streufert, *The Milton S. Hershey Medical Center/ The Pennsylvania State University*
Robert W. Swezey, *Science Applications, Inc.*
Judith M. Tanur, *State University of New York at Stony Brook*
Shelley E. Taylor, *University of California, Los Angeles*
Christine Timko, *University of Massachusetts*
Gary H. Winkel, *The Graduate School and University Center of the City University of New York*
Joanne V. Wood, *University of California, Los Angeles*

Preface

The development of a field or an area of inquiry is often marked by changes in measurement techniques, shifts in analytic emphasis, and disputes over the best ways of doing research. In many areas of psychology, a number of issues have characterized methodological evolution of the discipline, including questions regarding context and reductionism, or laboratory versus field research. For some of the newer areas in psychology, such as environmental or health psychology, this is not an issue of either/or. Although there has been some debate about these trade-offs, it is generally regarded by people in this field that some combination of the two approaches is essential. Depending on the question being studied, this balance may change. However, the questions asked are less likely to inquire ''which way is better'' and concentrate on how both may be used.

This observation serves to illustrate the fact that different research endeavors have different methodological issues. This volume explores some of the issues characterizing work on health, environment, and behavior. The issue of ecological validity in research is fully explored by Gary Winkel, who clearly establishes problem-based differences in research priorities and airs several sides of debates on these problems. Many of the issues raised lie at the heart of application of research findings, and the chapter invites integration of different approaches.

A number of problem-specific issues are also characteristic of research in these areas. Rosemary Lichtman, Shelley Taylor, and Joanne Wood consider some that are specific to studies of chronically ill patients. Institutionalized or not, these subjects are different from those typically studied in psychological research. Given the relationships between environmental variables and chronic illnesses, it is clear that these populations should and will be studied. Conceptual and methodological allowances must be made, and this chapter explores many of them.

Ronnie Janoff-Bulman and Christine Timko consider a different specialized population—victims. Many of the stressors and mishaps that affect health and define environmental influences on behavior involve victimization, albeit at varying levels. Though not all forms of victimization are as powerful as paralysis, rape, or cancer, some appear to be (e.g., the Three Mile Island or Love Canal experiences). In addition, victimized populations have special needs and variants of interaction with the environment that require consideration.

The fourth chapter, by Siegfried Streufert and Robert Swezey, shifts gears somewhat. Here the emphasis is less on the subject and more on methodological innovation that permits controlled study of topics without sacrificing their context. Simulations are discussed as one way of accomplishing this, and the advantages and disadvantages of this approach are explored.

Epidemiological research is little used and often poorly understood by psychologists. Because of its direct relevance to the study of behavior and health and environment, however, it is an extremely important approach for researchers in these areas. Stan Kasl discusses a number of issues involved in studying behavioral factors and health, providing a basis for understanding and perhaps conducting related work.

One of the primary tools of researchers studying the relationships between environment, behavior, and health is the survey. To the novice, this seems straightforward enough. Write some questions, type them up, and you've got a study. Judy Tanur, in her discussion of survey research methods, paints a different picture. Using environmental examples, she traces many of the basic rules and assumptions of survey studies and a number of interpretive pitfalls. In the final chapter, Andrew Baum, Raymond Fleming, and Jerome E. Singer discuss problems of studying environmental stress, noting possibilities beyond survey studies in field work. Using data collected from the Three Mile Island situation as an example, we argue for simultaneous measurement of multiple responses.

As with any volume like this, we invited people who we thought were the best to write the chapters we wanted and were dependent on their wisdom for a meaningful volume. We think that they have provided us with an important collection and are grateful to them for this (and for their good cheer toward a couple of hurried editors). We are also indebted to the constant, rather incredible indexing, proofing, record keeping and support of Martha Gisriel, without whom we would both be 10 years older.

Andrew Baum
Jerome E. Singer

1

Ecological Validity Issues in Field Research Settings

Gary H. Winkel
Environmental Psychology Program
City University of New York

INTRODUCTION

One of the more interesting challenges posed by the study of person–environment transactions involves the development of methodologies that will aid us in understanding the complexities of people's lives in different settings. Because settings are an integral aspect of our endeavors, the nature of the field as a research site presents opportunities and uncertainties. My intent is to address the conceptual and procedural issues that represent problematic elements in various forms of field research.

In the course of my discussion, I try to show that the nature of the ecological arrangements in different locales requires the adoption of flexible investigative strategies sufficient to meet field demands. Flexibility in research design, of course, complicates the evaluation of the validity of findings generated in the field. Yet validity issues comprise a central aspect of research planning, as well they should.

An enduring aspect of the validity problem stems from efforts to reconcile the demands of laboratory-based research design to the irregularities and uncertainties encountered in field research. The obstacles faced by investigators who wish to move from laboratory to field can be explained only partially by the latter's complexity. To a significant extent, these difficulties can be traced ultimately to the assumptions that set the framework for conditions that are asserted to be necessary for validity. These assumptions, however, cannot be transferred readily to the organization and operation of many field settings. As I show later, the procedures that have been developed by those practiced in the art of field work are based on a set of assumptions that differ from those guiding the work of

1

researchers trained within the hypothesis-testing tradition of most laboratory workers (Bogdan & Taylor, 1975; Filstead, 1970; Glaser & Strauss, 1967, Lofland, 1971; McCall & Simmons, 1969; Schatzman & Strauss, 1973). As a consequence, the procedures and approaches to analysis employed by these investigators appear to be confusing and unfamiliar.

An undesirable effect of these differences regarding valid knowledge has been a polarization of opinion regarding the legitimacy of different types of research design. Field researchers have often accused laboratory investigators of trivializing the explanation of important questions (Weiss & Rein, 1969). Laboratory researchers have countered by arguing that field researchers are insufficiently sensitive to the problems of the validity and reliability of data based on field studies.

These disputes seem to have their own internal dynamics. As a result, too little attention has been given to the substantive issues that demand attention when we attempt to explain the complexities of the settings in which people organize their lives. I try to show that there are complementarities and contributions that representatives of each position can bring to environmental research. I also propose that the concept of ecological validity may enable us to link elements of these two general orientations to data generation. The necessity for a consideration of ways to develop research designs that can be adapted to different research problems grows directly out of the somewhat unique challenges that environmental researchers confront.

THE FIELD AS A SETTING FOR RESEARCH

There are many reasons prompting a researcher to use field settings as study sites. One of the more common of these involves a desire to estimate the generality of a set of findings regarding some phenomenon or theoretical system across settings, situations, and persons. Because it is often assumed that the social and behavioral processes that are investigated within the laboratory constitute simulations of the same or similar processes operating in settings outside the laboratory, investigators may wish to determine the generality of laboratory-based findings. For example, a number of workers used laboratory-based research to examine the effects of ambient noise levels on reading ability (Bronzaft & McCarthy, 1975; Cohen, Glass, & Singer, 1973), attentiveness to social cues (Cohen & Lezak, 1977), environmental awareness (Korte & Grant, 1980), and helping behavior (Page, 1977). Others have drawn upon the work in cognitive consistency theory to examine its role in the explanation of environmental action (Heberlein & Black, 1981). Dissonance theory has been advanced to account for differential perceptions of environmental hazards (Shippee, Burroughs, & Wakefield, 1980). Saegert (1978) has provided a comprehensive review of research that has been conducted on density effects in both laboratory and field settings using an information-processing model.

There may be conditions in which the problem under study cannot be transferred easily into the laboratory. Field sites are then chosen as settings in which it is possible to examine the operation of variables that relate to a process of interest. For example, Mazmanian and Sabatier (1981) were interested in possible relationships among liberal political attitudes, environmental concerns, and partisanship as they affect public policy making. They used the proceedings of the California Coast Commissions as the content of their investigation. Costantini and Hanf (1972) sought an explanation for differences in environmental concern based upon the perceptions, backgrounds, and attitudes of major decision makers in Lake Tahoe. Sewell (1971) wished to link differences between engineers and public health officials in their environmental perceptions and attitudes regarding water purification to training and professional experiences. In each of these instances, it would have been impossible to answer the research question had the study been conducted in a laboratory. These investigators focused on actual judgments that the participants in their studies made with regard to various environmental policy questions.

Field research may be required as an essential preliminary step prior to working on a particular problem in a more systematic fashion. Usually the research question is not defined well enough to be pursued either in the field or in the laboratory. For instance, early environmental investigations of wayfinding in the built environment (De Jong, 1962; Gulick, 1963; Lynch, 1960) relied heavily on people's cognitive images of existing environments as revealed by maps drawn by the users of these settings. Much of the early work in this area was not guided by any particularly compelling theoretical model. It has been only recently that efforts have been made to understand this phenomenon within a theoretical framework (Chase & Chi, 1981; Kuipers, 1978).

Ethical issues may preclude the investigation of some questions within a laboratory setting. The only alternative may be the ongoing field context. For example, in a study of the role that environmental diversity and degree of participation in self-care might play in the recovery of coronary patients, it was obviously not feasible to assign coronary patients to a laboratory for study (Cromwell, Butterfield, Brayfield, & Curry, 1977). Nor would it be possible to examine the effects of exposure to long-term stressors as factors in the development of cardiac malfunction in a laboratory (Gentry & Williams, 1979; Siegrist & Halhuber, 1981).

The nature of the problem under investigation may be so intimately tied to the scale of the environment within which it operates that it would be impossible to simulate it at a lesser scale. Clearly, urban renewal projects (Fried & Gleicher, 1961; Gans, 1962; Hartman, 1966; Schorr, 1966), highway construction programs (Fellman & Brandt, 1970), assessments of special living environments for the elderly (Cantor, 1975; Carp, 1966; Hyde, 1980; Lawton, 1975), the social impacts associated with the creation of flood control districts (Harloff, Gump, & Curry, 1981), or the study of community protest growing out of the construction of a public facility (Francis, 1975) all represent aspects of the general environment that could not be transferred to a laboratory.

Field research is often required when the sponsors of the study have a vested interest in understanding a phenomenon as part of an ongoing setting. Even though it might be possible to model the problem of interest so that it could be explained in the laboratory, the sponsor may insist that generalizability will be guaranteed when using an intact setting. For example, much of the research conducted on learning in classrooms could be conducted in a laboratory. Frequently, however, school boards and parent groups are much more concerned with the consequences of these programs within ongoing school operations. When this is the case, data generated under controlled conditions may be very helpful to an investigator who must now venture into the field. For example, Bransford, Stein, Shelton, and Owings (1981) employed laboratory-based research in their studies of the conditions that aided children learning how to learn in school settings.

In many of the examples just cited, it is clear that the nature of the problem considered by the investigator required the use of a field setting. What is not clear are the factors that prompted the choice of the different research designs that were employed in these studies. In just this brief listing, it is possible to find examples of experimental, quasiexperimental, descriptive, correlational, survey, and participant observation studies. It is appropriate to ask whether the demands of the setting and/or the problem yielded a set of criteria that led to the choice of one approach rather than another. In some cases, this might have been so. In others, however, the selection criteria may have been related to the investigator's position regarding the epistemological status of the methods and procedures that were employed.

One person may assert that a qualitative, holistic design is most appropriate for a wide range of person–environment problems. Another may suggest that some form of quasiexperimental quantitative procedure would be most germane. Still a third may argue that it is only possible to understand the phenomenon using a descriptive, almost journalistic account.

Unfortunately, labels such as these often conceal the assumptive systems that lie behind them. Before we can assess the utility of any one or combination of procedures in research, it is critical to clear away the definitional confusion that abounds in descriptions of field research studies.

A central element of this process involves the identification of the assumptions that guide the construction of these research procedures. Once this has been accomplished, it will then be possible to discuss ways in which various designs might be related to one another and to the central problems in person–environment relations.

For the novice and even for those with some experience, the key phrases that appear to create the most confusion are "hypothesis-testing research," "qualitative research," "quantitative research," "holistic research," "field research," and "laboratory research."

THE LABORATORY AS A SPECIAL FIELD SETTING

It is relatively pointless to draw an artificial distinction between field settings and the laboratory. With regard to data generation and interpretation, both locales can be dimensionalized in terms of a common set of issues relating to information flow and regulation to and from researcher and those who are participants in the research effort. Because the laboratory has been used most frequently as the place in which reliable and valid knowledge presumably is generated, we can use it as our reference point in the analysis that follows. In this framework, it is important to remember that the laboratory, as a special type of field setting, operates within a definite assumptive base with regard to what constitutes valid knowledge.

In the broadest sense, the laboratory is a space that is set aside as a special purpose setting possessing certain characteristics. There are both functional and symbolic factors that account for the special status of the laboratory designation. Functionally, unwanted information from the exterior is excluded in a systematic manner. For example, in studies of the electrical activity of the nervous system, special precautions must be taken to rule out factors from outside that might interfere with the electrical recording devices or that might contribute unwanted noise to the data. In studies of social interactions, efforts are made to use the space to create mini social dramas varying in their complexity and guided by a script called the experimental protocol.

The objects that may be found in the laboratory can also serve a functional purpose in the operation of a study (chairs, tables, desks, equipment, writing materials, and so on). The organization of the laboratory's artifacts may also be used to affect the outcome of an investigation (Rosenthal, 1966).

Although not usually considered, the location of the laboratory within the context of other settings may be important in creating participant expectations and may guide subsequent behavior. If the laboratory is located in a university, an office building, or general health facility, it is plausible to suggest that these aspects of the setting may have clear symbolic referents for the participants. It is these symbolic qualities of the research site that represent another attribute of such specially designated locales.

It is assumed that when participants appear at the laboratory, they are prepared to adopt the role of research subjects whose activities are of interest to the investigator. The meanings that participants attach to the role of laboratory subject, however, may be partially a function of the manner in which they have been inducted into this role. In a considerable body of psychological research, the participants are college students who have either been required to participate in a certain number of studies and/or have been offered some incentive to cooperate. The manner in which they have been inducted into the study obviously can affect the nature of their subsequent behavior. People enter the laboratory study with expectations, uncertainties, beliefs and attitudes with regard to their participation, the researcher's expectations and desires, and the outcomes associated with their involvement in the procedures. It is, of course, these aspects of the research enterprise that have formed the basis of studies that have been conducted on demand characteristics (Orne, 1962), experimenter biasing effects (Rosenthal, 1966), and so on.

These characterizations lead to another potentially significant aspect of the laboratory as a special setting—the differentials that exist in the role relationships between researcher and researched. Generally it is the case that the researcher adopts a privileged position as far as information about the setting and its procedures are concerned. The investigator essentially controls both the sequence and duration of the information flow that transpires during the course of the study.

The participant, of course, also possesses some measure of power in that his or her behavior is the subject of presumed interest. Depending on the set with which the person enters the study, he or she may choose to cooperate, to withhold information, to second guess the intent of the research, and so on. Whether such behavior is important to outcome is obviously tied to the study design.

Another critical feature of the laboratory involves the extent to which the events that transpire there are under the direction and control of the investigator. In laboratory settings, of course, the researcher has developed a plan that dictates the types of treatment conditions that are administered, which participants receive which treatment condition, what measuring instruments are to be employed (including some estimate of their reactivity), what types of instructions are to be given, the nature of the relationship that is supposed to exist between researcher and participant, and so on.

A final component that is less relevant in the laboratory but is certainly important in other field settings involves the question of where the research might fit within a sociopolitical context. Clearly, there may be instances in which research data are gathered under politically controversial conditions and/or where the data and the interpretations attached to them could generate conflict. When these possibilities exist, they must be included as part of the research design.

I must also point out that whereas this characterization of the laboratory has focused primarily on the informational qualities of this special purpose locale as they relate to research methods and procedures, it is not possible to ignore the potential interactions that may exist between the content of the hypothesis being examined and the procedures that are used. This aspect of research planning has been given too little attention. As I show later, depending on how such interactions are conceptualized, it is then possible to increase the flexibility of the designs that are used in various settings.

For the moment, however, it is sufficient to note that the following elements are critical to design in *any* field setting (including the laboratory):

1. The nature of its boundaries, the material objects that may be found there, and its symbolic aspects.

2. Its place in the context of other settings that constitute its surroundings.

3. The degree of familiarity that participants using the setting have with it.

4. The spatial and temporal extensiveness of the participants' total activities within the setting.

5. The symbolic associations given to the locale and the activities that transpire there.

6. The conditions surrounding the induction of participants into research within the setting and the expectations, beliefs, and commitments they bring to the research endeavor.

7. The nature of the relationships that exists between and among the investigator and the participants during the course of the study.

8. The degree to which the researcher may be able to regulate and control the informational exchanges that occur in the setting.

9. The sociopolitical context surrounding the conduct of the research and the interpretations and uses to which are made of the resultant data.

When planning a study, these issues are crucial in *any* setting, regardless of whether it is designated as a laboratory, a supermarket, a classroom, a neighborhood residential block, a suburban park, or a wilderness trail. The critical difference between the laboratory and these other locales, of course, is how these components are conceptualized and incorporated into the procedures that are employed.

The laboratory is chosen as a research site primarily because it is assumed that it is possible to exercise control over those aspects of the setting that may be expected to contribute unwanted variance to the phenomenon being investigated. Through procedures such as randomization, employment of control or comparison groups, instructional sets, introduction of different types of treatment or experimental conditions, and regulation of space and time, the investigator hopes to rule out or minimize the operation of systematic components of variance that are considered irrelevant to research intent.

It should be obvious by now that these procedures have been developed for a purpose. It is assumed that the outcome of research conducted in this manner is to develop laws of behavior that can be generalized across time, space, situation, and person. The goal is to construct systems of explanation that are minimally contingent on factors beyond those that constitute the range of the existing theoretical system purporting to describe some phenomenon of interest.

Although there has been a growing recognition of the necessity for situationally constrained explanations of behavior (Bem & Allen, 1974; Bem & Funder, 1978), the fact is that the procedures that have been developed for the conduct of laboratory research are based on an epistemological model that aims for generality through the control or elimination of unwanted variance components. The fact that the researcher presumes to have control over these facets of the research design, however, does not mean that the laboratory is not a field setting. It is simply a special type of field setting explicitly designed to achieve a narrow set of goals. Both the goals and the transactions that occur in the laboratory may be characteristic of only a very few settings beyond it.

QUALITATIVE VERSUS QUANTITATIVE RESEARCH

Another distinction, possessing both a substantive and a trivial content, is drawn between so-called qualitative and quantitative research (Cook & Reichardt, 1979; Filstead, 1970). The trivial aspect of this differentiation involves the presumption that nonexperimental research must be nonquantitative in nature. It is important to stress that the use of quantitative measuring instruments in field research is entirely possible and, in some circumstances, desirable. As we have pointed out elsewhere (Ittelson, Proshansky, Rivlin, & Winkel, 1974), there are a number of descriptive field studies that have employed quantitative measures.

Conceptually, it would appear that the distinction is used to describe studies that rely upon a descriptive, almost journalistic, orientation to the characterization of a set of sociophysical processes. Amir's (1972) work on community opposition to the construction of the Hudson River Expressway offers a good example of this type of qualitative research. Amir consulted participants in the controversy and interviewed them about their experiences, used articles from the local newspapers, summarized the results of various public hearings conducted on the proposed highway, and analyzed the minutes of meetings held by different protest groups. His goal was to document the procedures used by at least one set of community groups to prevent the construction of an unwanted facility. Virtually no data were provided that were drawn from quantitative measures of community attitude toward the highway, the protesters, or the various agencies responsible for planning the facility. Because the aim of the research was to provide as full a description of the various phases of protest activity as possible, it is not completely unfair to say that the project involved an N of 1, i.e., the set of groups who mounted and persisted in their efforts to prevent the expressway's construction.

But there is another, more important reason prompting the use of the term *qualitative* that does have implications for field research. This involves the question of whether it is possible to use quantitative measures of a construct across settings, particularly when the meaning associated with the setting may affect the meaning of the construct itself. Qualitative researchers apparently believe that differences in context, as indexed by different meanings, result in qualitative differences both in settings and the behaviors and affects expressed there. It is further believed that these qualitative differences render comparison and interpretation of quantitative measures suspect. To illustrate this problem, consider for a moment the following applied research question that we are currently investigating.

Suppose a hospital administrator is interested in the identification of those aspects of an emergency room in a general hospital that might affect the level of patient distress. Suppose further that the emergency room is heavily used and that patients, depending on their illness or injury, experience different waiting times prior to treatment. As part of the analysis the investigator suggests that it might be possible to classify factors that affected patients through an examination of the organization of patient–staff contact, environmental variables related to the waiting experience and possible differences in patient characteristics (such as age, sex, ethnic background, frequency of hosptial use, and so on). As part of the assessment procedure, the investigator had previously developed two measures of patient distress—one associated with the degree of subjectively experienced worry or upset that the person reported feeling and the second measuring the degree of annoyance that patients reported as a consequence of waiting.

Because of the differing nature and seriousness of the presenting illness and injuries, the professional staff established an emergency area and a walk-in clinic. The clinic was designed to treat less severely ill or injured people. Occasionally, however, the number of patients that could be seen there far exceeded the number of staff available to treat them. When this occurred, the nurse who made decisions regarding the treatment setting to which patients should be assigned would inform them that they should remain in the emergency room. From a medical perspective, however, either place would be appropriate.

When the investigator gathered data on patients in the two settings, he or she found that there were significant differences in the degree of distress reported by the same pool of potential patients in the two settings but no difference in the degree of annoyance they reported in connection with the wait. In addition, the pattern of variables that contributed to the distress and annoyance in the two settings differed from one another.

If we can assume that decisions regarding assignment to the two settings occurred in a relatively random fashion, does it make sense to compare the scores for these two groups of patients? Because patients were assigned in a quasirandom manner, the quantitative investigator might respond in the affirmative. The qualitative researcher, on the other hand, might argue that the meaning of the scores in the two instances was different because of qualitative differences in the two settings. One possible explanation of the findings would be that if a patient was sent to the walk-in clinic, he or she might conclude that the problem was less serious than would be the case if asked to remain in the emergency room. The term *emergency* conveys a meaning that is different from the term *walk-in clinic,* and, as a result, the stress or upset felt by the two groups of patients was not quantitatively comparable. To put it another way, the factors that related to the upset or stress experienced in the emergency area were different from those that related to the upset reported in the walk-in clinic. The differing nature of these factors (which would presumably include being labeled as an emergency rather than a clinic patient and the different experiences in the two settings) would mean that a model developed to account for patient distress in the walk-in clinic might differ from a model developed to account for distress in the emergency area, even though the physical conditions of the patients in these two settings were roughly comparable.

There are two aspects to this problem. The first involves the dimensionality of the term *upset,* which relates to its context of use. The second involves the nature of the construct system that is invoked to account for the reported affect in the two settings. Clearly, many words that are employed in everyday language cover an array of experiences none of which may map directly and completely onto the chosen word. It is for this reason that the qualitative researcher would want to explore the different meanings associated with the term upset as used in these two settings.

The qualitative researcher would also wish to understand how the events that transpired in these two settings contributed to the different affective components that were summarized in the use of the word upset. From an environmentalist's perspective this issue is important because of what has been called the *ecological fallacy problem* (Robinson, 1950). A model linking the sociophysical components of these two settings to upset (whether dimensionalized or not) might very well include variables that would not be significant if each setting were analyzed separately. A qualitative researcher would argue that it might be inappropriate to develop a general model purporting to account for the variance in reported upset if the elements of such a model could not adequately capture the degree of reported upset in each setting separately. In other words, the qualitative researcher would ask about conditions that would have to exist for the general model to have any particular usefulness.

The qualitative researcher would approach the problem differently. He or she would attempt to determine whether it was substantively possible to pool the data from two different settings. This researcher might argue that the more appropriate comparison would involve the walk-in clinic with other types of clinics in the hospital rather than the emergency room. If the structural relationships among the variables in different clinics were comparable, then it is legitimate to develop a more general model. As far as the emergency room data were concerned, the more appropriate type of approach would be to locate other types of emergency situations for possible comparison purposes.

The appropriate type of research design for such a qualitative analysis would be one that focused on the dimensionality aspect of both the upset that might be reported in a setting and those aspects of the setting that could be linked to the dimensionalized upset. It is these designs that represent a major aspect of the field research literature.

HOLISTIC VERSUS HYPOTHESIS-TESTING RESEARCH

Of the various terminological distinctions drawn between laboratory and non-laboratory field research, I believe that the dichotomy between hypothesis testing and holistic research represents the most crucial of the differences considered thus far. Holistic investigators typically link their discussions of design to a set of philosophical assumptions regarding the types of knowledge that are possible in the human sciences. Although there might be quibbles regarding the ordering of these concerns among representatives of the holistic school, it is fair to say that there is general agreement in the basic outline of their position.

One of the major intents of any research endeavor involves the explanation of selected aspects of the phenomenologically diverse world that comprises the domain of concern of the human sciences in general and environmental researchers in particular. Various phenomena such as community protest against physical facilities siting, alienation in public housing residents, participation in neighborhood organizations, service delivery to populations that differ in social class standing, wayfinding in the built environment, and so on represent the central focus of concern. Rightly or wrongly, holistic researchers contrast their interests with those of investigators who are primarily interested in testing hypotheses generated from some theoretical system. Holistically oriented researchers argue that those working on testing theory are often far more interested in the theory than they are in the phenomena that these theories purport to explain (Glaser & Strauss, 1967). Holists believe that phenomena are embedded in different social and physical contexts within which these phenomena operate. Phenomena and context are indivisible and they must be studied simultaneously.

Holistic investigators concentrate on the analytic description of complex social and physical organizations (McCall & Simmons, 1969). Within this tradition, the goal of research is understanding, not prediction and control (Filstead, 1979). In the course of an analytic study of a field setting, components may be singled out for study, but only within the grounded conditions that characterize the locale's ongoing processes.

Returning to the emergency room example discussed previously, the holist might not even focus on patient distress as an issue in and of itself. If the intent was to describe the emergency room environment as a sociophysical system, patient distress might represent only one component of the description. The holist would attempt to provide a detailed account of the experiences of the various participants in this setting through observation, interviews, records of transactions among participants, and so on (Lofland, 1971).

In the course of developing categories into which various events could be classified, it might turn out that distress on the part of both staff and patients constituted a significant organizing feature of this setting; that is, both patients and staff might be seen to engage in integrated activities whose purpose is stress management. Thus, control over patient–staff contact, the development of coping systems for handling unruly patients, and environmental manipulations such as the use of screens to conceal particularly gruesome injuries might all be employed in an effort to manage stress.

The significance of these aspects of the environment may be gauged in terms of how much time and energy appear to be expended in this direction. Such a judgment might grow out of the analysis of the policies and procedures that were developed in the emergency room. For the holist, such an analysis might permit an assessment of the likelihood that an investigation of patient distress would tap into a central or peripheral aspect of the emergency room experience and what variables might be expected to have some explanatory impact on measures of distress. The focal hypotheses of the applied researcher or the theoretician interested in the stress concept would be of less importance to the holist except as those issues helped to illuminate the operation of the setting as a whole.

Holists believe that such an orientation to data generation is warranted on two grounds. First, it is premature to expect that social scientists are in any position to develop very elaborate theoretical models such as those that characterize the physical sciences. Historically, physical scientists proceeded on the basis of sensitivity to grounded empirical data that were integrated into theoretical models possessing rather powerful explanatory capabilities. Although social scientists might aim toward such models, our knowledge at the moment is too limited. We have not been able to develop general theories of behavior in various settings. At this point we are more likely to construct the types of explanatory systems to which we aspire if we employ research strategies designed to keep us as close as possible to the contextually embedded phenomenon that we wish to explain.

The second essential element of importance to the holistic researcher concerns the ways in which social data are to be interpreted. The phenomenologist Alfred Schuetz (Wagner, 1970) argued that there is a fundamental difference between social and physical scientists in terms of the construct systems they employ. The physicist does not have to be concerned with the meanings that molecules, atoms, or any set of subatomic particles may attach to the natural world. The social scientist, on the other hand, deals with "social reality," which has a specific meaning and relevance to the person situated in a sociophysical setting. It is on the basis of these meanings that "common sense" has developed into an integrated framework that defines the spaces and social organizations within which people act. If we are to understand these actions, we must appreciate the assumptive meaning systems that people use in different settings. In this context, the methodologies that are most appropriate for the development of the social sciences are those that take into account the nature of meanings that are shared and not shared.

Within Schuetz's framework, any methodology claiming adequacy must begin with people's commonsense interpretations of reality. This demand in turn implies that methodology must remain as faithful as possible to the empirical data that comprise the person's experiences. Hypothetical deductive procedures are limited in that typically they cover only a very limited range of experiences in the world. As a consequence, they do violence to an adequate theory of social reality.

Such a theme has been taken up by other holistic investigators who argue that a preoccupation with the proper canons of scientific research (statistical tests, the operationalization of constructs, and so on) interferes with the validity of the research (Filstead, 1970). By validity, however, Filstead means a concern for the richness of the empirical data that are to be used in the development of an explanatory system. Filstead is most dismayed by what he calls a literal positivism—the tendency to find a situation, preferably testable within a laboratory, in which all measures of the concepts employed can be given operational meaning even though it may not be clear that the resulting materials relate in any way to the person's phenomenal experiences as they operate in the world outside the laboratory.

For purposes of holistically oriented research design, it must be remembered that meanings, interpretations of social acts, and patterns of goals in different settings represent central elements in accounts of the phenomenally diverse behaviors we observe.

For example, suppose an investigator wished to know whether the availability of formal procedures for the regulation and control of physical change in a neighborhood could account for decisions to participate on the part of neighborhood residents. Suppose further that the municipal officials responsible for these local control agencies felt that some operated quite effectively in terms of involving people in the neighborhoods, whereas others did not do so. After having determined a suitable set of indicators for ''effective participation,'' the researcher finds that there are indeed some differences. Assuming that these findings are reliable, it is clear that some simple model positing a one-to-one linkage between control mechanisms and participation rates is simply not sufficient to account for the observed differences. A holistically oriented investigator would attempt to determine how different people interpret participation and nonparticipation, what meanings they assign to the act of participation, their perceptions of the agencies responsible for decision making, what goals they bring to living in neighborhoods, and how these relate to possible participation in the activities of neighborhood decision-making agencies.

Within a holistic framework, then, the identification of the multiplicity of factors that may influence participation as an outcome is considered a central aspect of *both* theory formulation and research design. Glaser and Strauss (1967) advocate the use of comparative research approaches to understand phenomena as they are revealed in various settings. The use of the comparative framework, however, is not for the purpose of testing theory. Rather, comparisons permit an investigator to augment the complexity of the theoretical system as a consequence of the comparison groups and settings that are selected.

Any variations in the structural conditions that account for phenomenal diversity in other contexts represent the elements comprising the groundedness of the theory. It is presumed that these may be organized drawing upon the richness of the immediate situation under study. In hypothesis-testing approaches, on the other hand, the simultaneous operation of many variables is not incorporated explicitly into theory. Rather, theory is constructed and elaborated through the accretion of a few variables added to the structure at a time. Contemporaneous events are evaluated primarily as potential sources of unwanted variance that require control or elimination through the use of a comparative research design.

Thus, the holistic investigator plunges immediately into the complex tangle of events that characterize most research settings. The research design and analytic orientation are directed toward the organization of simultaneously occurring events into categories of explanation that capture as many of the diverse phenomena observed in the setting as possible.

It is presumed that the resulting grounded theories, although initially applicable only to a single field setting, possess greater generality. As McCall and Simmons (1969) suggest, the purpose of analytic (i.e., categorical) description is not necessarily to test theory because only a single case may be available. These authors go on to point out, however, that *"This is not to say that participant observation studies cannot be used to test theory.* That test of theory comes in comparing such analytic descriptions of complex cases when these are available in sufficient number and variety'' (p. 3; italics in the original).

It is precisely this aspect of holistic research that proves worrisome to hypothesis-testing investigators. Holists frequently proceed on the assumption that the grounded theories they have constructed should include all factors that are relevant to the phenomena they have observed in a particular setting. In addition, the validity of their explanations rests upon the unfolding of a convincing set of plausible arguments. Once this has been accomplished, the research task is completed. Although not often stated explicitly, holistic researchers assert that what they have accomplished (if successful) is the identification of the underlying social-environmental structure of a setting that gives it coherence and internal organization. Having identified the structure, it is useless to replicate the study because the presence of structural similarities in other settings will result in very similar outcomes. For example, Goffman's (1962) work on institutions has led to the formulation of the conditions that would have to hold for any particular setting to be so categorized. Depending on the existence of these conditions, all the characteristics of institutionalization would, of necessity, be found. The epistemological foundation for this approach to research was first put forward by Znaniecki (1934).

From the hypothesis-testing perspective, the accounts put forward by holistic researchers can be faulted on at least three counts. The first involves the uncertainty associated with the use of a single case. The grounded categorical description or theory generated through the use of holistic procedures appears to allow no degrees of freedom for hypothesis testing because all degrees have been used to generate the explanation.

The second involves the nature of possible comparisons among the complex cases that are presumed to describe the same phenomenon or social structural arrangement. If multiple case studies are to be used for this purpose, it would seem that the variations in conditions from case study to case study would have to be minimal. Otherwise, it would be very difficult to make the comparisons in any quantitative sense; that is, if variability occurred in multiple subsystems of a general system simultaneously, the theorist might be hard pressed to determine which of the subsystem components accounted for the observed processes. Although this problem is not insurmountable, it complicates the descriptive work considerably.

The third objection is concerned with the problem of replication. Repeatability implies prediction, which some holists disavow as a legitimate criterion for scientific research. Of course, not all holists share this perspective. Glaser and Strauss (1967), for example, argue that a properly conducted holistic analysis is much more useful in applied settings than is a research emphasis confined to the behavior of a single set of variables. Because holists have recognized the multiple components defining a system, they are in a much better position to know where a specific change or intervention will fit within the overall operation of the setting under analysis. This comprehensive description provides a differentiated information map, both for the holist and potentially for the hypothesis-testing investigator. It is the latter who is constantly faced with the paradox of attempting to contextualize hypotheses that have been designed to be decontextualized (i.e., they are supposed to represent general explanations of relationships among variables). Yet generality demands the testing of these hypotheses in multiple settings whose contextual conditions can be expected to shift.

The complementarity of the results of holistic investigations to hypothesis-testing problems is irrelevant only for those who hold that the purpose of knowledge generation is the construction of transsituational generalizations about behavior. For those who believe in the necessity for a warranted or contingent generalization, it should be clear that field settings possess contextual features that may and often do have a crucial bearing on the hypothesis being tested as well as upon the structure of the research design itself.

It is thus possible to consider holistic procedures as a means for providing an information map of a particular research site. The interrelationships that exist among the contextual features of the setting that provide its organization can have a bearing on the hypotheses that may be assessed there. If the information map provides an adequate description of setting processes, it should also indicate what types of research procedures might be used. Because, as indicated earlier, each set of procedures is associated with a set of assumptions regarding what is to be considered true and error variance in the system, the information map may suggest ways of interpreting and possibly using potential sources of "error" as data for the explication of a theoretical structure or set of hypotheses growing out of an applied problem. The concept that I believe can be most usefully employed in research planning that uses both a holistic orientation and a hypothesis-testing framework is ecological validity (Winkel, 1977).

ECOLOGICAL VALIDITY

In research planning, an investigator must consider both strategic and tactical issues in the development of a research design. Tactical concerns relate to the particular data-gathering instruments that will be employed in the study. These data-capturing devices can run the gamut from primary to secondary sources of information and the instruments may range across the entire spectrum of reactivity (Webb, 1966).

Strategic issues in research design are concerned with the overall orientation that an investigator adopts when addressing a problem of interest. An integrated research strategy may involve experimental, quasiexperimental, descriptive, prospective, retrospective, or survey procedures. Obviously, depending on the problem, combinations of these strategies may be used.

With these preliminaries it is possible to define the ecological validity of an investigation as assessed by the extent to which the research strategy and tactics (i.e., both the form and content of the research plan) accurately capture or relate to the characteristics of the sociophysical setting as well as people's transactions within the setting.

A concern for ecological validity implies that an investigator will evaluate strategies in terms of their abilities to represent parameters of the sociophysical system being investigated in relation to the phenomenon being studied. A study's ecological validity involves clarfication of the relationships between the procedures and findings to the parameters that presumably account for the operation of the phenomenon embedded in its context.

In short, ecological validity should provide estimates of the likelihood that the research design employed, the construct system introduced or induced to account for some phenomenon, and/or the interventions(s) (treatments, experimental conditions) used resonate with the relevant parameters defining the overall operation of the system under study. It is important to realize that this definition of ecological validity refers both to the research strategy employed *and* to the explanatory system that is used to account for the findings. If either or both aspects of the project do mot map onto the sociophysical setting serving as the research site, its ecological validity may be jeopardized.

In the remainder of this chapter, I describe the assumptions that lie behind the use of the ecological validity notion, show how it can be used to extend and clarify the criteria used in experimental and quasiexperimental designs, and discuss techniques for its assessment.

ASSUMPTIONS GUIDING ECOLOGICAL VALIDITY CONCERNS

Phenomenon-relevant Research

Along with holistic investigators, I argue that the primary intent of environmental researchers involves the explication of the phenomenologically diverse world whose components and processes represent the domain of concern to the community of environmental researchers. Phenomena (defined here as comprising events of interest that are susceptible to scientific description and explanation) are distributionally organized in the range of settings that comprise the physical world that is the focus of our research. One of the intents of holistic investigation involves the explanation of which settings and under what conditions certain phenomena will be manifested. For example, if an investigator wished to understand the circumstances under which a person felt that he or she desired to communicate personal information about the self, there might be only a narrow range of environmental settings in which this phenomenon would become problematic. The environmental and social organizational structure that related to this intent on the person's part would, of necessity, be included in the explanatory system. It is equally the case that there might be settings in which the social exchange of what is considered personal information about the self is irrelevant. Finally, there are other settings in which such exchanges would be considered inappropriate.

The emphasis upon phenomena as the focus of inquiry is not meant to preclude either the development or testing of theory. On the other hand, I do not believe that an exclusive preoccupation with theory testing is likely to be most productive at this stage. There are relatively few theories that address issues of concern to environmentalists. Those that do exist have rarely been evaluated in terms of their ability to describe the distributional properties of the phenomena that the theories purport to explain.

Although obvious, it bears repeating that we do not engage in research for the sole purpose of testing theory. Theories, after all, have a *content*. That content is designed to explain something about the world. It is this range of "somethings" that constitute the phenomena that I believe are most significant at this stage in our development. The value of holistic research as a descriptive tool designed to locate phenomena within social and physical context represents one of its most important functions. Perhaps more significant, however, is its use in the generation of possible theoretical propositions (Glaser & Strauss, 1967).

Description and Intervention

I have already indicated that one of the major reasons that hypothesis-testing researchers do not trust descriptive accounts of phenomena depends on whether assertions that are made about causal relationships among the variables in a setting are based only on description. There can be little doubt that the manipulation of presumably causal factors across a range of settings and in contrast to other variables of interest is a powerful procedure for the development of differentiated explanatory systems. It is important to remember, however, that there is nothing inherent in holistic procedures that precludes the utilization of interventions or, more usually, the description of naturally occurring dislocations in the fabric of an ongoing sociophysical setting as a component of causal analysis (Glaser & Strauss, 1967). As suggested earlier, holists object to the use of interventions when the investigator provides no rationale for their appropriateness to the contextual features of the research site. It is this objection to which ecological validity is partially addressed. When an intervention or treatment condition is to be employed, sensitivity to the setting's characteristics in relation to the intervention is obviously required. In the absence of such an analysis, a perfectly plausible intervention may result in consequences that are either unintended or that do not appear to operate as predicted. When this occurs, the investigator who does not possess a good working knowledge of his or her research site may find the results of a study wholly uninterpretable.

Within the ecological framework, the utilization of interventions in field research can be a powerful technique for disentangling the connections that exist among the field's components. The uncoupling of these connections, however, is designed to permit a deeper understanding of how they operate in the undisturbed state and how they, in turn, affect some phenomenon of interest.

One of the better known examples of this difference in intent can be drawn from the research of Roethlisberger and Dickson (1946) on worker productivity. It was hypothesized that changes in the lighting levels of work stations should improve productivity. The changes, however, in no way seemed to account for variation in output. Because the phenomenon of interest involved productivity, these authors decided to examine more closely the ways in which worker groups organized themselves at the Western Electric plant. Their holistic investigations led to the following types of observations: (1) Some work groups were characterized by "a lack of ambition and initiative and a complacent desire to let well enough alone"; (2) the supervisory control that was set up by management to regulate and govern work output apparently exercised little authority; and (3) the employees believed that they would not be satisfactorily rewarded for any additional work they produced beyong that set by common agreement among the workers. These findings led to the development of the concept of informal groups within formal organizations resulting in possible barriers to communication among different levels of the organization. Whereas this conclusion has now been incorporated into the literature on organizational structure, the failure to understand the operation of these aspects of the work setting completely undermined the effectiveness of the intervention that was the original focus of study.

An investigator whose primary concern was centered on the development of physical equipment and its impact upon productivity might never have been led to pursue the conditions under which an intervention might be transduced effectively into the operation of an ongoing setting. An ecological framework, on the other hand, would motivate the investigator to expand and clarify a set of theoretical propositions relating some aspect of physical change to organizational structure. More important, the adoption of an ecological perspective alerts the investigator to the question of how a particular intervention (whether theory derived or growing out of demands for application) maps onto the setting into which it has been introduced.

Ecological Validity and the Problem of Meaning

Given the environmental researcher's interest in material objects and their interrelationships in various settings, it might be tempting to act as though people are simply black boxes who respond blindly to physical change. Clearly, material objects and their orchestration into spatial settings are assigned cultural, subcultural, and individual meaning in terms of which they may affect a wide range of human response. The meanings associated with these objects in the environment are also influenced by the contexts within which they are located. Their influences on human behavior can only be understood within those contexts.

For example, Casper and Wellstone (1981) document a controversy that arose in west central Minnesota regarding the construction of an extensive series of high-voltage transmission lines carrying ±400 kV of direct current from a generating station in North Dakota to a conversion station outside Minneapolis–St. Paul. The routing of the power lines cut across a number of counties in west central Minnesota resulting in a bitter controversy between the power companies and the farmers whose land would have to be seized so that the lines could be constructed. At one point in the sequence of events surrounding the project, uncertainties were voiced regarding the potential health effects that might be associated with the ionization of air molecules around the lines when fully operational.

If we confined the question of health impacts solely to the amount of ionization that occurred when the lines were transmitting full power and were able to determine, through physical measurements, the degree of ionization as a function of distance from the lines, prevailing weather conditions, amount of exposure, and so on, it would be possible to assign probabilities to the likelihood that there would be adverse consequences associated with these high currents. On the other hand, the bitterness of the controversy surrounding this environmental change was relatively widespread among residents of the affected area. In a number of interviews conducted with the participants affected by this project, it was clear that people did not evaluate the power lines solely in terms of the direct effects of air ionization on their health. Rather, the lines were considered symbolic of the extent to which the farmers who opposed them had been powerless either to halt construction or change the routing. What is more, the transmission towers and lines served as constant reminders of the extent to which the farmers felt betrayed by representatives of the state agencies whom they felt should have adopted a more adversarial role with regard to the power companies. Even if a definitive case could not be made for the direct effects of the current on resulting illness complaints, the lines could be appraised as threatening and the resulting stresses could have led to the appearance of physical symptoms. Efforts to deny the legitimacy of these perceptual aspects of possible illness events would not be warranted within the persepctive of current stress research (Baum, Singer, & Baum, 1981; Monat & Lazarus, 1977).

We have also seen the pervasive role that meaning plays in opposition to other forms of environmental change. Schorr (1963) has pointed out that efforts to define slums for purposes of urban renewal programs solely in terms of physical characteristics of housing and neighborhoods often disregard the social meaning of these environments for their inhabitants. It is these meanings that are influential in the various levels of protest that are mounted when physical change is to be introduced. They can also account for the puzzlement expressed by technicians who see only the obvious physical conditions of the environments for which they are planning and cannot understand why people would stand in the way of what they believe are obvious improvements. The technicians' assessments may be closer to those of residents who view their physically deteriorated housing as a temporary expedient and who plan to leave as soon as practicable. These evaluations may be contrasted with those provided by people who have formed extensive social networks and for whom neighbor and kin relationships are central to their assessments of any proposed physical changes.

Environments are Spatially and Temporally Organized

It should be obvious that environments possess both temporal and spatial extensiveness. Each of these environmental characteristics interact with people's experiences. For example, Baum, Gatchel, Aiello, and Thompson (1981) present evidence to show how learned helplessness develops over time in residential settings differing in density levels. They provide evidence to show how the helplessness phenomenon would be assessed differently depending on the temporal duration of exposure to setting conditions.

McCarthy and Saegert (1979) have shown how the scale of the environment affects perceptions of safety, control, privacy, and social support among low-income residents. Depending on the scale of the living environment, they found marked differences in residents' assessments of these perceptual aspects of the housing experience.

Finally, Barker and Gump (1964) have also shown how environmental scale relates to social organization. When the number of possible social roles in a setting exceeds the number of residents, people will do more things, work harder, feel more committed, and like group involvement more. Just the reverse will be found under conditions in which the number of people exceeds the number of activities possible.

Summary

The basic assumptions underlying the ecological validity notion are that the phenomena of interest to environmentalists operate in a context of material objects and their relationships located within a temporal–spatial context. These phenomena possess multiple linkages to the material conditions that comprise the context within which they may be located. The magnitude of these linkages may shift depending on the spatial and temporal constraints that exist at or during the time an investigation is undertaken. Finally, settings, the people who use them, and the activities that occur within them must be understood within a framework of cultural, subcultural, and individual meanings that people assign to them.

With these preliminary assumptions as background, we can now turn to the problems of research planning and design from an ecological perspective.

ECOLOGICAL APPROACHES TO RESEARCH DESIGN

There are a number of techniques that can be employed in the determination of matches among setting characteristics, construct systems, and research procedures. We have considered various holistic strategies that would allow a mapping of a setting's organization. Both Bogdan and Taylor (1975) and Lofland (1971) provide extensive references to a wide range of holistic investigations conducted in various field settings. Although these studies are informative, it is unfortunate that the majority of these studies are not concerned primarily with environmental issues.

One of the most pressing challenges for the future is related directly to the theoretical specification of the environmental characteristics that are most relevant to the different construct systems that we employ in our work. Recently, efforts have been made (Stokols & Shumaker, 1981) to describe, at a somewhat abstracted level, those factors that would be relevant to a wide range of person-environment transactions. Whereas these classification schemes suffer inevitably from their generality and exhaustiveness, they do have a heuristic function. When combined with aspects of information regulation required for the construction of a research protocol, they can assist an investigator in assessments of the adequacy of the strategies chosen for answering a set of research questions. The construction of these systems in the future, however, must be grounded more specifically in the characteristics of settings in relation to particular construct systems.

A good example of an approach that might be taken to the problem of matching construct system to field characteristics may be found in Saegert's (1980) paper on the social and psychological concomitants of settings categorized on the basis of density variations. In her efforts to describe how one would go about choosing a setting in which density issues could be investigated, Saegert examined various parameters that would be involved in this type of field research. Because of the obvious significance of different setting characteristics, Saegert recounts research she and Roberts conducted to identify both locales and conditions that appeared to be perceptually connected to stressful experiences associated with crowding.

This form of retrospective analysis represents another option available to the investigator who is concerned with the discriminating factors that guide the choice of a research site. In this type of study, the researcher starts with a phenomenon and attempts to reconstruct the possible variables that might have a bearing on its differential manifestations. Settings are then assessed on the basis of clusters of variables that are presumed to be salient to the phenomenon. Reliance on verbal report alone involves obvious risks. In Nisbett and Wilson's (1977) terms, it is hoped that it would be possible to ascertain influential rather than just plausible aspects of the experience that are potentially discriminating and predictive.

Of course, it is not necessary to rely solely on verbal reports in a retrospective study. For example, Appleyard (1969) wished to identify physical form variables in the built environment that might contribute to explanations of why certain buildings are remembered by residents in their attempts at wayfinding. Rather than develop an a priori scheme that catalogued plausible formal elements, Appleyard chose to work backward from frequency counts of remembered buildings taken from resident maps of Ciudad Guyana, Venezuela. Once having chosen a sample of residents based on selection criteria such as age, sex, education, and place of residence in the city, respondents were asked to draw maps of the city. Working from those buildings that residents recalled, he and his colleagues photographed and scaled them on the basis of possible attributes that could be hypothesized to account for their memorable qualities. These attributes were then intercorrelated and regressed on recall scores to determine which sets accounted for those sites mentioned most frequently.

This type of research procedure is frequently used in medical studies and is subject to the same criticism that has been voiced regarding the validity of the subsequent explanations (Anderson, Auquier, Hauck, Oakes, Vandaele, & Weisberg, 1980). Clearly, the results of Appleyard's work would have been more convincing if the variables identified as significant in the earlier phase of the research had been employed in a prospective investigation. Such a procedure was used by Carr and Schissler (1969) and illustrates how this can be accomplished.

Given the obvious importance of this type of preliminary field investigation, it is unfortunate that more references are not available describing how a focused holistic reconnaissance could be adapted to the needs of the investigator who wished to conduct comparative hypothesis-testing research. Usually, this type of research (if it is conducted at all) is done as preliminary or pilot work and never reported. When the results of a comparative field study are published, the reader can often detect that prior work was undertaken both to clarify the phenomenon and to describe field conditions that could have a bearing on the outcomes of interest.

To illustrate this point I refer to some recent work by Seligman, Kriss, Dorley, Fazio, Becker, and Pryor (1979) on the attitudinal variables that might be predictive of summer energy consumption. In this study, the authors apparently realized that energy consumption decisions were made by more than one member of a family. They gathered data on the attitudes of both husband and wife and used both attitude sets as predictors of energy use. Their results demonstrated a clear improvement in the amount of variance which they could account for, compared to predictions based on data from either family member alone. Unfortunately, we do not know what type of preliminary research was conducted that led to this decision.

The fact that prediction was improved in this case points to a more general observation that can be made about the clarification of a phenomenon. Such clarification can suggest possible extensions of relevant construct systems. Occasionally it is possible to accomplish this simply through careful analysis and a set for discovering ways in which methods may be adapted to advance a set of theoretical issues. This can be illustrated by some work reported by Reich and Robertson (1979). In this study, the authors wished to test hypotheses growing out of reactance theory (Brehm, 1972) in a field setting. The problem chosen involved various types of antilittering messages.

In their initial study, conducted at a swimming pool frequented by minority children and teenagers, they designed two types of requests. The first was constructed to arouse reactance behaviors ("Don't litter"). The second was worded to prompt a social norm regarding littering ("Keep the Pool Clean"). It was hypothesized that the directiveness of the "Don't litter" message would activate counterattitudinal forces because choice was constrained. The authors predicted that this message should lead to an increase in littering behavior. Their data were congruent with the hypothesis.

In an effort to extend the research and to replicate the findings, Reich and Robertson designed a second study in which they used the same two messages plus three new instructions. The first of these was even more directive; "Don't you dare litter." The last two were included to provide a broader range of general social norm messages relevant to the setting. The pool users were asked to: "Help keep the pool clean" and reminded that "Keeping the pool clean depends on you." In this study, however, the pool selected by the investigators was used mainly by white middle-class adults and some younger patrons. Analysis here, however, revealed no differences in amount of littering associated with the different instructions. In an effort to clarify these unexpected results, the authors conducted a third study.

Because previous investigators had reported that younger people and minorities were more likely to indulge in littering, the authors repeated the second study at the original pool site. They found that the data were again congruent with the reactance hypothesis. Reich and Robertson concluded that the reactance notion received some support but that its predictive value was not as general as might have been expected. How might an investigator who was interested in ecological validity as used in this paper have proceeded?

Consider first the sites selected for the investigation. All three studies were conducted at swimming pools. It seems plausible to suggest that swimming pools are settings in which greater freedom of action is possible and is tolerated. At least by formal definition, a swimming pool is a recreational setting in which participants may feel that they have greater latitude for playful behavior. Although not totally unconstrained, many behaviors are tolerated that might not be allowed in other settings such as a classroom or even a park. If an investigator was able to compare a swimming pool to other settings, using potential freedom of choice as a differentiating variable, it seems plausible to suggest that this setting would activate attitudes that would be particularly sensitive to reactance manipulations. In their paper, however, the authors did not provide any rationale for the choice of the sites. Such an omission would be acceptable if the reactance construct was not conditional on site characteristics. Yet it should be clear that this represents a hypothesis, not a foregone conclusion. Clearly, the construct validity of the reactance notion requires a set of statements regarding those circumstances under which it would be expected that reactance would operate in the predicted fashion. The ecological perspective forces the investigator to examine the organizational and meaning structure of different sites to determine whether the utilization of a construct system is appropriate or inappropriately applied in that setting. If these conditions were specified in the theory, the choice of setting would be simplified considerably. In addition, construct validity would be advanced through the possible extension of the theoretical structure surrounding the concept.

Next, consider the differences between the second study compared to the first and the third. At the second site, the authors report that the swimming pool was more likely to be frequented by adults and younger patrons. It is entirely possible that littering on the part of younger users of the pool would be affected by the presence of adults who would tend to enforce social controls against littering. To determine whether the presence of adults might have any influence on the amount of littering, it would have made more sense if the analysis had proceeded separately under conditions in which adults were present and absent. Internal comparisons of this sort are often quite possible within settings characterized by turnover in users, and such comparisons may allow the investigator to generate differential predictions regarding the validity of hypotheses of major concern.

Although not stated explicitly by the authors, it appears that the littering data were summed over all people in the settings without regard to age. The reasons for doing so might be connected to the assumption that the reactance concept was general enough so that it was not thought necessary to consider possible limits to its generality. An investigator concerned with the ecological validity of the theory, however, might be very interested in the extent to which ongoing field processes (such as the presence of adults who might exercise a social control function) would interact with the construct under investigation. In short, are predictions from reactance theory most likely in settings that are characterized by minimal social control conditions?

If an investigator believed that social control variables should be incorporated into the explanatory system, their ecological distribution and testing in different settings could advance the validity of the overall theory. Now let us consider the role that subcultural differences might have played in this study. It should be obvious that there may very well have been a set of subcultural norms that operated with regard to the legitimacy of requests for behavioral constraint. If the black teenagers who were the subjects of investigation in the first and third studies behaved more congruently with a reactance hypothesis than did the whites who were the subjects in the second study, it would have been important to determine what the reactance construct would say about these differences (particularly because the procedures and methods employed in the second and third studies were equivalent). Are some people more likely to be sensitive to reactance manipulations?

Is the crucial issue for the reactance construct race or social conditions that place a premium on rebelliousness as a way of establishing peer acceptance? If a swimming pool could be found that was used by white working-class teenagers, it might be possible to provide some preliminary information about race and class. Once more, comparisons between older and younger patrons would permit a test of the age variable.

Finally, let us examine the procedures employed in this study. The handbills with different messages printed on them were handed out to the pool users on a quasirandom basis. A different message was handed out to each person who approached the pool concessionaire. Thus, two individuals entering the pool at the same time would have received a different message depending on which set was used at that point in the study. If this happened with any regularity, it could have some effect on the outcome because treatment conditions presumably should occur without cross communication from condition to condition. Whether cross communication represents error in the design, however, is another question.

There are two conditions under which it might be considered error. In the first, cross-treatment communication might impair or enhance the effects being sought. If what was called a social norm message was received by one patron and a reactance message by the second, the latter might be more likely to discard the handbill because comparison of messages could accentuate the reactance instructions to refrain from littering.

The second possible source of error is connected to the first. Suppose the investigators wished to apply the results of their study. They recommend the antilittering instruction that appeared most effective. If cross-treatment communication accounted for some or all of the observed outcomes, the use of the most effective antilittering message *alone* might have no effects whatever on littering in other settings.

The utilization of an ecological perspective, however, could shift thinking away from the treatment of cross-intervention communication as unwanted error variance. After all, one of the ecological characteristics of many pool settings is various forms of social interaction. If the theoretical network surrounding the reactance construct specified that various group communications might result in predictable behavioral differentials, then internal comparisons could be used to evaluate these alternative predictions. Such studies would involve, among other things, observations of any communications among the recipients of different messages. The first group of observations would involve comparisons of people in group to single individuals. Later observations might require contrasts between different groups (e.g., mainly younger people contrasted to older users and so on). If the investigator believed that groups could pressure individual members toward nonconformity to rules and found that, when cross-treatment comparisons were made, littering increased, there are both applied implications to such a finding as well as the possibility of extending the theoretical system relevant to reactance.

Thus, systematic variations in the implementation of the research design itself (individual versus group receipt of the messages) could be used to test possible extensions of the construct system to map onto a wider range of ecological variations encountered in the field. Such research would require systematic departures from the requirements of appropriate research design in an effort to determine how the social conditions represented by these departures might be related to the nomological network (Cronbach & Meehl, 1955) of the reactance construct.

I have purposely chosen to spend some time discussing this study because it illustrates how a judicious combination of field-setting process conditions can be translated into multiple tests of hypotheses that grow out of a particular construct system. The similarities of the procedures being advocated here to those of the holistic investigator should be clearer by now. If we focused only on single instances of variation in field conditions, it is obvious that we would not possess sufficient degrees of freedom to test multiple hypotheses. When repeated observations can be made (either of different people or the same people over time), however, many opportunities for replication and cross comparison frequently exist.

Holists further claim that their analysis possesses the virtue of descriptive comprehensiveness. Similar options are available to the person interested in hypothesis-testing research if only he or she changes conceptual sets and gives serious consideration to observed variations in field conditions as a source of theoretical diversification. In this process, research procedures that might otherwise be the source of potential error can be pressed into the service of theory generation.

The type of analysis just described can often be accomplished within a relatively short time prior to the onset of the main study. This is especially true for relatively circumscribed environments whose scale is readily grasped by the investigator or for settings with which the investigator has personal experience. Unfamiliar research sites may be rendered comprehensible through the use of informants who can serve as guides. Suggestions for the creation of research partnerships with informants may be found in McCall and Simmons (1969) and Filstead (1970).

Archival data relevant to a wide variety of field settings can also be found in a diverse set of secondary data bases. An excellent guide has been prepared by Miller (1977). Finally, a concentrated period of field reconnaissance can be exceptionally helpful in research design.

For example, in a study of wayfinding problems encountered by visitors to the Museum of History and Technology of the Smithsonian Institution, Winkel, Olsen, Wheeler, and Cohen (1977) first reviewed whatever data had been gathered by prior investigators at the Smithsonian that had any bearing on orientation issues. The museum administrator's initial statement of the problem was that both visitors and staff lost their way in the building. To deal with this problem they also wished to implement and test various orienting devices.

Although such abbreviated problem descriptions are common in applied research, it has been my experience that the researcher can often design a more informative study if the dimensions of the problem are articulated more finely. In this case, we spent some time simply trying to understand what was meant by "orientation problems." Adopting a holistic perspective, we asked ourselves where orientation fit within the overall experience of visiting the Museum of History and Technology. One alternative we considered was that visitors might think of the museum primarily as entertainment. If that was true, then people would be satisfied with anything they experienced and problems in wayfinding would be limited to obvious issues such as locating exits and public facilities. Had we not considered this possibility, we might have developed a set of orientation indicators, designed some devices relevant to these indicators only to find that they were not "effective." Their ineffectiveness could then be due to the unimportance of wayfinding issues with the result that people just disregarded our guides. The obvious point is that an "important" question for the researcher and/or sponsor of research is not necessarily important to the users of the setting. It is, therefore, essential to ascertain where the problem fits within the ongoing setting structure.

Our reconnaissance effort was therefore organized in phases. First, was orientation a problem for visitors and where did it fit within the visit? Second, where do wayfinding problems fit within the other components of the setting's operation? Third, assuming that wayfinding was important to the visitors' overall experience, could orienting information be designed to enhance the experience as a whole? Fourth, given the spatial and temporal components of the visit, when and where is orienting information required?

Data relevant to our first question were taken from existing surveys conducted by museum staff in the past. We also devised an informal observation study to document whether entering visitors sought out orienting information. If they did, we recorded the kinds of questions they asked. To accomplish this aspect of our preliminary research plan, we stationed assistants at various information desks and recorded people's questions verbatim. In this study, and in recent research on the development of a hospital information system, we have found that this form of unobtrusive data gathering is exceptionally informative. Not only can we obtain a partial map of the distribution of information seeking, we can also document how people organize their communications regarding information being sought.

Various museum administrators were interviewed also. Rather than use questions that focused only on obvious wayfinding problems, our interviews were expanded to include administrator perceptions of effective communications to visitors and how they would like these to be realized. It was only later in the discussion that we asked about possible linkages between their intentions and various orienting aids that might be used. On the basis of this material we could categorize orienting problems into six broad classes.

The data generated by our literature review, observations, and interviews with staff provided a set of performance criteria that various orienting devices would have to meet. These criteria formed the basis for alternative approaches that could be taken to the design of specific orienting aids. Staff could then guide us in the choice of which devices they would prefer to have implemented.

Possible locations for our orienting aids were determined through an extension of our observational procedures. It was plausible to assume that orientation problems were most likely to occur when people confronted choice points in the setting. Our wish to remain unobtrusive led to the development of possible behavioral indicators of disorientation problems. These included group conferences at choice points, consulting with security personnel, stopping to look around (e.g., down halls or into rooms), and so on. We also conducted short tracking studies of visitors noting when people appeared to be lost. When these observations were mapped on floor plans of the museum, we could then make some reasonable inferences about probable points at which orienting information might be helpful.

This step was important because, unlike the laboratory setting, whatever changes were introduced had to fit within competing sources of information from the ambient environment. Through the arrangement of the devices we could better ensure that they would communicate effectively. The validity of the research design rested upon the location of the interventions within the existing ecological arrangements of the museum. Clearly, to the extent that interventions represent hypotheses growing out of a construct system or the demands of an applied problem, those interventions must mesh with other events operating in the field. An intervention might be quite effective as long as it is noticed and engages, in some fashion, with ongoing behavior.

The possibility that the interventions might not have been effective due to poor location could be considered a potential source of error associated with the research design. Consistent with our earlier discussions of the cross-treatment communication problem in the Reich and Robertson research, however, we applied this form of analysis in the current study. The question we posed involved those conditions under which it would be likely that informational sources in the environment might not be noticed due to competing information. As part of our research design, then, we systematically varied the location of our devices to test various hypotheses appropriate to this interest. We arranged our data collection procedures so that we could compare the use of the devices at different levels of traffic flow. Our assumption here was that competing information associated with the presence of greater numbers of people would differentially affect the percentage of people who could gain access to the aids, and that under higher density levels people would be less likely to notice the devices. We also moved the devices to different locations to test our inferences regarding those points in the spatial context where information would be more likely to be sought. Finally, we wished to compare the use of people as information guides to the use of impersonal sources of information such as maps.

Whereas all of these comparisons are relevant in the early stages of an empirically grounded theory of information seeking in the environment, they are also intimately linked to the ongoing ecology of this setting. Ecological validity demands required such comparisons.

The interactions among the criteria that the different orienting approaches had to meet, the spatiotemporal nature of the visit and wayfinding constructs, represents another aspect of the research design. We can illustrate this using two of the criteria. The first stated that people required an overview of the area they were considering for a visit, and the second required that people not be forced to backtrack on their path to an exhibit group.

To meet the first criterion, we had designed overview maps of the major halls in the museum. In addition, we provided additional pictorial information about the types of exhibits that would be found there. Had we relied only on the maps, however, we would have had to make a number of problematic assumptions about the translatability of map data into memory. The use of maps alone required us to assume that: (1) This abstracted information could be stored cognitively; (2) map information would be matched to existing environmental cues regarding directionality and turns; (3) verbal labels attached to the maps could be translated into the visual forms associated with the exhibits (whose names were not immediately obvious); and (4) regardless of the distance to be traveled, there would be no reduction in the clarity of the map image.

The last assumption was directly relevant to the requirement that people not be forced to backtrack. The possibility that the maps might not have been effective in communicating a vivid image that would remain constant over time led us to introduce various prompts at different locations in the hall under study. We could then compare the effectiveness of the maps and the prompts in terms of reducing backtracking.

The centrality of space–time factors in field settings thus involves both elements of research design (how will the intervention operate over space and time) and construct development (how do space and time affect the operation of the construct). Hence we are not confined only to questions of construct and internal and external validity in field research. Each of these components interacts with one another, and it is this type of interaction and its interpretation that is central to ecological validity concerns.

The spatial–temporal issues in this setting had a direct bearing on our research design. The components that appeared salient to our analysis of orientation suggested a staged procedure that would enable us to differentiate among different ways of presenting orienting information. Because questions had arisen regarding the role that maps and signs (singly and in combination) might contribute to effective wayfinding, we decided that it would be most appropriate to use a base-line condition in which minimal orienting information was available. We were fortunate in this regard. The handout maps that the museum generally employed were being revised and were not available to visitors. Visitors could obtain assistance only by asking staff at the two main entrances, consulting a list of exhibits located there or asking security officers.

Being a public facility, it was also possible to introduce an element of randomness into the study. Obviously, we could not assign visitors randomly to conditions. We could, however, control the introduction of the various orienting interventions we employed over the course of the study. In this setting, visitor turnover was a constant element that would probably be characteristic of other museums. Thus special precautions did not have to be taken when assessing the generalizability of this aspect of the study to other settings of a similar kind.

Visitor turnover also meant that cross-treatment communication was not a problem. In addition, the experimental interventions were blended into various parts of the temporal and spatial flow of the visitor's movement through the building. Thus, the intervention was viewed as a legitimate part of the museum experience. We could then inquire about these devices in ways that seemed appropriate to the setting's context.

This example illustrates the use of preliminary field reconnaissance guided by a combination of holistic procedures and hypothesis-testing concerns. By using three investigators it was possible to conduct this work in 2 weeks. Once the issues had been identified and the various internal comparisons had been integrated into a comprehensive design, the data gathering required only 10 weeks. We believe, however, that the 2 weeks were crucial to our development of an ecologically relevant study.

Although these and other forms of holistic analysis can improve an investigation's ecological validity, we have not given formal consideration to the problem of possible confounds or plausible alternative explanations that might be used to explain the results of a field study. In the museum example, possible differences in familiarity with the setting could have accounted for whatever differences we found in testing the orientation devices. Although we could randomly assign treatment conditions to the ongoing operation of the setting, we had no guarantees that the statistical distributions for a familiarity would be similar from condition to condition. It is to this issue that we now turn.

The Problem of Confounds and Plausible Alternatives in Field Research

In my earlier analysis of the laboratory as a field setting, I suggested that information regulation and the control of social relationships represented two dimensions that guided these special purpose settings. The utilization of the various procedures employed in the laboratory is based on a model of knowledge that proceeds by uncoupling interrelated variables under controlled conditions. It is assumed that such a process will lead to the development of a set of generalizable "laws of behavior." It is further assumed that these laws will be interrelated gradually over time. The resulting complexity will then summarize the diverse behaviors that represent the focus of investigation. The success of this venture rests upon the validity of each of the components that comprise the whole.

Because of our understandable concern for clarity of explanation as a function of good research design, it is not surprising that much has been written concerning validity issues in experimental and quasiexperimental studies (Campbell & Stanley, 1963; Cook & Campbell, 1979). These discussions have tended to focus on so-called "threats" to validity that stem from failures in research design and analysis. It is not necessary to summarize these because they have been discussed thoroughly by Campbell and his associates. An even more elaborate set of such threats in the context of field research in clinical medicine and epidemiology may be found in the work of Sackett (1979).

Although these threats have been considered primarily in the context of research design, I argue that the majority of them are not methodological at all. Many so-called methodological problems are traceable directly to the nature of the problem being studied and to the settings within which these problems and phenomena manifest themselves. As long as the investigator continues to conceive of field research as a problem of potential methodological artifact, it is small wonder that the complexities encountered there appear as insurmountable obstacles. What is the nature of these obstacles considered as threats?

Ordinarily the notion of "threat" is treated as systematic variance that operates concomitantly with the variance that is to be attributed to the constructs that generate the hypotheses under examination. The presence of such concomitant variation renders interpretation problematic, because it is not possible to decide which of two or more factors may have contributed systematically to observed outcome.

The problem of concomitant variation, however, is not an issue that is peculiar to field settings. Even with the powerful array of information-controlling procedures available to the laboratroy researcher, improper problem conceptualization can almost be guaranteed to lead to the presence of plausible alternatives.

To appreciate the commonalities among various field settings (which include the laboratory as a special case), I suggest that we ask ourselves two questions with regard to presumed "threats" to validity. First, to what extent are the "threats" that can be identified as part of the operation of various field settings *directly relevant* to the content of the theories that we wish to develop? And second, do various "threats" represent legitimate operating characteristics of field settings that require us to phrase our theoretical statements so that they hold only in a conditional or contingent fashion? Thus we might be required to say that X explains Y, subject to a set of other contingencies that might also be present.

Answers to these questions are related to the level of analysis chosen by the investigator to account for a particular phenomenon. The level of analysis involves the substantive content of a particular explanatory system. For example, are the constructs conceptualized primarily in the domain of some discipline such as psychology, sociology, economics, biology, biochemistry, and so on? Or is there some combination of constructs drawn from different disciplines that represents the content of explanation?

If an investigator chooses one level of analysis, variation attributable to the operation of variables that comprise the explanatory content of another discipline may be relevant to outcome but irrelevant to theory construction at the level specified by the investigator. For example, if someone is interested in the use of specially designed learning materials to account for differences in cognitive performance, the biological fact of maturation may be relevant to the outcome but irrelevant to the construct system employed by the cognitive theorist. To suggest that maturation represents error associated with research design, however, represents a misunderstanding of error. The problem is traceable to a specification of the level of theoretical analysis that precludes biological explanations. This is a theoretical decision on the part of the investigator, not a methodological problem. Obviously, the failure to consider maturation as a potential explanatory element may be translated into the type of research design that is employed. That failure, however, is not considered properly as a methodological artifact.

A more interesting example of the level of analysis issue can be taken from the work of Casper and Wellstone mentioned earlier. If an investigator chose to confine analysis to the physiological effects of exposure to ionized air molecules (considered as a physical process), it might be impossible to account for differential illness rates using just this bounded range of variables. The use of psychological concepts relevant to perceived threat and its role in stress reactions might provide a better account of observed illness rates. If the research design did not include measures anticipating this possibility, any outcome might be uninterpretable because stress represents a plausible alternative that is not only directly relevant to outcome but that may be theoretically required. Once more, however, any omission of this sort is not a methodological artifact. It is a problem of theoretical misspecification.

Many of the substantive concerns of environmental researchers are influenced to a significant extent by the social organizational characteristics of the settings within which research is conducted. I believe that careful analysis of the threats to validity that are commonly discussed in the research design literature will reveal that these threats are directly traceable to social organizational issues. To the extent that this is true, then, it may be possible for researchers who wish to conduct field studies to reconsider their research problems as potential theoretical issues that require resolution. To illustrate the possibilities inherent in this position, consider the following examples.

In their investigations of the effects of differential densities on dormitory dwellers, Baum and Valins (1977) reported that those residents living in high-density conditions who considered themselves friends experienced fewer negative consequences associated with high-density living. If a researcher interested in density effects randomly assigned individuals to dwelling units, this methodological decision might very well enhance the consequences of high density by uncoupling existing social relationships that would mitigate its stressful qualities. Failure to randomize or only partial randomization might be considered as a methodological artifact when attempting to understand differential consequences associated with varying density levels.

It should be emphasized that effective randomization may be characteristic of a rather narrow range of settings. Indeed, if this were not the case, one might wonder why the laboratory as a research setting was ever invented. Given the possibility that randomization (or lack thereof) as a salient environmental operating characteristic may be a socially based decision, the investigator must inquire about the degree to which the antecedents and consequences of randomization are directly relevant to the phenomenon being investigated and hence must be considered as a possible candidate for the theoretical system being employed.

Even Cook and Campbell (1979) admit that randomization as a strategy for the assignment of treatment conditions can have either demoralizing or energizing effects upon those who, as a result of such a social decision, either receive or are denied access to a favored or socially desirable program. From the researcher's perspective, the issue becomes whether this particular component of research decision making must be included as part of the theoretically relevant systematic variance that might account for differential behaviors.

Let us return to density research for another example of the problem under consideration. Suppose an investigator was interested in the amount of cooperation and mutual assistance that residents exposed to different density levels might provide. Because of a desire to employ a measuring tool that had been widely used in studies of cooperative behavior, assume that he or she attempted to induce residents in high- and low-density settings to participate in a prisoner's dilemma game. Suppose, further, that the research found that whereas there were differences among residents in the two settings more people in the high-density setting either refused to participate or, after having agreed to participate, dropped out of the study. Any claims regarding density effects might be discounted as due to differential mortality in the environments under study. It is entirely possible, however, that the fact of differential mortality might be a consequence of the social atmosphere associated with the two settings. If this was the case (and a good theoretical argument can be made for differential amounts of social-withdrawal, which is one component of mortality), this "testing" confound or threat could very well be considered as a theoretically relevant outcropping of the phenomenon of interest. Under these circumstances it might make better sense within the ecology of the field setting to utilize tasks that would be considered appropriate to them and would be subject to different levels of participation. The scores for differential participation could then be used as a substantive outcome variable used to evaluate theoretical predictions regarding the effects of differing density levels. Utilizing this approach, Bickman, Teger, Gabriele, McLaughlin, Berger, and Sunaday (1973) were able to demonstrate some very convincing effects. These investigators used a variant of the lost letter technique and also asked residents to save milk cartons for students who needed them for an art project. In both instances there were consistent and strong effects for these measures of differential participation.

To illustrate the so-called measurement problem further, consider a study reported by Ley and Cybriwsky (1974). In this project the authors were interested in the effects that a local social control system would exert on the expression of deviant behavior. They used the stripping of abandoned cars as an indicator of a rather minor form of criminal activity. Ley and Cybriwsky argued that environments whose cues indicated few social sanctions for deviant behavior would be likely sites for finding abandoned stripped cars compared to areas in which social control cues were available (e.g., blocks containing occupied houses, stores, and apartments). Congruent with their hypothesis, the authors found differences in predicted patterns of abandoned and stripped cars.

One plausible alternative for the results was that cars were abandoned and stripped in front of apartments, houses, and stores just as frequently as elsewhere but that police tow trucks were more likely to remove these eyesores from those locations. The authors provided evidence that ruled out this alternative. Suppose, however, that the alternative was not eliminated—the police did indeed have a selective system of towing abandoned cars. Would this represent an error in research design (i.e., differential measurement error)? At a bare minimum the answer would be yes. If, however, further inquiry revealed that abandoned and stripped cars were just as likely to be found in front of apartment houses and stores, this outcome would cast doubt upon the adequacy of the construct system used by the authors. Thus, what might constitute an error in research design could be turned to theoretical advantage.

Next consider the problem of self-selection into environments. This possibility is often used to discount research results. In a recent paper, Stokols and Novaco (1980) described a project designed to investigate the relationship between the distance people traveled to work and any stress that might relate to different commuting times. In their data analysis, the authors found that a number of people had reported moving to a different house, in part to compensate for the stresses involved in work journeys. Under some circumstances these accounts might be interpreted as a problem of environmental self-selection that would be confounded with commuting time. On the other hand, it would be somewhat conservative to argue that a finding such as this was not germane to the hypothesis. It might complicate the data analysis relevant to the hypothesis under study, but it would be difficult to argue that this represented a methodological problem.

The museum orientation problem discussed earlier also illustrates the points being raised regarding the interpretation of plausible alternatives. It is recalled that we were concerned with the possibility that nonrandom assignment of visitors to the intervention conditions might be correlated with differences in the degree of familiarity visitors had with the museum. If such differences existed, we might have encountered problems in understanding the role that the interventions played in affecting orientation.

The decision to introduce the devices randomly was guided partially by a desire to reduce any possible systematic differences in the comparison conditions that might be traced to differential familiarity levels. It seemed implausible to us that alternating the days and hours at which different interventions would be used would be likely to result in a systematic variability in familiarity. Familiarity is an ecologically distrubuted variable and is obviously relevant to theoretical explanations of orienting differences. In this study, randomized introduction of the orienting devices was designed to increase the variability associated with this possibility so that its effects could be assessed as part of the analytic treatment of data.

Potential mortality differences in response to our questionnaires represented another possible difficulty. Our preliminary investigations had revealed that there were limits in the amount of time that people would give us, even though they were willing to cooperate. Because some of the orienting devices were complicated in their design, we needed to ask a range of questions to assess component effectiveness. We handled this problem by using a central set of questions that assessed the orienting effectiveness of each device. We then altered the questionnaire to include small sets of questions relevant to each component being tested. Because of visitor turnover, it was possible to build a pool of responses to the major questions (answered by all respondents) and small subsets of responses to specific aspects of the devices. Thus, we reduced the mortality rates under all conditions to a minimum.

In summary, the investigator should give careful consideration to the interpretation provided for plausible alternatives. Extant field conditions represent systematic variance that may or may not affect some outcome issue of research interest. If they are systematic, they must be evaluated in terms of their potential theoretical significance. Regardless of whether they are germane to the construct system, they must be handled if they influence outcome. Thus, research design must anticipate these contingencies.

But the conditions they represent are not in the research design as a methodological problem generally. They are part of the conceptualization of the problem that is subsequently represented by the design of the research and the analytic approaches that are taken when the data are gathered.

Before closing this chapter, I briefly discuss approaches that may be taken to assess the ecological validity of research.

Approaches to the Estimation of Ecological Validity

It would, of course, be desirable if it were possible to obtain some numerical index of the ecological validity of an investigation. As Brunswik (1956) has suggested, however, numerical indices of the ecological validities of cues relevant to some response are dependent on the relationships of the cues to other cues in different settings. Given the ecological distrubutions of processes that might be relevant to the explanation of a phenomenon of interest, it would be reasonable to suppose that different numerical estimates for these processes would be obtained, depending on the setting and its contextual features. Clearly, what is required is the development of theoretical systems that leads to predictions regarding possible values that different processes might assume in different settings. Under some circumstances the investigator might expect very weak relationships among variables. Such an outcome is acceptable as long as theoretical considerations can explain these differences. For example, comparisons of nonrandom to random assignments to living conditions might lead the researcher to conclude that the predicted effects of high-density living compared to low densities would be absent or reduced if the nonrandomness of assignment meant that friends could live together in the higher-density settings.

In the approach being advocated in this chapter, the distinction between theory-relevant and irrelevant plausible alternatives suggests that research designs must be capable of treating both possible sources of variance. The adroit use of experimental and quasiexperimental research designs to rule out theoretically irrelevant alternatives does not seem warranted to me in many instances. The elimination of theory-"irrelevant" variance could easily lead to the judgment that most of the reliable variance of an outcome measure should now be classified as unexplained, whereas the included variables account for only a fragment of the remaining variance. Such a result is not uncommon (Sarason, Smith, & Diener 1978). Yet, if our theoretical systems can only account for a minimal amount of the variance associated with the phenomena in which we are interested, does this not raise some rather serious questions concerning the adequacy of our theoretical models? Although the point cannot be pursued here, it seems reasonable that the failure to take the ecology of field settings seriously is related precisely to recognition of the possibility that we are condemned to marginal explanations of marginal phenomena.

Concluding Remarks

The principles and issues put forward in this chapter should be considered as a starting point for further discussion of the problems of environmental field research. My intent has been to reconsider the apparently irreconcilable differences that have been alleged to characterize holistic and hypothesis-testing research. I hope that the reader will come to appreciate the contributions that our colleagues following the holistic tradition may be able to contribute to problems of mutal concern. If I have been successful, the concepts addressed in this chapter will allow hypothesis-testing researchers to read accounts of holistic research design and perhaps adapt them to their own needs. I hope that holistic investigators will appreciate the possibilities that the ecological validity notion might provide in their efforts to deal with the complex set of issues that comprise the contextual aspects of the problems they wish to address.

I believe that the ecological validity notion will provide assistance to investigators who are occasionally overwhelmed by the complexity of the problems that seem to characterize many field settings. With careful consideration of the intent of a research enterprise, the reconceptualization of what constitutes error, the utilization of so-called threats to validity to contribute to theoretically relevant systematic variance, and a sensitivity to the organizational integrity of various settings, it should be possible to explore how far ecological validity considerations may be able to carry us as we deal with the central problems of environmental research.

Aside from the question of the range of applicability of ecological validity concerns, this notion raises a number of important issues for the environmentalist. We have touched very briefly on the means that might be used to assess ecological validity, and this clearly is an area that requires much further work. We must also consider the problem of the disentanglement of complex treatment conditions that may be used in intervention studies. When an intervention is made up of integrated components, the configural properties of the totality may not be capable of additive decomposition. If this is the case, there are some important conceptual and analytic problems that must be addressed. We also need to address the criteria that are important in the determination of when a plausible alternative explanation is directly, contingently, or totally irrelevant to some phenomenon of interest. Finally, we must give much more serious consideration to the quantitative techniques that need to be employed when analyzing field data. These are matters for the future, however.

REFERENCES

Amir, S. (1972). Highway location and public opposition. *Environment and Behavior, 4,* 413–436.

Anderson, S., Auquier, A., Hauck, W., Oakes, D., Vandaele, W., & Weisberg, H. (1980). *Statistical methods for comparative studies: Techniques for bias reduction.* New York: Wiley.

Appleyard, D. (1969). Why buildings are known: A predictive tool for architects and planners. *Environment and Behavior, 1,* 131–156.

Barker, R., & Gump, P. (1964). *Big school, small school.* Stanford: Stanford University Press.

Baum, A., Gatchel, R., Aiello, J., & Thompson, D. (1981). Cognitive mediation of environmental stress. In J. Harvey, (Ed.) *Cognition, social behavior, and the environment.* Hillsdale, NJ: Lawrence Erlbaum Associates.

Baum, A., Singer, J., & Baum, C. (1981). Stress and the environment. *Journal of Social Issues, 37,* 4–35.

Baum, A., & Valins, S. (1977). *Architecture and social behavior: Psychological studies of social density.* Hillsdale, NJ: Lawrence Erlbaum Associates.

Bem, D., & Allen, A. (1974). On predicting some of the people some of the time: The search for cross-situational consistencies in behavior. *Psychological Review, 81,* 506–520.

Bem, D., & Funder, D. (1978). Predicting more of the people more of the time: Assessing the personality of situations. *Psychological Review, 85,* 485–501.

Bickman, L., Teger, A., Gabriele, T., McLaughlin, C., Berger, M., & Sunaday, E. (1973). Dormitory density and helping behavior. *Environment and Behavior, 5,* 465–490.

Bogdan, R., & Taylor, S. (1975). *Introduction to qualitative research methods.* New York: Wiley.

Bransford, J., Stein, B., Shelton, T., & Owings, R. (1981). Cognition and adaptation: The importance of learning to learn. In J. Harvey (Ed.), *Cognition, social behavior, and the environment.* Hillsdale, NJ: Lawrence Erlbaum Associates.

Brehm, J. (1972). *Responses to loss of freedom: A theory of psychological reactance.* New York: General Learning Press.

Bronzaft, A., & McCarthy, D. (1975). The effect of elevated train noise on reading ability. *Environment and Behavior, 7,* 517–528.

Brunswik, E. (1956). *Perception and the representative design of psychology experiments.* Berkeley, CA: University of California Press.

Campbell, D., & Stanley, J. (1963). *Experimental and quasiexperimental designs for research.* Chicago: Rand McNally.

Cantor, M. (1975). Life space and the social support system of the inner city elderly of New York. *The Gerontologist, 15,* 23–27.

Carp, F. (1966). *A future for the aged: Victoria Plaza and its residents.* Austin: University of Texas Press.

Carr, S., & Schissler, D. (1969). The city as a trip: Perceptual selection and memory in the view from the road. *Environment and Behavior, 1,* 7–36.

Casper, B., & Wellstone, P. (1981). *Powerline: The first battle of America's energy war.* Amherst: University of Massachusetts Press.

Chase, W., & Chi, M. (1981). Cognitive skill: Implications for spatial skill in large scale environments. In J. Harvey (Ed.), *Cognition, social behavior, and the environment.* Hillsdale, NJ: Lawrence Erlbaum Associates.

Cohen, S., Glass, D., & Singer, J. (1973). Apartment noise, auditory discrimination and reading ability in children. *Journal of Experimental Social Psychology, 9,* 407–422.

Cohen, S., & Lezak, A. (1977). Noise and inattentiveness to social cues. *Environment and Behavior, 9,* 559–572.

Cook, T., & Campbell, D. (1979). *Quasi-experimentation: Design and analysis issues for field settings.* Chicago: Rand McNally.

Cook, T., & Reichardt, C. (Eds.). (1979). *Qualitative and quantitative methods in evaluation research.* Beverly Hills, CA: Sage.

Costantini, E., & Hanf, K. (1972). Environmental concern and Lake Tahoe: A study of elite perceptions, backgrounds and attitudes. *Environment and Behavior, 4,* 209–242.

Cromwell, R., Butterfield, E., Brayfield, F., & Curry, J. (1977). *Acute myocardial infarction: Reaction and recovery.* St. Louis: Mosby.

Cronbach, L., & Meehl, P. (1955). Construct validity in psychological tests. *Psychological Bulletin, 52,* 281–302.

DeJong, D. (1962). Images of urban areas. *Journal of the American Institute of Planners, 28,* 266–276.

Fellman, G., & Brandt, B. (1970). A neighborhood a highway would destroy. *Environment and Behavior, 2,* 281–302.

Filstead, W. (Ed.). (1970). *Qualitative methodology: First-hand involvement with the social world.* Chicago: Markham.

Filstead, W. (1979). Qualitative methods: A needed perspective in evaluation research. In T. Cook & C. Reichardt (Eds.), *Qualitative and quantitative methods in evaluation research.* Beverly Hills, CA: Sage.

Francis, M. (1975). Urban impact assessment and community involvement: The case of the John Fitzgerald Kennedy Library. *Environment and Behavior, 7,* 373–404.

Fried, M., & Gleicher, P. (1961). Some sources of residential satisfaction in an urban slum. *Journal of the American Institute of Planners, 27,* 305–315.

Gans, H. (1962). *The urban villagers.* New York: Free Press.

Gentry, W., & Williams, R. (Eds.). (1979). *Psychological aspects of myocardial infarction and coronary care.* St. Louis: Mosby.

Glaser, B., & Strauss, A. (1967). *The discovery of grounded theory: Strategies for qualitative research.* Chicago: Aldine.

Goffman, E. (1962). *Asylums: Essays on the social situation of mental patients and other inmates.* Chicago: Aldine.

Gulick, J. (1963). Images of an arab city. *Journal of the American Institute of Planners, 29,* 179–197.

Harloff, H., Gump, P., & Campbell, D. (1981). The public life of communities: Environmental change as a result of the intrusion of a flood control, conservation and recreational reservoir. *Environment and Behavior, 13,* 685–706.

Hartman, C. (1966). The housing of relocated families. In J. Wilson (Ed.), *Urban renewal: The record and the controversy.* Cambridge, MA: MIT Press.

Heberlein, T., & Black, J. (1981). Cognitive consistency and environmental action. *Environment and Behavior, 13,* 717–734.

Hyde, J. (1980). Survival analysis with incomplete observations. In R. Miller, B. Efron, B. Brown, & L. Moses (Eds.), *Biostatistics casebook.* New York: Wiley.

Ittelson, W., Proshansky, H., Rivlin, L., & Winkel, G. (1974). *An introduction to environmental psychology.* New York: Holt, Rinehart, & Winston.

Korte, C., & Grant, R. (1980). Traffic noise, environmental awareness, and pedestrian behavior. *Environment and Behavior, 12,* 408–420.

Kuipers, B. (1978). Modeling spatial knowledge. *Cognitive Science, 2,* 129–153.

Lawton, P. (1975). *Planning and managing housing for the elderly.* New York: Wiley.

Ley, D., & Cybriwsky, R. (1974). The spatial ecology of stripped cars. *Environment and Behavior, 6,* 53–68.

Lofland, J. (1971). *Analyzing social settings.* Belmont, CA: Wadsworth.

Lynch, K. (1960). *The image of the city.* Cambridge, MA: MIT Press.

Mazmanian, D., & Sabatier, P. (1981). Liberalism, environmentalism, and partisanship in public policy making: The California Coastal Commissions. *Environment and Behavior, 13,* 361–384.

McCall, G., & Simmons, J. (1969). *Issues in participant observation.* Reading, MA: Addison–Wesley.

McCarthy, D., & Saegert, S. (1979). Residential density, social overload and social withdrawal. In J. Aiello & A. Baum (Eds.), *Crowding in residential environments.* New York: Plenum.

Miller, D. (1977). *Handbook of research design and social measurement.* (3rd ed.) New York: Longman.

Monat, A., & Lazarus, R. (Eds.). (1977). *Stress and coping.* New York: Columbia University Press.

Nisbett, R., & Wilson, T. (1977). Telling more than we know: Verbal reports on mental processes. *Psychological Review, 84,* 231–259.

Orne, M. (1962). On the social psychology of the psychological experiment. *American Psychologist, 17,* 776–783.

Page, R. (1977). Noise and helping behavior. *Environment and Behavior, 9,* 311–334.

Reich, J., & Robertson, J. (1979). Reactance and norm appeal in antilittering messages. *Journal of Applied Social Psychology, 9,* 91–101.

Roethlisberger, F., & Dickson, W. (1946). *Management and the worker.* Cambridge, MA: MIT Press.

Robinson, W. (1950). Ecological correlations and the behavior of individuals. *American Sociological Review, 15,* 351–356.

Rosenthal, R. (1966). *Experimenter effects in behavioral research.* New York: Appleton-Century-Crofts.

Sackett, D. (1979). Bias in analytic research. *Journal of Chronic Disease, 32,* 51–63.

Saegert, S. (1978). High density environments: Their personal and social consequences. In A. Baum & Y. Epstein (Eds.), *Human response to crowding.* Hillsdale, NJ: Lawrence Erlbaum Associates.

Saegert, S. (1980). A systematic approach to high-density settings: Psychological, social and physical environmental factors. In M. Gurkaynak & W. LeCompte (Eds.), *Human consequences of crowding.* New York: Plenum.

Sarason, I., Smith, R., & Diener, E. (1975). Personality research: Components of variance attributable to the person and the situation. *Journal of Personality and Social Psychology, 32,* 199–204.

Schatzman, L., & Strauss, A. (1973). *Field research: Strategies for a natural sociology.* Englewood Cliffs, NJ: Prentice-Hall.

Schorr, A. (1966). *Slums and social insecurity.* Washington, DC: U.S. Government Printing Office.

Seligman, C., Kriss, M., Darley, J., Fazio, R., Becker, L., & Pryor, J. (1979). Predicting summer energy consumption from homeowners' attitudes. *Journal of Applied Social Psychology, 9,* 70–90.

Sewell, W. R. D. (1971). Environmental perceptions and attitudes of engineers and public health officials. *Environment and Behavior, 3,* 23–60.

Shippee, G., Burroughs, J., & Wakefield, S. (1980). Dissonance theory revisited: Perception of environmental hazards in residential areas. *Environment and Behavior, 12,* 33–52.

Siegrist, J., & Halhuber, M. (Eds.). (1981). *Myocardial infarction and psychosocial risks.* Berlin: Springer–Verlag.

Stokols, D., & Novaco, R. (1980). Transportation and well-being: An ecological perspective. In I. Altman, J. Wohlwill, & P. Everett (Eds.), *Transportation and behavior.* New York: Plenum Press.

Stokols, D., & Shumaker, S. (1981). People in places: A transactional view of settings. In J. Harvey (Ed.), *Cognition, social behavior, and the environment.* Hillsdale, NJ: Lawrence Erlbaum Associates.

Wagner, H. (1970). *Alfred Schuetz: On phenomenology and social relations.* Chicago: University of Chicago Press.

Webb, E., Campbell, D., Schwartz, R., & Sechrist, L. (1966). *Unobtrusive measures.* Chicago: Rand McNally.

Weiss, R., & Rein, M. (1969). The evaluation of broad aim programs: Experimental design, its difficulties and an alternative. *Administrative Science Quarterly, 15,* 97–109.

Winkel, G. (1977). The role of ecological validity in environmental research. In L. van Ryzin (Ed.), *Behavior-environment research methods.* Madison, WI: Institute for Environmental Studies, University of Wisconsin.

Winkel, G., Olsen, R., Wheeler, F., & Cohen, M. (1977). *The museum visitor and orientational media: A comparison of different approaches in the Smithsonian Institution, National Museum of History and Technology.* New York: Center for Human Environments, Graduate Center, City University of New York.

Znaniecki, F. (1934). *The method of sociology.* New York: Holt, Rinehart, & Winston.

2 Research on the Chronically Ill: Conceptual and Methodological Perspectives

Rosemary R. Lichtman
Shelley E. Taylor
and
Joanne V. Wood
University of California, Los Angeles

Chronic illness has been the major cause of disability and death in the United States since the beginning of the 20th century (Graham & Reeder, 1979). At any given time, 50% of the population has some type of chronic condition that requires medical management, making the total number of individuals affected by chronic disease substantial (Gartner & Reissman, 1976). Research on chronic illness is therefore propitious. The consideration of the problems of chronic illness in a volume focused on environmental concerns is particularly appropriate. The importance of environmental factors in the etiology of chronic illness (Graham & Reeder, 1979) as well as in treatment and rehabilitation has been clearly demonstrated. For example, environmental stressors (e. g., air pollution, toxic wastes, and ingested substances) clearly have causal significance in the development of the two major chronic illnesses in our country, coronary heart disease and cancer (Cohen, Glass, & Phillips, 1979). Lifestyle has also been convincingly linked to chronic disease (e.g., Dembroski, Weiss, Sheilds, Haynes, & Feinleib, 1978).

Chronic illness, in turn, has an impact on the environment. The patient's lifestyle is irrevocably altered, which forces changes in the patient's social environment as well. His or her relationships with family members may be strained (Wortman & Dunkel–Schetter, 1979), and new individuals, such as medical personnel, figure prominently in the patient's life.

Because this chapter focuses on already-diagnosed populations, its interest is not in the environment's etiological role but rather on the psychosocial changes brought by chronic illness and its treatment. In particular, we focus on conceptual and methodological issues associated with chronic illness either when it is an object of study in its own right or when it is a vehicle for exploring other substantive issues. Conducting research with the chronically ill raises a host of conceptual and methodological issues, some of which are common to any field research, others of which are unique to the problems of illness itself (see Watson & Kendall, 1983). We focus on five main conceptual issues: short-term versus long-term focal problems, the temporal course of patient reactions, the relationship between researcher and patient, the importance of the physical nature of the chronic illness, and the patient's social system. We then turn our attention to methodological issues and focus especially on the following points: choice of research design, cooperation with medical personnel, time frame of the research, issues of sampling and generalizability, format of stimulus materials, problems of data collection, and ethical issues. In the following pages, we draw heavily on examples from research on cancer and coronary disease. This is both because they represent our own areas of expertise and because they are the two major chronic diseases and causes of death in our nation.

CONCEPTUAL ISSUES IN THE STUDY OF CHRONIC ILLNESS

Short-term versus Long-term Focal Problems

Research on chronic illness can be short or long term. Short-term studies often center around improving patient adjustment to particular treatments or illness-related events, such as chemotherapy for cancer patients, bypass surgery for heart patients, or self-administration of insulin for diabetics (see Johnson & Leventhal, 1974; Langer, Janis, & Wolfer, 1975 for examples of this approach). Long-term research focuses on the general changes experienced by patients in their lives as a consequence of their illness, rather than on specific events. Note that use of the terms *long term* and *short term* refers not to the research itself—indeed, we consider longitudinal versus single-session research later—but rather to the temporal range of the issues encompassed by the research.

Many researchers will find short-term studies and interventions highly compatible with their research training. Short-term intervention studies with the chronically ill may be very similar to laboratory studies. The researcher is often presented with highly specific events in which the independent variables are relatively easy to control and the dependent variables easy to measure. The time frame is short, there are few variables that may introduce noise in the data, and the relationships among variables are relatively clear. Yet, unlike laboratory work, research with the chronically ill provides the advantage of a real-world setting, and the results frequently have important practical implications for how to manage the chronically ill. Moreover, the fact that this research is short term does not mean that the intervention will necessarily have only a short-term impact on the life of the patient. For example, successfully intervening in the side effects experienced in chemotherapy can have a major impact on the cancer patient's quality of life, even though the aim of the work is to enable the patient to cope better with the specific chemotherapy session; more general effects on the quality of life are serendipitous consequences.

A great deal of social psychological work with the chronically ill has adopted this short-term intervention focus. A classic example is Johnson and Leventhal's (1974) study of coping with an aversive medical procedure. Patients awaiting an endoscopic examination (which involves swallowing a tube that takes pictures of the upper gastrointestinal area) were provided with information that was designed to enhance their feelings of control over the experience. It was found that when patients had information regarding the probable sensations they could expect and steps they could take to make the passage of the tube easier, they responded less emotionally to the treatment. A study by Burish and Lyles (1979, 1981) demonstrated that cancer patients who were taught self-hypnosis were able to take more hyperthermia treatments with less pain than were patients not instructed in self-hypnosis. From these kinds of studies, psychologists have learned a number of techniques that make chronic illness and its treatments less aversive to the patients. The payoffs in the reduction of noncompliance and in higher quality of life are potentially great.

Long-term issues of adjustment to chronic illness are harder to study. The time frame of the research is often longer, usually requiring other than experimental research designs, a topic that is covered more fully later in this chapter. Also, rather than a clear-cut situation with specific independent variables and dependent variables, one is instead faced with a general issue (i.e., the chronic illness) that is experienced idiosyncratically by each patient. Patients' reactions to illness are likely to be substantially influenced by a great many historical and contemporaneous factors such as personal history of illness, relationships with partner, family members and friends, and occupational history.

Many of the subsequent issues we take up in both the conceptual and methodological portions of this chapter are greater problems for long-term than for short-term studies. However, all the forthcoming issues are likely to arise in research with the chronically ill, regardless of the scope of the particular study and therefore merit consideration generally.

Patient Reactions to Chronic Illness: A Temporal Focus

A patient's whole life is often altered by a chronic illness. He or she is likely to undergo a great many changes, both physical and psychological. In addition, logistical requirements may lead to changes in activities. The consequence of this fact is that one cannot get an accurate appraisal of the effect of an illness on individual psychological functioning by studying one point in time. Rather, an individual's life will often change gradually in response to a chronic illness, and hence the psychological effects one documents may apply only for the particular time point of one's study. At the very least, then, one's conclusions must be temporally bounded (see Wellisch, 1981, for a discussion of this issue).

Note that this issue is conceptually distinct from the question of whether one adopts a longitudinal research design in studying the problems of chronic illness. It does not follow that the need for a temporal focus will of necessity point in the direction of a longitudinal methodological design. A temporal focus can be achieved through other research designs as well, as we note later. The conceptual point is that the patients' reactions at any point in time must be put into temporal context, in that reactions change as the nature of one's illness changes and as one moves farther from an illness episode (see Thomas, 1978). For example, early in the development of a chronic illness, psychological responses may be deceptively quiescent. Initial responses to the diagnosis of the chronic illness may be shock or even denial, as the patient questions whether or not the diagnosis and prognosis are accurate (Hackett & Cassem, 1969; Kubler–Ross, 1969; Quint, 1963; see also Silver & Wortman, 1980b).

Around the time of diagnosis, the patient is frequently under institutional management; that is, the detection of a suspicious symptom or problematic condition usually leads to multiple physician visits and/or hospitalization for at least a short time. That the patient is not in his or her own environment must be considered when interpreting the patient's behavior, because much of what one sees early in the disease process may be a reaction to institutionalization itself, rather than to the disease. The researcher must therefore attempt to assess the impact of physicians, nurses, and the entire medical setting on the patient to determine the meaning of particular psychological responses. Patients may react to their initial contacts with medical facilities with helplessness and dependence, or with anger or reactance (Leventhal, 1975; Taylor, 1979), which may have little or nothing to do with their feelings about being ill.

Were one to conduct research on the chronically ill some weeks after a diagnosis has been made, the psychological portrait might appear somewhat different. Reactions to diagnosis (Quint, 1963) or to specific interventions such as surgery are often delayed (Lindemann, 1941). Early in the illness process there are often many decisions to be made, treatments to be initiated, and appointments to be kept. It is difficult for the patient to develop any clear sense of what the illness means for his or her life. Once the initial poking and probing is over, the visitors have all gone home, and the patient has time to think about the meaning of the illness, its full implications may set in. Stroke patients, for example, may experience feelings of elation upon discharge from the hospital as they think about all the things they will be able to do when they get home. Once home, however, they may realize the extent to which their activities are limited by their stroke-related disabilities. The consequences may be depression and increasing dependency on those around them (Dahlberg & Jaffe, 1977). Responses to chronic illness, such as depression, may, then, be delayed (e.g., Croog & Levine, 1977; Quint, 1963).

Still later in the disease process, if the patients have come to terms with whatever restrictions the illness has made in their lives, they may come to feel that the implications of the illness are well integrated into their lifestyle. If there are no additional acute bouts with the illness, patients may come to feel "cured" or at least not under any immediate threat. Many such patients will no longer think of themselves as patients. For example, cancer patients 6 years away from the initial diagnosis of cancer with no signs of recurrence may not consider themselves cancer patients any longer. Similarly, a man who had a heart attack 4 years previously and is now maintaining a pleasant pain-free life-style may feel that he is no longer a heart patient. At this point the chronic illness may have a relatively small impact on the patient's psychological status. Examining a patient's reactions at this stage may be enlightening concerning the long-term impact of a chronic illness that is in remission, but it may say relatively little about the earlier impact of that illness. It also raises questions about the validity of retrospective reports about the early impact; the patient's retrospections may adopt the rosy glow that years free of symptoms provide. The mirror image of this situation is that patients who are not in remission but who are growing more ill, and whose conditions require active intervention, may provide a falsely negative picture. Distinguishing the impact of continued treatment, feelings of loss of control, and poor prognosis from merely having a chronic illness is critical.

The substantive content of adjustment to chronic illness also changes with time. Early in the illness process, issues relating to body image may dominate. During an illness bout, not only the area directly affected by illness is threatened, but the entire body image plummets (see Fisher & Cleveland, 1958; Schwab & Hameling, 1968). Body image is usually lowest immediately after diagnosis and improves subsequently as one adjusts to the implications of the illness. Later in the illness process, changes in vocational and avocational pursuits and threats to one's interpersonal relationships are of greater concern. These responses are delayed because it is often only after a period of time with chronic illness that an individual can resume close to a normal schedule, and only at this point are the threats to one's ongoing activities apparent. One may realize that one's energy level is considerably lower and that one can no longer accomplish as much in as short a period of time as one had previously (Dahlberg & Jaffe, 1977). One's friends may react negatively to the illness, causing social relationships to be at least somewhat altered. Patients may discover that they have to learn social management techniques both in letting other people know about their illness and in cueing their friends and family on how to react to them (Wortman & Dunkel–Schetter, 1979).

The consequences of these points for the researcher is that certain issues may appear falsely central in the adjustment process solely as a function of the time period of one's research. Were the same issues examined at a different time in the postdiagnosis period, they might not seem nearly as important. Clearly, then, whatever the nature of one's research, whether short term or long term, whether focused on particular issues or aimed more broadly at general adjustment, one must consider patients' responses in context: What is the prognosis of the disease, how disabling is it, and how far is the patient from an acute episode? Are the reactions more a consequence of the medical treatment than of the disease? What is the impact of the illness on one's relationships and job and is that impact temporary or permanent?

The Relationship Between Researcher and Patient

The examination of the psychosocial impact of chronic illness creates a unique relationship between the researcher and patient. Whether the research is short term, involving, for example, an intervention with a noxious medical procedure, or long term, such as an exploration of the coping responses, the patient, by participating in the research, permits the researcher a glimpse into some of the most private moments of her or his life. A very special, albeit temporary, bond between researcher and patient can often develop as a consequence, and the implication of this bond can be substantial.

Frequently, research with the chronically ill has powerful therapeutic implications (cf. Rubin & Mitchell, 1976). Long-term threat or disability raises issues that may create conflict, anxiety, or depression for the patient. Moreover, it may be precisely these issues that the patient wishes to discuss, regardless of the researcher's agenda. Therefore, it is advisable, when working with the chronically ill, to have some expertise in clinical psychological issues represented in one's research team. The absence of an understanding of the significance of these problems can produce either an unresponsive researcher who does a disservice to the patients involved, or a panicked researcher who is in over his or her head and does not know how to cope with the tears, anger, or frustration of patients. In addition to this clinical sensitivity and expertise in working with patients, one typically needs good referral services for those admittedly rare individuals who are having substantial difficulty coping with their illness. A diversity of recommendations including both clinics and private services as well as a range of specialties, such as psychiatry, psychology, and social work, permits the widest range of choice for the patient. A ready list of these resources can be gracefully left either with a particularly disturbed patient or with all patients interviewed.

A concommitant of this need for clinical sensitivity is the need to be alert to the meaning implicit in patient questions and to the meaning that can be extracted from one's own answers. Often these blockbuster questions are asked in an apparently offhand manner, such as a daughter's casual question, "Is cancer hereditary?" or a husband's apparently disinterested query, "Can you catch cancer?" Correct answers such as "Yes, many cancers have a substantial hereditary component" or "It is possible that some cancers can be related to infectious diseases" (e.g., the relationship between cervical dysplasia and genital herpes) are irresponsible in the context of a daughter's fear about her own chances of contracting cancer or a husband's concern about "catching" cancer from his wife. Under such circumstances, the factually correct answers need to be modified and set in a context that will not further threaten the questioner. Answers to these questions are often better left to the physician, and a carefully worded sentence to this effect can be appreciated by patients. A researcher who unwisely answers questions of this type may inadvertently damage the patient's and/or the researcher's relationship with the physician.

There are other reasons that the researcher should avoid giving medically relevant information to the participants. Often physicians are concerned that their patients will receive unsolicited information that conflicts with their recommendations and would prefer that no information be given out by people interacting with their patients. Information giving might also prove damaging to the research itself if it were given out in such a way as to bias the results of the study. A policy position should be taken on this issue by the research team prior to the initiation of the research, and it should be fully discussed with any hired interviewers.

Patients often have hidden agendae and seek confirmation for their private theories about their physical or psychological status. A cardiac patient who informs the researcher that, although he had a heart attack 3 years earlier, he now feels that he is cured may conclude his pronouncement with the words, "Don't you think?" A noncommital response, "You certainly seem to be in good health," assuming that that is true, can well solve the problem. In our psychosocial interviews with breast cancer patients (Taylor, Lichtman, & Wood, 1984a), it was clear that the majority of our patients had a vested interest in identifying any problems they might have as "normal" difficulties, and any favorable signs of adjustment they showed as "special" or "better than average." During the course of our interviews, many women sought approval for these perceptions. How is the researcher to deal with such obvious requests for validation of patients' psychological experience? Our operating assumption is that the researcher should reinforce these feelings of normality in areas of difficulty (as long as that difficulty *is* relatively normal) and of being special in good adjustment. For example, a brief bout with depression following a heart attack or a period of anxiety over the possible recurrence of cancer are both well within the normal range of responses for these disorders, and letting patients know this can often be very comforting to them. This should be done in such a way as to avoid biasing the results of the ongoing research if possible. For example, a comment can be made at the point of the patient's inquiry that the researcher would like to discuss this issue more fully at the end of the interview. At that time, the researcher can concentrate on the psychological needs of the patient and provide whatever reassurances seem necessary.

Interestingly enough, the same generalizations often apply to significant others, especially the spouse. In our interviews with the spouses of breast cancer patients, for example, we found that husbands had a strong interest in having their wives appear normal in their adjustment. When asked whether the wife had expressed any anger or depression following the cancer, the frequent response was a defensive, "No more than would be expected," or a more evasive, "Wouldn't anyone under the circumstances?" Spouses and other family members, then, can also benefit from the reassurance that the patient's reactions are well within the normal range of what would be expected, and such reassurances can in turn lead to more open responses (Lichtman, Wood, & Taylor, 1982).

A more serious issue in this context is the fact that patients often develop strong defenses against the realization that they have a serious illness or the fact that their illness is life threatening. For example, a common belief is that the actions one is now taking on behalf of one's health (e.g., changes in diet or attitude) are sufficient to prevent a recurrence. More seriously, one patient we interviewed in our breast cancer study flatly denied she had breast cancer, despite the fact that she had had a mastectomy; instead, she believed she had been treated for a nodule under the breast. In a clinical psychological practice where one is seeing patients who present the therapist with psychological complaints, an appropriate procedure would be to challenge these defenses, albeit gently at first, in the hopes that the patient could eventually relinquish them. Such challenges are not, however, appropriate for the researcher working with those who present with physical complaints. One must respect the fact that patients often need these powerful defense mechanisms to keep threatening emotional fantasies in check (Wellisch, 1981). The need for these defenses waxes and wanes; the patient sometimes behaves as though his or her chances for cure are substantial and at other times acknowledges that they may be considerably less than that (Kubler–Ross, 1969). Nonetheless, it is the researcher's responsibility not to challenge these mechanisms that are necessary for the patient's emotional survival.

In summary, the study of chronic illness involves a new relationship between researcher and subject that differs substantially from that in other research settings. The relationship requires a special sensitivity and respect for the patient's needs and private agenda. The researcher always has certain goals around which research questions have been designed, and these may overlap less than perfectly with the patient's interest in participating. Thus, frequently the research will be sidetracked by the patient from its otherwise predetermined course. It is the responsibility of the research to show some tolerance for patients' agendae and to respect their wish to discuss these issues. The research contract involves an implicit bargain that the patient will extract meaning and aid from the research, just as the researcher will extract useful information. It is, then, the obligation of the researcher to provide some time during the course of the research for discussion of these issues so that the implicit bargain with the patient is fulfilled. However, it is also the case that one must protect both one's own and the patient's relationships with the patient's physician as well as the research enterprise itself. Consequently, content and timing of information must be carefully considered. These issues should also be discussed in interviewer meetings, so that standardization of procedures is maintained.

Understanding the Chronic Illness

In order to do competent research on the chronically ill, the researcher needs to be well grounded in an understanding of the particular disease under investigation: its etiology, physiology, treatment, and prognosis. This is not to say that the researcher must be a physician or even medically trained. Rather, some very basic facts about the illness and its management must be known. Without this information the researcher's credibility can be damaged, and errors can be made in decisions about what issues to pursue as well as how to interpret the results. Is the disease progressive? Are there disabilities that occur, and if so, what kind? What is the ultimate prognosis? What is the time frame of the illness? Does disability or deterioration occur at different rates during the time period? What are the treatments that are used to deal with the illness and what are the expected effects of them? What are the likely effects of both long- and short-term medication and treatment?

Knowing these facts is necessary, first, to gain entry into a medical setting. Physicians and nurses are unlikely to cooperate with the plans of researchers who are blatantly ignorant about the illness they are studying. Such knowledge is also critical not only to establishing one's credibility with medical personnel, but in understanding what they say. A physician approached regarding his willingness to make patients available for a study will likely ask, "What kind of patients do you want?" The researcher without an idea of the parameters of patient populations will likely be turned away without any patients. For example, is a cancer study to include only stage one patients, or should it include stage two, stage three, and stage four patients as well? Is a study of coronary artery disease to include only MI patients, or should angina patients also be included? The researcher must have established answers to these questions before approaching medical personnel. It is useful, too, to learn the jargon and shorthand that inevitably develops around the treatment of any illness to appear credible, to facilitate rapport, and simply to communicate with the medical staff.

The researcher must be conversant with chronic illness and its treatments in order to deal appropriately with patients and their families. If one betrays ignorance about the illness and treatments, one loses credibility with them as well. Moreover, one may not understand the information provided by patients (e.g., specific details about radiation treatments or chemotherapy drugs) without basic preparation. Even more important is that one may actually miss the significance of information provided during the research. For example, when one of our patients was asked how she was faring with her chemotherapy, she indicated that when the chemotherapy got to be too much for her she occasionally had a few drinks before the forthcoming session. She then winked. To the casual observer, this incident would appear to be nothing more than taking a couple of swigs to muster up one's courage. In fact, this information is far more significant. Alcohol reduces one's white blood count, often to a point that a chemotherapy session must be cancelled. Close examination of our interviews revealed that a few of our breast cancer patients were, in fact, using alcohol to avoid chemotherapy, a very subtle form of noncompliance (Taylor, Lichtman, & Wood, 1984b). Knowing what questions to ask patients and understanding how to interpret what they say, then, can depend substantially on familiarity with the course of the illness and its treatments. Similar issues arise with families and significant others. Often family members' reactions to the chronic illness of a spouse, child, or parent are as tied to specific events in the illness sequence as are the reactions of the patient him or herself (Lichtman, 1982). Knowing what kind of surgery a breast cancer patient had, for example, and thereby understanding what the scar probably looks like can place the husband's emotional reactions to the scar into context (Lichtman et al. 1982; Wellisch, Jamison, & Pasnau, 1978).

Once the data have been collected, failure to take into account various aspects of the illness can lead to errors in interpretation. For example, our recent study of breast cancer revealed that many patients went through a period of depression some weeks after their surgery. Because stage models of adjustment have been prominent in recent years (e. g., Bowlby, 1961; Gunther, 1969; Guttman, 1976; Klinger, 1975, 1977; Kubler–Ross, 1969; Schulz & Aderman, 1974; Shontz, 1975; see Silver & Wortman, 1980a, for a review), it was tempting to conclude, as other work had, that depression is simply a delayed reaction to cancer, predictably late in the emotional sequence of responses. However, chemotherapy is often initiated at this point, and chemotherapy itself produces debilitating side effects, such as hair loss, nausea and vomiting, or difficulty in sexual functioning. It is entirely possible that depression may be more specifically tied to these situation-specific factors than to a more general psychodynamic model of psychological adjustment.

The Patient as Part of a Social System

No patient experiences chronic illness in isolation; rather, the patient is part of several social systems, all of which are affected by the illness. The major one, of course, is the patient's immediate family. Two out of every three American families will have to cope with some form of cancer in a family member, and virtually every family will have to cope with some kind of chronic illness at some time (Wellisch, 1981). Viewing the patient as part of a social system alerts the researcher to issues that affect the patient as well as issues that have an impact on the family (Litman, 1974).

Many issues that would seem to be addressed satisfactorily by considering the patient as an individual in fact *require* a broader systems perspective. Level of adherence to medications, for example, is substantially affected by family support and encouragement (e.g., Becker, 1976; Davis, 1968). A patient's self-esteem is likely to be substantially determined by his or her partner's sexual and affectional response following diagnosis (e.g., Gates, 1975). Even short-term specific interventions such as those that enhance feelings of personal control (e.g., Langer & Rodin, 1976) often depend on interaction with the patient's social milieu to achieve and sustain their effects.

The impact of one family member's chronic disease is substantial in many areas of the family's functioning (Wellisch, 1981). The family is almost always affected *economically,* in that chronically ill patients often require continual treatments that can strain or drain family resources. Like the patient, the family must adjust to the *treatment regimen.* Many wives, for example, assume responsibility for remembering medications, and all family members must adjust their schedules and car use to accommodate a seemingly unending series of appointments with physicians (Davis, 1968). There are many *interpersonal* changes that may arise within the family as a consequence of chronic illness. A common one involves alterations in dependency relationships. Often, the patient becomes at least temporarily more dependent and the spouse more dominant than may have previously been the case. Michela's (1981) study of married couples' reactions to heart attack revealed that husbands close to their heart attacks were more dependent on their wives and were less influential in the family (e.g., they made fewer decisions), compared with those farther from their heart attack. Loss of power or equity in the relationship may be expected to the extent that the patient requires aid or resources from the spouse. *Sexual functioning* is frequently disturbed by chronic disease (Ray, 1980). Cardiac patients, for example, are often afraid to resume sexual activity once they have had a heart attack, and indeed many are warned by their physicians not to do so (Croog & Levine, 1977). Treatments such as chemotherapy may lower one's libido or reduce sexual capacity by interfering with lubrication or the ability to maintain an erection.

The family as a *support system* is also often affected by chronic illness. Cancer patients may be victims within their own families and circle of friends. The threat of some illnesses is so great that it is difficult for others to cope with it effectively; hence they may "cope" by isolating and rejecting the patient (e.g., Wortman & Dunkel–Schetter, 1979). Even when family members do not reject the chronically ill patient, they will often avoid discussing the illness or the possibility of recurrence at all costs, maintaining that it is morbid or negativistic to focus on what is in the past. Patients, in contrast, may have a need to discuss these issues (Lichtman, 1982).

Many chronic illnesses have a *hereditary component,* and, accordingly, when a family member develops an illness, the meaning of that illness is far greater on the family than is the direct impact it has on the patient's health and the family member's activities. The threat it poses for other family members, particularly children, can be substantial (Wellisch, 1979). For example, our own work on breast cancer (Lichtman, Taylor, Wood, Bluming, Dosik, & Leibowitz, in press) revealed several daughters who, once they realized their substantial risk of contracting breast cancer, withdrew from the family, particularly the mother, in some cases leaving the family setting altogether. It is critical, then, that this genetic and hereditary problem be considered when understanding the dynamics of family interaction.

The social context beyond the patient's family also introduces important variables to take into account when studying chronic illness. Single patients, for example, clearly have different problems than do married ones. A patient who has been treated for breast cancer with a mastectomy and who is trying to negotiate a new interpersonal and sexual relationship may find it extremely difficult to do so and may not be certain about how to disclose the fact of her illness. Age may influence how difficult it is to deal with an illness. Older people may be more prepared for a chronic illness, and it may not interfere as significantly with their lifestyle as is the case for younger patients, particularly those with children (Grandstaff, 1976). Ethnic background influences such factors as the interpretation of symptoms, the meaning attached to particular illnesses, and even the ability to withstand pain (Zborowski, 1958; Zola, 1966). Social class may influence what concerns are foremost in a patient's mind. Working-class people may be seriously concerned with the money problems resulting from expensive treatments and time lost from work, whereas upper-class people have the luxury of dwelling on less mundane concerns (Litman, 1974).

What, then, is the methodological significance of conceptualizing the chronically ill patient as part of a social system? At least two major consequences follow from this perspective. First, the patient's reaction to the illness and treatment cannot be understood without knowing the impact of the illness on the social environment, especially family members. Second, when developing research designs for the study of chronic illness, it is useful to consider broadening the investigation to include other individuals such as family members, so that perspectives other than the patient's can be brought into one's research results.

METHODOLOGICAL ISSUES RAISED BY THE STUDY OF CHRONIC ILLNESS

A number of methodological issues arise when the researcher begins to study chronic illness, some representing problems whose impact may be controlled if they are anticipated. Some of these problems are to be found in any field study, whereas others are peculiar to the health setting involving chronically ill or institutionalized patients. The following areas are some of the main methodological issues one encounters in doing research on the chronically ill: choice of research design, cooperation with medical personnel, time frame of the research, issues of sampling and generalizability, format of stimulus materials, problems of data collection, implementation of research findings, and ethical issues.

Choice of Research Design

The first methodological issue presented by the study of chronic illness is the choice of a research design. This decision will be heavily determined by whether one selects a short- or long-term problem. Short-term problems, as noted earlier, often present situations very similar to laboratory research conditions and hence may best be examined through an experimental design. For example, if one wishes to study the effect of different kinds of coping techniques, such as imaging versus relaxation on adjustment to chemotherapy, the best design is an experimental one in which subjects are randomly assigned to the two conditions and assessments are made after a number of chemotherapy sessions, preferably both before and after they have learned the coping technique. For some problems after-only designs are more appropriate than pre–post designs, because the treatment will not be repeated. Surgery studies, for example, fall into this category in that subjects usually receive only one surgical intervention (e.g., Egbert, Battit, Welch, & Bartlett, 1964). It is not, of course, always possible to have random assignment to condition when working with chronically ill populations. Sometimes one treatment group must come from one facility and another from another facility. Sometimes control subjects must be run before or after subjects in an intervention group for practical or ethical reasons (Dracup, Guzy, Taylor, & Barry, in press). In these and similar instances, a variety of quasi-experimental designs (Cook & Campbell, 1979) are available to approximate as closely as possible the inferential power that one obtains with a randomized, prospective clinical trial (i.e., a true experimental design).

For more long-term and general issues of adjustment, the choice of research design is more problematic. This choice is particularly important for the study of chronic illness, because there are many psychological and social factors involved that act in a cumulative fashion to influence the adaptive process. Ideally, to best understand psychosocial adjustment to chronic illness, one needs to research both the range of problems occurring at different points in time during the course of the disease, as well as the cumulative effects of adjusting to the disease over its entire course (Turk, 1979). Although questionnaire and brief interview studies are sometimes utilized to examine such issues, a better choice is naturalistic observation or intensive interview in order to provide for a full understanding of the adaptive process (Cannell & Kahn, 1968; Turk, 1979; Weick, 1968).

In selecting the research design, a number of issues merit consideration. We review each of several designs, considering the advantages and disadvantages of each. Each, of course, is appropriate for somewhat different issues, and understanding the strengths and weaknesses of each method can help one decide upon an issue-design match.

Longitudinal research allows one to focus upon a group of individuals over an extended period of time. Its advantages are that one can determine the cumulative effects of illness and can determine whether effects are in fact due to the course of the illness as opposed to transient situational factors. Longitudinal designs are well suited to studying delayed or long-term effects of an intervention done early in the course of illness. Furthermore, certain kinds of topics can be studied only longitudinally, such as compliance with long-term treatment regimens.

There are a number of disadvantages of longitudinal designs as well. They demand a lengthy time investment by the researcher and are usually quite expensive. The sample one studies longitudinally may be biased (e. g., they may be less busy or less sick), because one must secure permission from them in advance for the multiple sessions during which they must cooperate. Any sampling errors that occur initially are, of course, perpetuated in the follow-up sessions, to which must be added biases due to attrition. Death, relocation, change in health status, loss of interest in the study, and other reasons for dropping out can greatly alter the original sample. Furthermore, once a longitudinal study has been designed it is difficult to add new measures, in that measurement comparability over time is an important advantage of longitudinal designs. Accordingly, longitudinal designs often include a great many questions and different types of measures in order to be certain that variables are measured successfully. Finally, a longitudinal design may be reactive in that multiple measurements on patients undoubtedly produce effects of their own.

In a cross-sectional design, the same individuals are not studied across time; instead, groups of individuals drawn from different time points on the illness continuum are studied at once. This allows one to study a range of issues occurring over time without the expense of the longitudinal design. Its particular advantages are, then, that it is less time-consuming and logistically easier. There is less probability of reactivity due to repeated measurements and less likelihood of atypical samples in that subjects must agree to participate only once. One can select the maximally effective measuring techniques at any given time rather than being wedded to measures that were developed on the sample some time ago. A cross-sectional design also enables one to develop a theoretical model more quickly, in that one does not have to wait as long a time to see the nature of one's results (Bell, 1953).

A variation in the cross-sectional design is the blocked, retrospective design. In this design, data are collected at only one point in time, but subjects are stratified over time, so that one has data representing each time point during the temporal period of interest (i.e., cross-sectional design); in addition, subjects' reconstructions and retrospections regarding their responses during previous time periods are collected. These retrospections may then be used to construct a model of long-term adjustment that can be validated either by comparing patient retrospections with the results of the cross-sectional design, or by comparing the retrospective results with a subsequent longitudinal study. Whether or not the model holds up against the cross checking, patients' perceptions of their reactions during earlier episodes of the illness can be interesting in their own right. Disadvantages, of course, are that one cannot observe developmental sequences and cumulative effects of illness on individuals, and long-term models constructed from cross-sectional or retrospective data may be wrong, due to uncontrolled factors present at the specific time of data collection.

Lazarus's (1978) ipsitive-normative model involves the in depth study of a small number of participants. The idea behind the ipsitive-normative approach is that intensive study of a few individuals over time and across situations can reveal processes underlying changes following exposure to a stressor; these processes are themselves the microprocesses that characterize the more general cause–effect relationships that are typically unearthed in studies of large samples of people adjusting to the same stressor (the normative approach). The kinds of situations for which the ipsitive-normative design is suited are different from those used for a cross-sectional or longitudinal research. It is most appropriate for studies in which the goal is a delineation of the specific transactions that occur between an individual and the environment in response to a stressor. For example, Lazarus (1978) has suggested that this approach provides the best way to research stress-specific hypertension. Using this strategy, one would study people who have a symptom pattern of significant elevation in blood pressure (hypertensives) compared to normotensives across a variety of situations that may be stressful. One then examines the individual's reactions to stressful events on blood pressure elevation and eventually extrapolates to the physiological, psychological, and social processes underlying hypertension. One disadvantage of the ipsitive-normative approach is that the group, by virtue of being small, may be biased. Furthermore, individuals who agree to be studied in such an intensive fashion may be unusual in other ways as well (e.g., they may be less ill). The ipsitive-normative approach further requires a lengthy time, money, and logistical investment by researcher.

The convergent design developed by Bell (1953) is an accelerated longitudinal approach that estimates changes over a long period of time from data gathered in a much shorter period of time. The essence of the convergent design is a series of cross-sectional studies of several analogous groups at equally spaced time intervals from the onset of the illness; repeated measures of each group are then taken so that they overlap. Hence, each small group validates a portion of the data obtained from the two adjacent small groups. This design could be used to study, for example, juvenile diabetics and their coping with the disease and therapy during their adolescent and young adult years or the reactions of multiple sclerosis patients over the years of increasing debilitation from their disease. The convergent design has many of the advantages of a longitudinal approach without the disadvantages of a lengthy time commitment. Furthermore, it allows for cross validation at overlapped points. One disadvantage of the approach is that it still involves considerable time investment by the researcher, albeit a shorter one than for a true longitudinal design. Furthermore, the groups must be comparable for the design to work, which may be difficult to guarantee with patient groups. If attrition occurs differentially across groups, the validity of the estimated cumulative effect may be questionable.

In choosing any particular research design, one needs to weigh the requirements particular to the focal research problems and then determine which of the preceding designs is the best one for exploring that issue.

Cooperation with Medical Personnel

One of the biggest stumbling blocks in research with the chronically ill that arises well before data collection gets underway is convincing gatekeepers and caregivers to allow the study to be carried out. At the very least, in order to gain access to a sample of chronically ill patients, one needs the approval of a physician. More commonly, more than approval is required, such as aid in enlisting the sample of patients to participate and cooperation in the conduct of the study, as in prescreening patients for their suitability for participation in the study or rating physical and psychological adjustment. These are data that can be obtained only from the individuals who work directly in the physical management of patients. So formidable can these problems be that we have sometimes elected to find the setting first and then practically design the study around it! One may develop a general idea of the issues one wants to study, but before pinning down precisely the nature of the research protocol, it is often advisable to determine exactly the nature of the setting and patient sample one has and then modify the protocol to be appropriate for that setting and sample. The unhappy alternative may be to invest considerable time and effort into a literature review, written conceptualization, research design, and construction of measures, only to have the study never get off the ground. This places the researcher in a fundamental dilemma: If one does not have a complete research plan in tow, one may not be able to garner the medical cooperation required to gain access to patients; at the same time such preparation is unwise before a sample is guaranteed. The wise course is to work simultaneously on the cooperation necessary for the setting and the conceptualizations necessary for a good study.

The cooperation of medical personnel is hard to achieve for several reasons. Medical personnel typically have a different orientation to health-related problems than the psychological researcher has, a difference that is manifested in several ways. First, health-related professionals are primarily concerned with the physical management of the patient and with what techniques will work to improve a patient's health. Their concerns are making the patient feel physically more comfortable, or bringing the chronic illness to a state of stable management or actual cure. Psychologists, in contrast, are frequently interested in the emotional state of the patient and what factors correlate with or lead to beneficial physical or psychological outcomes. A second difference in orientation is that medical people are very action and application oriented. Psychologists, in contrast, are typically more theoretical; their research is often more basic than applied and not necessarily oriented toward health outcomes. A corollary difference is that in their action orientation medical professionals are looking for physical and psychological prescriptions to use with their patients, whereas psychologists are often more tentative in the hypotheses they advance and in the conclusions they draw. Hence, whereas the physician may look for practical advice on how to alter behavior for the better psychological management of patients, the researcher is often unwilling to provide such hard and fast rules. Because the researcher is not necessarily in a position to provide something of specific benefit to the patients, the physician may sincerely feel that participating in the study would not be worthwhile for his or her patients. Physicians may also fear that participation would be physically and emotionally taxing for certain patients, or they may simply shy away from associating with a project that will place new demands on their test-weary patients. Some physicians may fear reprisals via malpractice suits if patients feel they have been harmed by participating in a psychologist's study that they recommend. As a consequence, the physician may quite logically refuse the researcher access to his or her patients.

Sometimes the goals of the researcher and those of the physician are actually in conflict. For example, some of our own research has centered around understanding the attributions that people make for their illness, especially cancer (Taylor et al., 1984a). In our interviews we have asked a series of probing questions regarding the specific attributions that patients make for their cancer, as well as whether they attribute their cancer to themselves, some other person, the environment, or chance factors. During the course of the research it emerged that our goals were in direct opposition to those of the physician, who had apparently spent considerable time with individual patients trying to get them not to blame themselves for their cancer. When he discovered that we were asking about the possibility of self-blame, and furthermore that several of his patients were indicating that they blamed themselves, an awkward moment was created. He clearly wanted to know the names of those patients so that he could convince them that they were not to blame for their cancer, and he was generally leery of our investigation of this issue.

Physicians or other physical caregivers who attempt to arrange entree for a researcher may overestimate the amount of power they actually have and may accordingly overestimate their ability to ensure medical cooperation and availability of patients. A physician in one of our studies estimated that he had approximately 1800 patients that he could make available to us. The reality of the situation turned out to be 185. In a study of cardiac patients, a cardiologist assured a dissertation level graduate student that he could get him access to four or five cardiac rehabilitation programs for his thesis, an assurance upon which the student's thesis and subsequent orals were based. As it happened, the physician was not able to provide access to any of the programs.

Physicians and gatekeepers are not the only individuals who may advertently or inadvertently scuttle a research project. Nursing personnel and other staff may not cooperate or may even sabotage the project for a variety of reasons. Often a research project requires that these personnel do extra work, such as screening patients or making patient adjustment ratings, work that is resisted when it is added to what is already usually a very heavy schedule. Alternatively, medical personnel may feel that the research is not good for the patient and thereby undercut the recruiting effort of the researcher. Frequently the staff will dislike a particular treatment in the protocol, such as the control group, but strongly approve of another condition in the research, such as the experimental manipulation, and convey this information to patients, urging them to insist upon being members of the experimental group. For example, in one cardiac rehabilitation project involving the comparison of an exercise program with relaxation training, the nursing staff, all of whom were solidly behind the exercise rehabilitation program, subtly communicated to patients that they were better off if in the exercise group. Patient willingness to continue in the relaxation condition was jeopardized.

Even when a researcher luckily finds an eager and cooperative nursing staff, a lack of research expertise can interfere. Nurses may not realize the importance of filling out a behavioral checklist at each and every prescribed interval, for example. An eager nurse who helped in one project suggested that she could personally select "good" patients for our sample.

Finally, medical personnel may actually react with distrust to a psychological researcher, because of feelings of territoriality and/or differences in status. Medical caregivers often feel that the physical and mental health of their patients is their own exclusive province, and should not be invaded by a psychologist. Furthermore, research psychologists are not held in terribly high esteem by many medical personnel, because they do not directly contribute to the physical care of patients. Therefore, the belief that a psychologist actually has something to contribute to the understanding and/or management of the chronically ill may be doubted.

Often the best solution to this problem is to have a multidisciplinary team conduct the research on the chronically ill (Taylor, 1978). Such a team is best able to do effective research in a setting involving chronic or institutionalized patients because it provides diverse expertise. Each individual will have a different perspective on the patient and will be able to provide information unique to that perspective. Physicians, for example, typically know a great deal more about the physical management and treatments of the patient than do other members of the team. A psychologist may have more insight into the existence of and reasons for particular psychological responses to illness. Nurses may be privy to private thoughts that patients voice and to the interaction of patients with family members. By pooling all information, one often develops a more effective research project. Enlisting the cooperation of medical caregivers by involving them in one's research means that the previously noted logistical problems are lessened, because the physician and other medical personnel are committed to the work and able to run interference (see also Dracup, Guzy, Taylor, & Barry, in press).

Team approaches to research problems are not without their headaches. Coordination among the team is frequently a problem and should be anticipated. Often a clear time frame, schedule of meetings, and set of agendae for these meetings may alleviate coordination difficulties. Because research materials often must be developed by all members of the team, there are frequently time delays in the preparation of these materials. Conflicts may develop because researchers trained in different disciplines may have different biases about the most appropriate measures to employ or approach to take. Nonetheless, overall, the advantages of a team approach usually outweigh their disadvantages.

Time Frame of the Research

Another set of issues that arises in research with chronically ill patients is the need to budget extra time for such research. For example, going through a human subjects committee often takes a great deal longer than would be required for laboratory research, because there are so many potential ethical issues that come up. Because the psychologist–researcher conducting work on the chronically ill may not be located in medical school, often he or she must go through a nonmedical human subjects committee. Under such circumstances, one has individuals who are typically without expertise in the health arena evaluating the project. Often such well-meaning individuals have misconceptions about the impact of the disease and/or treatments on patients that lead them to suggest changes in the protocol that are impractical, unwarranted, or unfeasible. The consequence may be several contacts with the committee over a period of many months. For example, when we attempted to get approval to conduct our study of breast cancer patients, one human subjects committee member was so intent upon protecting potential patient participants from coersion that he suggested that the cover letter to patients accompanying the researchers' invitation to participate come not from the physician himself but from his accountant! The committee member seemed oblivious to the probability that patients would perceive this as terribly out of place and as a potential threat to their right of privacy. On the other hand, when one goes through a medical human subjects committee, its members are often not too conversant with or responsive to psychosocial foci of research, and hence, the same delays can occur.

Start-up time may also lengthen considerably when an institutional health setting is involved. The researcher may have to appear before several committees or revise protocols several times to satisfy that setting's administration. The researcher is thereby dependent on the setting's schedule.

The logistics of gathering data usually take longer than is intially planned. Often one must depend on the cooperation of a great many disinterested individuals. As noted earlier, for example, patients may need to be prescreened by nurses, who are not members of the research team and for whom this task is an extra burden. Not surprisingly, then, they do not make such screening a top priority. Too, a forecasted stream of patients may turn out to be a mere trickle.

Scheduling also presents difficulties; for example, interviews are often put off because patients' daily lives intrude. Some of these intrusions are treatment-related (for example, chemotherapy or reactions to it can interfere with the scheduling of an appointment), but many are due to the simple vagaries of existence such as holidays, friends or relatives coming in from out of town, or other things getting in the way. When one recruits through an institutional setting, the patient may suddenly be scheduled for medical tests and may have to cancel or not show up for the research. Data from studies on chronic illness are rarely as clean or clear-cut as those derived from laboratory investigations, and as a consequence, data analyses, too, may take a great deal longer and be more cumbersome than in other kinds of research.

Issues of Sampling and Generalizability

A fourth set of issues that arises when conducting research with the chronically ill and/or institutionalized concerns the sample on which one conducts one's research and the ability to generalize to other populations. Some generalizability restrictions are introduced by the needs of the study in that certain kinds of studies require only certain kinds of patients. Clearly, one is always sampling only individuals identified as having the disease and as being treated for it. Those individuals who have not yet been diagnosed, or those who have dropped out of treatment, virtually always escape the sampling net. Certain kinds of research, such as lengthy interview studies, require patients that are alert and verbal and physically able to participate in the study. Accordingly, patients who are not particularly verbal, not English speaking, not alert, or who are advanced in the illness are often excluded from the research. Any time one is researching a patient group, one is obviously always interviewing survivors. This fact in itself produces bias.

The setting from which one recruits a sample or conducts the research may also introduce biases. Accessing patients through an urban clinic will result in a different sample than will contacting patients through a physician's private practice. Frequently, arbitrary restrictions are introduced by the treatment setting regarding the patients that one can use for research, and these arbitrary restrictions may limit generalizability. One may be restricted to using patients who come to a medical facility on particular days. In one study, patients from particular letters of the alphabet could be used, because only physicians treating those "letters" had agreed to the study; this may also introduce selectivity: A story among Boston researchers, whether apocryphal or not, maintained that a sample heavily drawn from the A's, B's, or C's would be disproportionately Italian, whereas one drawn from the F's, G's, and H's would be more heavily WASP. In addition, typically one has access only to volunteers even when a physician makes available a set of patients, and so all the problems of volunteerism emerge in this self-selection process (Rosenthal & Rosnow, 1969).

A restricted range of the illness itself is almost always included in one's sample. If one recruits from a hospital setting, one may get patients who are somewhat sicker or closer in time to an acute episode than if one recruits from an outpatient practice. Physician or nurse prescreening of patients is likely to eliminate the most ill potential volunteers. Patients themselves self-select according to certain dimensions; for example, patients who are currently free of illness may not want to label themselves as chronically ill and may therefore not participate, and patients who are very ill may not have the energy or stamina to take part in the research. Likewise, psychological adjustment may determine self-selection. Research may be skewed toward those who are poorly adjusted because, when a psychological project is available for participation, some individuals take advantage of the apparent opportunity for psychological help. Alternatively, those who are especially healthy may want to "show off" their well-adjusted state and disproportionately participate. Because one does not have access to the nonvolunteers, it is frequently difficult to ascertain which, if any, of these biases may have been introduced into one's work.

A very important sampling issue involves understanding patients' motives for participating in one's study. A variety of possible motives exists. One common motive is pleasing the physician; that is, if contact with a patient sample is initially made through a letter or verbal contact with a physician, patients may believe, erroneously or not, that the project has the endorsement of the physician. Accordingly, they may see their participation in the project as something that will please him or her. A variant of this motive is that some patients will conclude, when they receive, from their physician, a letter or an invitation to participate, that their physician has particularly selected them to participate in the research. They may, for example, conclude that the physician feels they are a particularly good example of someone who has adjusted well to their situation; hence, they may participate because they want to fulfill the physician's expectations and thereby distort their responses in the direction of those perceived expectations.

A number of patients participate in research for social comparison purposes. Because there is still so little written for patients about the psychosocial aspects of chronic illness, they often know very little about how others react to the condition they have (Wood, Taylor, & Lichtman, 1982). Patients may therefore conclude that participating in a research project will provide them with information about others' responses to illness so that they can learn whether they have adjusted successfully and/or differently than other patients.

Some patients participate in research because they have pathological conditions independent of research, and, as just noted, the psychologically oriented research provides them with a nonthreatening environment in which to express this pathology. We see this as a request for help and accordingly attempt to provide such individuals with referral services to help them explore the problems they are experiencing more thoroughly. Other patients participate because they have developed some pathology as a consequence of their particular illness. They may, for example, have trouble adjusting to the restrictions that the chronic illness imposes on their lives and need to talk these factors out. Again, referrals to therapists with knowledge of the patient's physical problems is advisable. Finally, a great many individuals participate in psychological research projects because they believe that by doing so they will help others facing the same problem later on.

These are only a few of the potential motives that patients have when they agree to participate in research probing these most personal aspects of their lives. Other more idiosyncratic ones may also exist. In any case, the problems presented by such motives are that the resulting data picture may be distorted, and generalizability of findings to other samples accordingly may be limited. The initial contacts with potential patient subjects, then, must be carefully constructed so that they do not inadvertently attract patients with particular motives. Interpretation of patient responses should further be enlightened by knowledge of possible patient motives.

Format of Stimulus Materials

Deciding on the format of the stimulus materials to be used is a crucial element in designing research with the chronically ill. Materials used in past studies run the gamut from open-ended interview protocols to standardized psychological test batteries, each with its own set of problems. The advantages and disadvantages of each should be carefully considered when making a final decision.

Data gathered in open-ended interviews often provide rich insight about the nature of problems that people encounter when facing chronic illness. However, there are potential problems with such methods. Questions are often idiosyncratic to a particular research investigation, making generalization to other investigations or populations difficult. Coding schemes may be ill specified or difficult to use without extensive training, and inferences drawn may be based on qualitative, not quantitative, data. Hence, the information drawn from such methods may be unusable or uninterpretable for other psychologists.

A format that collects closed-ended data also has advantages and disadvantages. Closed-ended data, such as standardized psychological tests (e.g., MMPI) or researcher-prepared questionnaires, are easier to handle and may facilitate the use of appropriate and enlightening statistical analyses. Their forced-choice format may, however, strip the phenomena of the richness provided by open-ended techniques.

In many studies, a mix of the two formats is desirable. This mix provides both the richness and the precision desired for describing and interpreting the phenomena. When the focus of the research is on theory building, the mix might be weighted more heavily toward open-ended data. For more circumscribed theory testing, the more rigorous analyses call for the collection of more closed-ended data.

Problems of Data Collection

Typically, there is less precision in the administration of stimuli and in the collection of outcome measures in studies with the chronically ill than can be the case in the laboratory. This is true first because one has less control over the environment and the conditions of data collection. One may decide to interview patients in their own homes, for example, which vary from each other in innumerable ways. Or, if the study is conducted in a hospital, many individual nurses, working on both day and night shifts, may be involved in the administration of dependent measures. Around-the-clock supervision to insure standardization is usually impossible.

Furthermore, chronic illness interacts with other aspects of the patient's life and hence introduces variability as a function of the patient's background and life situation more than is the case in the laboratory. This variability means that participants do not always understand the questions in the same way. In addition, patients who do not read and write in English very well will have difficulties completing a questionnaire or standardized test that may be part of an interview followup.

A third factor muddying health research is that in some cases the ideal research design may have to be bent to fit the demands of the situation. For example, if an experimental treatment condition is clearly better for patients than the control treatment, medical personnel, patients themselves, and human subjects committees will often agitate to provide as beneficial an experience for control patients. The two conditions may, then, become very similar. Although morally correct, this solution presents methodological and statistical frustrations.

The fact that research on the chronically ill often needs a longitudinal perspective raises certain problems as well. There is the usual attrition in a longitudinal design due to subjects' not being able to continue in the study. These problems are exacerbated when one has a health focus, because patients may deteriorate or die during the course of the research or may recover to a point where they no longer wish to consider themselves as having the disease. They may, too, develop other illnesses that distort the picture of effects from the original chronic condition. This is often the case of older patients who are victims of multiple chronic illnesses.

Another methodological difficulty may arise when researchers choose techniques of data collection that are not second nature to them. Studies in the chronic illness domain frequently involve methodological techniques such as interviewing that are learned by clinicians but not necessarily by researchers. Until researchers become adept in the technique, it may be an uncomfortable situation for researchers and patients alike.

Implementation of Research Findings

The outcome of the research may also create difficulties for the researcher. Typically, a great deal of time must be invested in a project before any products in the form of publications are realized. This may be frustrating to (and dangerous for) a young researcher who sees productivity of laboratory-dwelling colleagues as higher than his or her own. A more important and frustrating consequence can be that the hard-earned results may not have any impact on procedures, even when they point to such changes. Decisions about changes in medical procedures usually involve concerns other than possible psychological benefits to the patient such as medical outcome for the patient, convenience for the staff, or other values held by medical caregivers. Hence, when a strong recommendation for intervention results from psychological investigation, it may not be implemented. Despite these problems, investigating chronic illness does present the researcher with exciting opportunities. Under some circumstances, one's results *will* lead to implementation of a new policy, and there can be few greater rewards than having made a positive difference in the emotional and physical adjustment of patients.

Ethical Issues

Particularly troublesome ethical issues arise when one is conducting research with the chronically ill. Because the subjects are not sophisticated college sophomores and because the research touches personal, enduring aspects of the participant's life, the researcher must be especially cautious. One must be mindful of two main areas of concern: (1) the responsibilities vis-à-vis one's position as researcher, and (2) the possible unintended consequences of the research. We discuss both areas of concerns in turn.

The responsibilities of the researcher include those that are present in other types of research, but some issues are especially critical when studying the chronically ill. These center around privacy, confidentiality, informed consent, and the patient/researcher relationship.

The very nature of research on the chronically ill introduces threats to the patient's privacy at all stages of data collection. It can be considered a violation of privacy simply to get the names of patients from their physicians without the patient's knowledge. This problem can be circumvented by employing staff nurses to go through files, select appropriate research candidates, and mail a cover letter introducing the study. Interested patients may then contact the researchers directly. Possible sample biases resulting from this procedure do, of course, need to be considered.

Next, the research may be expressly directed toward the most private areas of patients' lives; one may probe into their religious preferences, their sexual relationships, their home lives or marriages, and their innermost thoughts and feelings surrounding their illness. The first step to protect the patient's privacy is through informed consent—subjects should be forewarned of the personal nature of the study as well as the specific areas to be probed, to the extent that that is possible. During the course of the research itself, participants may be informed that an upcoming series of questions is particularly personal and that they may wish to decline answering. These guidelines should also apply to the use of medical chart data in that patients' consent should be obtained before chart materials are used.

During and especially after data collection, steps to insure subjects' anonymity and confidentiality become pivotal in protecting their privacy. The usual methods of insuring anonymity through the use of coding schemes are helpful. At the same time, however, this procedure becomes difficult when several different kinds of measures are taken at different time points. Still, only one investigator need have the information identifying each coded set of data. The use of case examples in later written reports must also be judicious in that patients reading through them may stumble across their own cases.

The use of other informants, such as the spouse or the physician, brings special issues of confidentiality. Specifically, each individual should be told that only group-level information about the study will be available and not data on individual cases. For example, in our work on reactions to breast cancer we interviewed both patients and their spouses to attempt to assess the effect of illness on family functioning. In several cases, either patients or their spouses asked what the other had said during the interview. Our rule was not to divulge any confidences one spouse provided to the other, and it was sometimes awkward to maintain this position in the face of persistent pressure to reveal what the other had said. Under some circumstances, the researcher may be privy to information that the patient chooses not to disclose; for example, patient charts may indicate alcoholism, psychological impairment, medications for nervous disorders, or other physical or psychological problems that patients chose not to raise with the researcher. Protecting the confidentiality of the patient data can, then, extend to the patient him or herself. Under other circumstances, the patient may disclose information to the researcher that he or she wants kept from the physician. This desire should be respected. A persistent physician who desires information about individual patients should be reminded of the initial agreement to provide only group information and not details about individual participants.

In terms of informed consent, three major requirements are involved: competence, knowledge, and volition (Kazdin, 1980). All three assume special importance when studying the chronically ill. First, as to competence, the researcher should be aware that the ability to make an informed decision can be threatened when one's subjects are suffering a chronic illness. Illness may produce physical distress that distracts a patient from making a competent decision. It may also produce emotional distress such as a depression that likewise can affect the ability to consider information in a systematic manner. This issue is especially problematic with groups such as children, the elderly, and those suffering some mental impairment. Hence, caution in what research issues are explored and full, clear, and jargon-free informed consent forms are especially important.

Competence, then, leads into the second issue of knowledge. In order to obtain truly informed consent, the informed consent form must detail all procedures and spell out all potential risks to the subject. The researcher may feel pressured to exaggerate the harm that may befall a subject, while nonetheless simultaneously believing that most patients benefit from participating. Because it is obviously important to make all potential risks clear, it is equally valuable to stress these potential benefits, so that potential participants can make a truly knowledgeable decision.

The issue of providing knowledge becomes especially thorny in experiments when treatment effects are unknown; that is, potential risks and benefits are as yet unknown, and one can only guess what they are likely to be. Thus, this uncertainty itself must be mentioned. Even when full knowledge is possible, the subject's knowledge of other treatment conditions may contaminate the research or lead the subject to prefer another group assignment. Withholding particular treatments from subjects is an ethical problem itself, but one that can often be remedied by offering those treatments to control group subjects at the conclusion of the study.

In research on the chronically ill, the most difficult ingredient of informed consent is volition. Even when great pains are taken to represent the research as separate from the medical institution, patients often have difficulty making this distinction, This is especially true when the research is being conducted in an institution such as a hospital, and when the researcher could be seen as having some power or status over the patient. Patients may believe that the quality of their follow-up care could be jeopardized by refusing to participate. These issues are best handled by dealing with them directly. Subjects must also have full assurance that they can withdraw from participation at any time with no penalty of any kind.

We have already discussed the special relationship between researcher and subject that exists in health research. The nature of this relationship adds weight to every ethical issue we highlight in this section. As mentioned earlier, the patient's perception of the researcher's power and status, whether veridical or not, may induce the patient to participate. Once the study is underway, the prestige or importance of the scientific research may make the subject feel that she or he cannot balk at particular questions or procedures (Kelman, 1972). Earlier we listed possible motives for participation that add to the researcher's ethical responsibilities, motives such as a desire for medically relevant information or for therapy. One should be alert to these possible motives and private agendae in order to understand the meaning behind a respondent's veiled queries and to address these with sensitivity, should that be warranted. The special relationship may cause the patient to freely confide in the researcher, sometimes excessively so. The researcher may have to set limits on these disclosures as well as guard carefully the subject's privacy. The special researcher/patient relationship may have a role in producing possible unintended consequences of the research for the patient participant, to which we now turn.

Chief among these concerns is the need to protect the patient from the possibility that the research may exacerbate the patient's physical condition and/or the patient's psychological reactions to that condition. On the issue of physical adjustment, the patient may not be feeling well at the time the research is scheduled and the researcher therefore must weigh the ethical decision of whether participation would be too draining for the subject against the researcher's desire for standardized timing of procedures or the ability to obtain the data at all. Another potential problem is the possibility that the research will lead the patient to question or doubt some aspect of medical treatment and thereby drop out of treatment, leading to worsened current health or prognosis. For example, asking questions about reactions to a particular noxious therapy (e.g., chemotherapy for cancer) may lead patients currently in the midst of that therapy to draw conclusions regarding a cause–effect relationship about possible future ill effects. Wishing to avoid unpleasant future side effects, they might choose to discontinue the therapy. It is easy to overstate such risks, and in fact such reactions may be unusual. Nonetheless, the possibility should be anticipated by the researcher.

One must consider, too, the possibility that the research intervention can create a psychological impact on the patient that can aggravate the physical course of illness. For example, a recent study that taught cardiopulmonary resuscitation to the families of heart attack victims revealed that the long-term impact of such training was in *increase* anxiety and depression, not only in family members but in patients as well. Because these emotional conditions can aggravate heart conditions, the need to design an offsetting intervention was substantial (Guzy, Taylor, Dracup, & Barry, 1982).

Protecting the patient's psychological well-being is often more difficult than protecting physical well-being. The research may subject patients to stresses that they would not face otherwise or may exacerbate already existing stressors. In our interviews with breast cancer patients, for example, we asked about patients' theories regarding what caused their cancer and about the changes they had made in their lives. In the process, we may have implied some possible causes that a subject had not considered previously. Another possibility is that some questions may have awakened a realization of a connection between a woman's theory and a particular life change. If a patient thinks that being overweight has caused her cancer, for example, the question as to whether she has made any changes in her dietary or exercise habits may arouse anxiety or guilt. We took steps to prevent such occurrences; we asked questions about theories and those concerning life changes in separate sections of the protocol, and we also gave a full debriefing that indicated that very few causes of cancer are known with certainty.

More generally, untoward consequences may occur due to the often distressing nature of health research. Researchers often ask patients to discuss painful details of their lives. In the process they may relive earlier periods of fright and depression, or questions may reawaken fears that patients had been trying to put behind them. Long after the researcher has packed away his or her protocol kit and gone home, the respondent may be reflecting on issues rekindled during the interview. That the patient is part of a social system makes these concerns especially keen. The research participation may bring about new soul searching, a reevaluation of relationships, and more open disclosure between the patient and others (cf., Rubin & Mitchell, 1976). This can, of course, have beneficial effects, but researchers should always be mindful of the potential impact of their probing.

The implicit bargain between researcher and respondent dictates that the researcher will provide all subjects with some report of the study's findings. There, too, one must be cautious. When one provides patients with general summary statements about the findings of the research, it is important to consider the impact these results may have on the patients themselves. A patient will be able to see where he or she falls on a particular answer and may be able to use the statistical information to infer, correctly or incorrectly, information about physical or psychological status.

Finally, another potential consequence the researcher should protect against is possible damage to the relationship between the patient and the medical professional. Frequently, for example, patients will use research as an opportunity to vent their frustrations against the medical establishment, including particular physicians or medical care givers with whom they have had unpleasant experiences. By concurring with a patient's negative assessment of his or her physician, one may contribute to the deterioration of the relationship. A noncommittal response may be better, and, indeed, continued cooperation from the professional may depend on it.

We have purposely overstated the case for the protection of the participant and overestimated the likelihood that participation in a research project will harm the patient. In reality, the probability that cooperation with research psychologists will significantly stress the patient is small. Compared with the stress that the illness itself may bring, the strain of participation in an interview and/or questionnaire study is not likely to be significant. The researcher can generally be guided by his or her common sense and compassion and restructure the research session when the patient appears distressed.

CONCLUSION

We have summarized what we see as the main conceptual and methodological decisions and issues facing the psychologist doing research on the chronically ill. Before closing, some comments on practical issues surrounding this kind of research should be made. The study of chronic illness continues to be an area of priority and significance on the national level. At times when other resources for psychological investigation are shrinking, the opportunities for research on chronic illness have been largely maintained. Not only are resources generally more available for studying these kinds of problems than others, but receptivity within the medical establishment to psychological and social foci on chronic illness is increasing. As the role of psychological factors in both the etiology and the successful treatment of chronic illness has become apparent, the willingness of medical people to pay attention to psychological factors has clearly increased (Taylor, 1978, 1983).

One remaining worry is that our lengthy discourse on the problems that arise when studying the chronically ill has sent any initially interested researchers scurrying to the laboratory in fear. Although we set out to discuss these issues frankly, we would be remiss if we did not conclude with some brief attention to the benefits of researching the chronically ill. In the introduction to this chapter we discussed the significance of chronic illness to our society. Here we emphasize how rewarding it can be to find that theoretically meaty work can be done on issues of such real-world importance. The data can often be surprisingly rich in their theoretical implications.

One caveat is warranted: Research on chronic illness is often hard on the researcher. It can be depressing and emotionally draining to deal with people who are chronically ill and/or dying. The research is not easily put out of one's mind when one returns home. However, there are personal rewards as well; it can be uplifting to have contact with strong, courageous people. The writing of this chapter has prompted its authors to talk extensively about the lessons that have been learned from doing research on the chronically ill. We have concurred that, in the process of interviewing people who have had a bout with a life-threatening disorder, and who rearranged and managed their lives so as to accommodate to these problems, we have learned important lessons in how to manage the problems that we confront in our own lives. Research with the chronically ill, then, provides the researcher with a unique opportunity not only to study issues of increasing significance in the population but issues that are likely to be personally revealing and important as well.

ACKNOWLEDGMENTS

Preparation of this chapter was supported by a grant from N.I.M.H. (MH 34167) to the second author and by a Research Scientist Development Award (MH 00311) to the second author. The helpful comments of John Michela on an earlier version of the chapter are gratefully acknowledged.

REFERENCES

Becker, M. H. (1976). Sociobehavioral determinants of compliance. In D. L. Sackett & R. B. Haynes (Eds.), *Compliance with therapeutic regimens.* Baltimore: Johns Hopkins University Press.

Bell, R. Q. (1953). Convergence: An accelerated longitudinal approach. *Child Development, 24,* 145–152.

Bowlby, J. (1961). Processes of mourning. *The International Journal of Psychoanalysis, 42,* 317–340.

Burish, T. G., & Lyles, J. N. (1979). Effectiveness of relaxation training in reducing the aversiveness of chemotherapy in the treatment of cancer. *Journal of Behavior Therapy and Experimental Psychiatry, 10,* 357–361.

Burish, T. G., & Lyles, J. N. (1981). Effectiveness of relaxation training in reducing adverse reactions to cancer chemotherapy. *Journal of Behavioral Medicine, 4,* 65–78.

Cannell, C. F., & Kahn, R. L. (1968). Interviewing. In G. Lindzey & E. Aronson (Eds.), *The handbook of social psychology.* Reading, MA: Addison–Wesley.

Cohen, S., Glass, D. C., & Phillips, S. (1979). Environment and health. In H. E. Freeman, S. Levine, & L. G. Reeder (Eds.), *Handbook of medical sociology* (3rd ed.) Englewood Cliffs, NJ: Prentice–Hall.

Cook, T. D., & Campbell, D. T. (1979). *Quasi-experimentation: Design and analysis issues for field settings.* Chicago: Rand McNally.

Croog, S. H., & Levine, S. (1977). *The heart patient recovers.* New York: Human Sciences.

Dahlberg, L. C., & Jaffee, J. (1977). *Stroke.* New York: Norton.

Davis, M. S. (1968). Variations in patients' compliance with doctors' advice: An empirical analysis of patterns of communication. *American Journal of Public Health, 58,* 274–288.

Dembroski, T. M., Weiss, S. M., Sheilds, J. L., Haynes, S. G., & Feinleib, M. (1978). *Coronary-prone behavior.* New York: Springer–Verlag.

Dracup, K., Guzy, P. M., Taylor, S. E., & Barry, J. (in press). Consequences of cardiopulmonary resuscitation training for family members of high-risk cardiac patients. *Archives of Internal Medicine.*

Egbert, L. D., Battit, G. E., Welch, C. E., & Bartlett, M. K. (1964). Reduction of postoperative pain by encouragement and instruction of patients. *New England Journal of Medicine, 270,* 825.

Fisher, S., & Cleveland, S. E. (1958). *Body image and personality.* Princeton, NJ: Van Nostrand.

Gartner, A., & Reissman, F. (1976). Health care in a technological age. In *Self-help and health.* New York: New Human Services Institute, 17-45.

Gates, C. C. (1975). *Emotional impact of breast cancer.* Unpublished manuscript. Boston: Peter Bent Brigham Hospital.

Graham, S., & Reeder, L. G. (1979). Social epidemiology of chronic illness. In H. E. Freeman, S. Levine, & L. G. Reeder (Eds.), *Handbook of medical sociology* (3rd ed.) Englewood Cliffs, NJ: Prentice–Hall.

Grandstaff, N. W. (1976). The impact of breast cancer on the family. *Frontiers in Radiation Therapy Oncology, 11,* 146–156.

Gunther, M. S. (1969). Emotional aspects. In D. Ruge (Ed.), *Spinal cord injuries.* Springfield, MA: Charles C. Thomas.

Guttman, L. (1976). *Spinal cord injuries: Comprehensive management and research* (2nd ed.) Oxford: Blackwell Scientific Publications.

Guzy, P. M., Taylor, S. E., Dracup, K., & Barry, J. (1982). *Consequences of CPR training for families of cardiac patients.* Unpublished manuscript. University of California, Los Angeles.

Hackett, T. P., & Cassem, N. H. (1969). Factors contributing to delay in responding to the signs and symptoms of acute myocardial infarction. *American Journal of Cardiology, 24,* 651–658.

Johnson, J. E., & Leventhal, H. (1974). Effects of accurate expectations and behavioral instructions on reactions during a noxious medical examination. *Journal of Personality and Social Psychology, 29,* 710–718.

Kazdin, A. E. (1980). *Research design in clinical psychology.* New York: Harper & Row.

Kelman, H. C. (1972). The rights of the subject in social research: An analysis in terms of relative power and legitimacy. *American Psychologist, 27,* 989–1016.

Klinger, E. (1975). Consequences of commitment to and disengagement from incentives. *Psychological Review, 82,* 1–25.

Klinger, E. (1977). *Meaning and void: Inner experience and the incentives in people's lives.* Minneapolis: University of Minnesota Press.

Kubler–Ross, E. (1969). *On death and dying.* New York: MacMillan.

Langer, E. J., Janis, I. L., & Wolfer, J. A. (1975). Reduction of psychological stress in surgical patients. *Journal of Experimental Social Psychology, 11,* 155–165.

Langer, E. J., & Rodin, J. (1976). The effects of choice and enhanced personal responsibility for the aged: A field experiment in an institutional setting. *Journal of Personality and Social Psychology, 34,* 191–198.

Lazarus, R. S. (1978). A strategy for research on psychological and social factors in hypertension. *Journal of Human Stress, 4,* 35–40.

Leventhal, H. (1975). The consequences of depersonalization during illness and treatment: An information-processing model. In J. Howard & A. Strauss (Eds.), *Humanizing health care.* New York: Wiley.

Lichtman, R. R. (1982). *Close relationships after breast cancer.* Unpublished doctoral dissertation, University of California, Los Angeles.

Lichtman, R. R., Taylor, S. E., Wood, J. V., Bluming, A. Z., Doski, G. M., & Leibowitz, R. L. (in press). Relations with children after breast cancer: The mother-daughter relationship at risk. *Journal of Psychosocial Oncology.*

Lichtman, R. R., Wood, J. V., & Taylor, S.E. (1982, August). *Close relationships after breast cancer.* Presented at the American Psychological Association Annual Meeting, Washington, D.C.

Lindemann, E. (1941). Observations on psychiatric sequelae to surgical operations in women. *American Journal of Psychiatry, 98,* 132–137.

Litman, T. J. (1974). The family as a basic unit in health and medical care: A socio-behavioral overview. *Social Science and Medicine, 8,* 495–519.

Michela, J. L. *Perceived changes in marital relationships following myocardial infarction.* Unpublished doctoral dissertation. University of California, Los Angeles.

Quint, J. (1963). The impact of mastectomy. *American Journal of Nursing, 63,* 88.

Ray, C. (1980). Psychological aspects of early breast cancer and its treatment. In S. Rachman (Ed.), *Contributions to medical psychology* (Vol. 2). New York: Pergamon Press.

Rosenthal, R., & Rosnow, R. L. (Eds.) (1969). *Artifact in behavioral research.* New York: Academic Press.

Rubin, Z., & Mitchell, C. (1976). Couples research as couples counseling: Some unintended effects of studying close relationships. *American Psychologist, 31,* 17–25.

Schulz, R., & Aderman, D. (1974). Clinical research and the stages of dying. *Omega, 5,* 137–143.

Schwab, J. J., & Hameling, J. (1968). Body image and medical illness. *Psychosomatic Medicine, 30,* 51–71.

Shontz, F. (1975). *The psychological aspects of physical illness and disability.* New York: MacMillan.

Silver, R. L., & Wortman, C. B. (1980a). Coping with undesirable life events. In J. Garber & M. E. P. Seligman (Eds.), *Human helplessness: Theory and applications.* New York: Academic Press.

Silver, R. L., & Wortman, C. B. (1980b, September). *Expectations of control and coping with permanent paralysis.* Paper presented at the American Psychological Association Annual Meeting, Montreal.

Taylor, S. E. (1978). A developing role for social psychology in medicine and medical practice. *Personality and Social Psychology Bulletin, 4,* 515–523.

Taylor, S. E. (1979). Hospital patient behavior: Helplessness, reactance, or control? *Journal of Social Issues, 35,* 156–184.

Taylor, S. E, (1983). The developing field of health psychology. In A. Baum, S. E. Taylor, & J. Singer (Eds.), *Handbook of Psychology and Health* (Vol. 4). Hillsdale, NJ.: Lawrence Erlbaum Associates.

Taylor, S. E., Lichtman, R. R., & Wood, J. V. (1984a). Attributions, beliefs about control, and adjustment to breast cancer. *Journal of Personality and Social Psychology, 46,* 489–502.

Taylor, S. E., Lichtman, R. R., & Wood, J. V. (1984b). Compliance with chemotherapy among breast cancer patients. *Health Psychology, 3,* 553–562.

Thomas, S. G. (1978). Breast cancer: The psychosocial issues. *Cancer Nursing, 1,* 53–60.

Turk, D. C. (1979). Factors influencing the adaptive process with chronic illness: Implications for intervention. In I. Sarason & C. Spielberger (Eds.), *Stress and anxiety* (Vol. 6). Washington, DC: Hemisphere.

Watson, D., & Kendall, P. C. (1983). Methodological issues in research on coping with chronic disease. In T. G. Burish & L. A. Bradley (Eds.), *Coping with chronic disease.* New York: Academic Press.

Weick, K. E. (1968). Systematic observational methods. In G. Lindzey & E. Aronson (Eds.), *The handbook of social psychology.* Reading, MA: Addison–Wesley.

Wellisch, D. K. (1979). Adolescent acting out when a parent has cancer. *International Journal of Family Therapy, 1,* 230–241.

Wellisch, D. K. (1981). Intervention with the cancer patient. In C. K. Prokop & L. A. Bradley (Eds.), *Medical psychology: Contributions to behavioral medicine.* New York: Academic Press.

Wellisch, D. K., Jamison, K. R., & Pasnau, R. O. (1978). Psychosocial aspects of mastectomy: II. The man's perspective. *American Journal of Psychiatry, 135,* 543–546.

Wood, J. V., Taylor, S. E., & Lichtman, R. R. (1982). Social comparison processes in serious illness. Paper presented at the *American Psychological Association Annual Meeting,* Washington, DC.

Wortman, C. B., & Dunkel–Schetter, C. (1979). Interpersonal relationships and cancer: A theoretical analysis. *The Journal of Social Issues, 35,* 120–155.

Zborowski, M. (1958). Cultural components in responses to pain. In E. G. Jaco (Ed.), *Patients, physicians and illness* (1st ed.) Glencoe, IL: Free Press.

Zola, I. K. Culture and symptoms: (1966). An analysis of patients' presenting complaints. *American Sociological Review, 31,* 615–630.

3 Working with Victims: Changes in the Researcher's Assumptive World

Ronnie Janoff-Bulman
Christine Timko
University of Massachusetts, Amherst

Conducting research with victimized populations has a major psychological impact on one's life. This impact is usually far from expected and is one for which the researcher is generally unprepared. The research experiences of social psychologists commonly involve studies with populations (often college students) with whom there is little reason to feel discomfort. We are able to establish ourselves as "knowers" in the research enterprise, shaping our hypotheses and narrowing the range of experimental responses. There is ordinarily little room for experimental surprises and little possibility of being profoundly affected by our research endeavor. The major effect of our research in such cases is that of feeling positive or negative about the support (or lack thereof) of our experimental hypotheses. Such a process is not to be belittled, for it represents the normal course of scientific investigation. Its significance in the present case is in presenting a backdrop against which to compare the impact of research with victims, an enterprise that has an impact reaching far beyond that of our usual experience.

It becomes obvious early in one's research with victims that despite our attempts at grand theorizing and hypothesizing, we, the researchers, are the learners, and not the knowers. Although hypothesis testing remains a central part of the research process, much more is simultaneously being learned; people's experiences are being processed, new questions are being raised, fresh insights are being presented. There is a belief that not simply numbers will support or fail to support a theory, but that familiarity with the victims' experiences will provide the more important personal confirmation and validation of one's theoretical models. The unwittingly "arrogant" position as knower is impossible to maintain in the face of individuals who are coping with events that are troublesome for most of us to even think about seriously. The respondents have lived through (or are living through) the very events that we try to avoid thinking about in relation to ourselves, the very events that we would find frightening were we to truly believe they would happen to us. The experiences and reactions of victims force the researcher to question his or her basic suppositions about the operation of the world and one's place in it. The psychological impact is extraordinary, going far beyond the realm of one's academic hypotheses about a phenomenon, to the realm of one's most basic personal assumptions. The research enterprise is alternatively depressing, anxiety provoking, humbling, and inspiring; it is a course marked by highs and lows and strong emotional upheavals. One's life is dramatically affected, for the ways in which the researcher views the world and him or herself change. This chapter represents an attempt to discuss these changes in the researcher's "assumptive world." Having conducted intensive interviews with several different victim populations, including paralyzed accident victims, rape victims, and cancer victims, we have gone through personal metamorphoses far greater than expected when embarking on the research enterprise.

OUR ASSUMPTIVE WORLD

The greatest impact of working with victims is felt at the level of one's basic assumptions about the operation of the world. Several psychologists have addressed the issue of the existence and importance of basic assumptions or conceptual systems in guiding our adjustment to our environment. Parkes (1975), for example, developed the phrase "assumptive world" to represent:

> the individual's view of reality as he believes it to be, i.e., a strongly held set of assumptions about the world and the self which is confidently maintained and used as a means of recognizing, planning and acting—Assumptions such as these are learned and confirmed by the experience of many years. They enable me to make correct predictions about the world and to order my own behavior accordingly. (p. 132)

Parkes' view of the assumptive world parallels Bowlby's (1969) conception of "world models," which Bowlby regards as working models of the environment and oneself that enable an individual to plan, set goals, and function effectively. For Parkes (1971), the assumptive world "is the only world we know and it includes everything we know or think we know" (p. 103). Thus Parkes does not distinguish different conceptual levels of our assumptive world; a general conception that the world is predictable is not recognized as distinct from the more narrow (albeit related) assumption that "the chair I sit on will not break."

The existence of such distinctions is apparent, however, in the work of Epstein (1973, 1979, 1980), who also argues that people require a complex conceptual system in order to direct their behavior. According to Epstein (1980):

The human mind is so constituted that it tends to organize experience into conceptual systems. Human brains make connections between events, and, having made connections, they connect the connections, and so on, until they have developed an organized system of higher and lower order constructs that is both differentiated and integrated. Whether we like it or not, each of us, because he has a human brain, forms a theory of reality that brings order into what otherwise would be a chaotic world of experience. We need a theory to make sense out of the world, just as a scientist needs a theory to make sense out of the limited body of information he/she wishes to understand . . . An individual's overall theory of reality includes sub-theories of what the individual is like (a self-theory), of what the world is like (a world-theory), and of how the two interact with each other. (pp. 33–34)

Epstein's "theory of reality" is organized hierarchically into minor and major postulates. Minor postulates represent narrow generalizations that are derived directly from experience, and these minor postulates are organized into major postulates, which are themselves organized into even broader, higher order postulates. An example provided by Epstein (1980, p. 35) of the hierarchy in an individual's self-theory is the following: "I am a good ping-pong player" (a lower order postulate), "I am a good athlete" (a higher order postulate), "I am a worthy person" (a much higher order postulate). Certainly, invalidation of one's major postulates has far greater consequences than invalidation of one's minor postulates. Yet, as Epstein (1980) notes, the major postulates are very broad generalizations and thus, unlike the more narrow, minor postulates, are further removed from the direct test of experience and therefore more difficult to invalidate.

The "structures of meaning" discussed by Peter Marris, an English sociologist, seem to be similar to Epstein's notion of major postulates. According to Marris (1975), in order to effectively function in a changing environment, we conserve the:

fundamental structure of meaning each of us has grown up to . . . The continuing viability of this structure of meaning, in the face of new kinds of experience, depends on whether we can formulate its principles in terms abstract enough to apply to any event we encounter; or, alternatively, on whether we can ignore or prevent experiences which could not be comprehended in terms of it (experiences where our expectations would be repeatedly and bewilderingly unfulfilled). The first is an extension of learning, the second a constriction of experience: both seek to make life continuously intelligible. (pp. 19–20)

All the terms mentioned here—*assumptive world, world model, theory of reality, structure of meaning*—appear to refer to the same conceptual system that we have developed over time in order to provide us with viable expectations about ourselves and the world so that we may function effectively. For the purposes of this chapter, the term *assumptive world* is used to represent this conceptual system.

Changing Our Assumptive World

The similarity between the notion of "assumptive world" and that of Kuhn's (1962) "paradigm" is probably apparent to the reader. Just as a paradigm provides a framework within which to conduct "normal science," the assumptive world provides the framework within which to conduct normal (i.e., day-to-day) living. According to Kuhn (1962), a paradigm is a set of beliefs (p. 4), a map (p. 108), an organizing principle (p. 120), and a way of seeing (pp. 117–121; see Masterman, 1970), which are all perspectives consistent with an assumptive world. It is thus instructive to consider Kuhn's perspective on a paradigm shift and the circumstances that engender a change in one's very basic working assumptions.

Whereas scientific activity is usually characterized by "normal science," in which there is general acceptance of a paradigm, occasionally "particularly pressing" anomalies appear that lead to crises. The response to a crisis of this sort is a scientific revolution, in which a new paradigm is embraced and substituted for the old. Although Kuhn is not explicit regarding the conditions of these anomalies, his book is rich with historical examples. Kuhn (1962) does suggest that such a pressing anomaly might "clearly call into question explicit and fundamental generalizations of the paradigm . . . Or an anomaly without apparent fundamental import may evoke crisis if the applications that it inhibits have a particular practical importance" (p. 82). It is essential to note that not all anomalies result in abandonment of a paradigm. Many anomalies are eventually assimilated or bring about relatively minor adjustments in one's assumptions, or paradigms, in a manner paralleling the Piagetian acquisition of knowledge via assimilation and accommodation. Thus, for Kuhn, awareness of anomaly is necessary for scientific discovery, but anomalies need not always lead to crises. In noncrisis situations, there is extended exploration of the area of anomaly, and such exploration is terminated when the paradigm theory, according to Kuhn, has been adjusted "so that the anomalous has become the expected" (p. 53); this involves an "additive adjustment of theory" rather than an entire shift in theory. In these cases, unlike those engendering crisis, the paradigm theory itself has not "been pushed too far." When, however, a crisis occurs, Masterman (1970) states: "the paradigm itself goes bad on you, it is stretched too far, producing conceptual inconsistency, absurdity, misexpectation, disorder, complexity and confusion" (p. 83).

In the scientific realm, then, a shift in paradigm seems to come about when the old paradigm can simply no longer account for the data of one's scientific experience; so, too, one's "assumptive world" changes when it can no longer account for the data of one's life experiences. This process of change is accompanied by considerable stress and anxiety (cf. Epstein, 1979; Horowitz, 1979), resembling a Kuhnian state of crisis. Perhaps the most common bases for changes in one's assumptive world are life crises that render one's old assumptions obsolete. Parkes (1971, 1975) discusses at length such "psychosocial transitions." He writes:

> Among the various categories of events which are often classed as 'stressful' are those major changes in the life space which give rise to the need for a person to give up one set of assumptions about the world and to develop fresh ones . . . Relocation of urban slum dwellers, amputation of a limb and bereavement by death are examples of psychosocial transitions which have been systematically compared . . . psychosocial transitions are often turning points in life and adjustment. (1975, p. 131)

Psychosocial transitions do not include, according to Parkes (1975), maturational changes such as developing in size or appearance, for these transitions occur gradually and thereby involve barely (if at all) recognized changes. Rather, psychosocial transitions generally are "lasting in their effects," "take place over a relatively short period of time," and "affect large areas of the assumptive world" (Parkes, 1975, p. 103). Such events, involving dramatic loss or life changes, will lead one to question old assumptions and develop new ones (see also Horowitz, 1979). "Grief work" following loss, for example, involves a thorough review of old assumptions and a restructuring of one's assumptive world (Parkes, 1975; see also Marris, 1975).

A major personal life crisis need not be the only road to changes in assumptions, however, as other routes to change are available. The process of therapy can readily be regarded as a process of becoming aware of and then reshaping one's old assumptions (cf. Parkes, 1975). Further, there may be situations in one's life when anomalies become readily apparent and when the cumulative effect of such anomalies is too great to ignore. For us, such a situation arose through our research with victims. Ordinarily, we might choose to ignore (or at least not attend to) anomalies, those events that cannot be easily assimilated or explained on the basis of our theories of reality. We certainly are unlikely to seek out further, similar anomalies in light of the anxiety that is apt to be engendered. Yet, when we conduct research, we are involved in an enterprise with a life of its own, one that we are motivated to complete and see through to the end, and it is this great desire that literally forced us, despite great discomfort, to confront an accumulation of instances that could not be explained within the framework of our individual assumptive worlds. As researchers in the area of victimization, we experienced changes in our theories of reality, even though we did not directly experience a psychosocial transition of the sort discussed by Parkes (1971, 1975). No doubt the changes undergone by those experiencing psychosocial transitions are more sweeping and far reaching, but we too experienced a change in important aspects of our assumptive worlds. Parkes (1971) notes that at times:

> some change in the life space may cause me to 'question an assumption'; to objectify the assumption and examine it much as one might question a witness in a

court of law. Such examinations are painful because of the threat which they represent to the established assumptive world. (p. 105)

Conducting research with victims represented such an experience that led us to objectify our assumptions and question their viability in the face of the evidence we were confronting. In the end, we found that our assumptive worlds had to change.

The Assumptions of Invulnerability and Meaningfulness

In examining the aspects of our assumptive world that changed as a result of conducting research with victims, it is important to note that this assumptive world is not necessarily readily accessible. In fact, the very nature of our theories of reality is such that we operate on the basis of these assumptions constantly, even though we are not generally aware of these assumptions. Epstein (1980) believes one's theory of reality is "not a theory that a person is normally aware of and can describe" (p. 35); the theory is implicit, not explicit, and most individuals would be unable to report on their personal theories if asked to do so. Parkes (1971), too, contends that there are areas in one's assumptive world that are "relatively inaccessible to introspection." It is not a simple task to describe the makeup of one's assumptive world, because to a large measure such assumptions or theories must be inferred from one's actions and behavior. For Epstein (1979), emotions are the key clues to theories of reality: "Whenever an emotion occurs, it can be assumed that a postulate of significance to an individual's self-system [theory of reality] has been implicated" (p. 49).

Thus, an understanding of one's assumptions involves a process of inference and reconstruction. That we at times "question an assumption" and thereby "objectify it" (Parkes, 1971) suggests that some event or series of events may invoke an examination of assumptions, perhaps by making us feel very uncomfortable and anxious emotionally, or perhaps by forcing us to confront a situation that we truly do not want to believe. In such instances we are led to consider why we feel uncomfortable or don't wish to believe what we are seeing, and it is in these instances that we can most readily reconstruct particular aspects of our assumptive world. Working with victims led us to reconstruct aspects of our assumptive world, for we were extremely uncomfortable with what we saw and did not want to believe what was becoming increasingly evident—that truly innocent victims were suffering tremendously.

In order to fully explain what changes may be brought about by researching victimization, it is helpful to briefly discuss the changes in self- and world views that are brought about by victimization itself (for a more in-depth treatment of this topic, see Janoff-Bulman & Frieze, 1983). Researchers who have described the psychological reactions of victims to their misfortune have pointed out that a primary response is the loss of a perception of invulnerability (Bard & Sangrey, 1979; Janoff-Bulman & Frieze, 1983; Janoff–Bulman & Lang–Gunn, in press; Lifton & Olson, 1976; Notman & Nadelson, 1976; Perloff, 1983; Weisman, 1979; Wolfenstein, 1957; Wortman & Dunkel–Schetter, 1979). As Wolfenstein (1957) states, a victim is likely to experience a sense of ''helplessness against overpowering forces . . . [and] apprehension that anything may now happen to him. He feels vulnerable'' (p. 159). It appears that, in the absence of personal victimization, the assumption of invulnerability is a very basic assumption, reflecting our belief in a relatively safe and secure world in which one can live free from misfortune. Thus, although we all acknowledge that bad things happen in this world, we simultaneously assume that bad things are not going to happen to us. Experimental evidence for the proposition that people maintain an assumption of personal invulnerability in their everyday life was found in a study by Janoff–Bulman, Madden, and Timko (1980). In this study, college students estimated the extent to which a series of negative events (including cancer, mugging, senility, car accident) was likely to happen to them and the extent to which the same negative events were likely to happen to ''the average person your age.'' Respondents consistently rated their own vulnerability to misfortune as significantly lower than that of others. Similar experimental findings have been obtained by Weinstein (1980; Weinstein & Lachendro, 1982), who has demonstrated that people have a tendency to be unrealistically optimistic about future life events, underestimating the probability of negative events happening to them and overestimating the probability of positive events.

Victims experience a change in their beliefs regarding personal vulnerability; misfortune has happened to them, and thus they are no longer able to function on the assumption that ''It can't happen to me.'' Victimization shatters not only the assumption of invulnerability, but the related assumption that events in the world ''make sense'' (Janoff-Bulman & Frieze, 1983; Silver, Boon, & Stones, 1983; Silver & Wortman, 1980; Taylor, 1983). The assumption of invulnerability rests, at least in part, on the belief that the world is comprehensible and orderly—that we know when and why certain events will happen. In order to preserve assumptions of meaningfulness and predictability, we construct certain theories or ''social laws'' of human events. Thus, in the case of misfortune, we believe that we can control personally relevant outcomes (cf. Seligman, 1975), and in our day-to-day existence we frequently operate on the basis of an ''illusion of control'' (Jenkins & Ward, 1965; Langer, 1975; Wortman, 1976). We further believe, perhaps following an early understanding of parental punishment, that if we are good people we will be protected from misfortune, an assumption discussed at length by Lerner (1980) as the ''just world theory.'' The world as we experience it is meaningful to the extent that events and outcomes can be accounted for by our theories of reality; it can make sense only within the context of what we believe and assume to be true. When we confront misfortune, and its ''distribution'' does not seem to ''fit'' our personally constructed ''social laws'' (e.g., justice, control), the event fails to make sense. Thus as Janoff–Bulman and Frieze (1983) write, ''Victims often feel a total lack of comprehension regarding the why's and wherefore's of their misfortune. Particularly if they regard themselves as decent people who take good care of themselves and are appropriately cautious, they are apt to find themselves at a loss to explain why they were victimized.'' (p. 6).

Changes in the victim's assumptive world are no doubt far-reaching and extensive; victimization would certainly fall within the boundaries of Parkes' (1971, 1975) ''psychosocial transition.'' What of the observer of the victims of misfortune? What of the researcher who is conducting a study with individuals who have been victimized? As already discussed, as researchers, we experienced changes in our assumptive world; these changes were surely less extensive than those undergone by actual victims yet, nevertheless, were psychologically unnerving and disturbing.

The most immediate major postulate that we were forced to objectify and examine was our own everyday assumption of invulnerability. This assumption was so very basic for us that we never realized the extent to which we operated on it on a day-to-day basis. In fact, prior to our research we might have described it as a Pollyanna perspective and certainly not seriously entertained by a modern individual. Although the experimental results already cited point to the existence of an illusion of invulnerability, the reality of this assumption for us was not apparent until we began to work with victims. We soon realized how much we had assumed ''It can't happen to us.'' When confronting our assumptive world, it was difficult to ascertain where such an assumption existed in our complex framework of theories. It became quite clear, however, that the assumption of invulnerability did not exist in an assumptive vacuum, but rather that it soon called into question many related postulates. Although the realization that confronted us was ''Oh no, it can happen to me,'' this forced us to grapple with many related issues, particularly those revolving around questions of meaningfulness. As mentioned earlier, one's assumptive world must be inferred and reconstructed, and thus it is not easy—or perhaps even possible—to construct an accurate picture of one's network of assumptions. Nevertheless, based on our own experiences with victims, it soon became clear that our sense of personal invulnerability was being threatened and with it our perceptions of a meaningful and predictable world.

The Process of Change in Working with Victims

Much of the social psychological literature on victimization has attempted to address the question of how others react to victims. In general, there appears to be a consensus that blaming the victim is a common reaction to innocent victims, and it is not difficult to recognize that such an attributional position is consistent with an attempt to maintain a belief in personal invulnerabilty. After all, if a misfortune was the fault of the victim, then the event was not random and is unlikely to happen to anyone who is distinguishable from the victim. Lerner's (1980) work on the just world hypothesis explains victim derogation by pointing to a need people have to believe that the world is just, that people get what they deserve and deserve what they get. Lerner asserts that there are two ways in which we can fault the victim. We can refer to the victim's behavior and thereby see the victimization as following directly from actions; if we are unable to point to behavior, we derogate the victim's character. In this way, according to Lerner, we are able to maintain a belief in a just world. Additionally, using Lerner's formulation, we are able to maintain a belief in a world in which we are essentially invulnerable, for we can either avoid the "unfortunate" behaviors of the victim or we can regard ourselves as better, more worthy people who are undeserving of "punishment." Other social psychological formulations provide further support for our beliefs in safety and security. Walster (1966) has argued that we blame victims so as to maintain a belief in a controllable (rather than a just) world. A controllable world is also one in which we can maintain an illusion of invulnerability.

One extremely salient aspect of conducting research with victims is that these theories regarding observers' reactions to victims begin to seem very real. They are no longer textbook theories; rather, they come to life. Perhaps the initial reaction to working with victimized populations is to try to establish dissimilarities between oneself and the victims, thereby distinguishing the self from those who are suffering. As researchers, we may attempt to see the victims as responsible, at least in part, by attributing the misfortune to their behaviors or their character; alternatively, we may emphasize superficial differences between ourselves and the respondents, differences such as age, gender, or appearance (cf. Weinstein, 1980). This may seem to be a sad commentary, but in light of our very basic assumption of safety and security, it should be less unthinkable. Further, this attempt to locate responsibility in the victims does not occur in the absence of a sense of deep concern and sympathy for the respondents. Instead, it appears to be somewhat of an automatic reaction, one tied very closely to our need to understand and make sense of the victimization. There is an intense need to know why the negative event happened, and the more similar the victim is to oneself, the greater the apparent need to know. In her initial study with victims, the first author interviewed individuals who had been paralyzed in freak accidents. Not only were the respondents similar in age to the researcher, but many had been victimized while engaging in activities commonly engaged in by the researcher (and probably most people)—activities such as diving into a pool or riding in an automobile. In such cases, the need to know why the accident happened to these people was particularly acute, as was the initial attempt to center responsibility on the victims themselves.

Private theories as to how these negative outcomes could have occurred were entertained and matched against each case. Was the person diving unfamiliar with how to dive, or was the individual too daring? Was the passenger in the vehicle driving with someone he or she knew was reckless, was the driver drunk, was the passenger encouraging high speeds? Were these accident victims basically careless, irresponsible, uncaring individuals? In retrospect, all these possibilities strike us as peculiar, reflecting a particularly just, controllable view of the world. Nevertheless, the theories were entertained in an attempt to maintain a belief in personal invulnerability; there had to be something to account for what happened to these people, or major assumptions about the world would have to be questioned. As we learned, this questioning would come in time.

The attempt to locate fault in the victim, or at least to explain the event in a way that could make the researcher immune, may be reminiscent of a reaction common to people who learn of unfortunate and potentially threatening news. The middle-aged man who learns that a heart attack has killed someone his age, or the woman who hears of another woman's mastectomy is very apt to respond with, "What happened?" Although this question seems benign and perhaps is loaded with concern, it is also hoped that the answer will provide some comforting news. Perhaps the heart attack victim was very overweight, or smoked heavily, or had a history of heart disease from an early age; or maybe the woman had ignored a lump for a long period of time, or had taken hormones for many years, or had a strong family background of breast cancer. To the extent that any of these was the case and the listener could both make sense of the event and distinguish him or herself from these antecedents, the event could be readily explained in a manner that would not threaten one's own sense of invulnerability.

Those victims in our work who had been engaging in activities that involved some "assumption of risk," no matter how minimal, were not threatening to our assumptive world. These included paralyzed accident victims who had been hang gliding or had been playing football for a high school team and rape victims who had been hitchhiking or had left a bar less than sober with men they hardly knew. For these individuals, volitional behaviors could be regarded as contributing factors to the victimizations. In the case of the cancer victims we interviewed, it was more difficult to point to behaviors that may have contributed to the victimization. However, because the mastectomy patients were often considerably older than ourselves or had a family history of breast cancer that put them at high risk for getting the disease, a nonthreatening explanation for their illness was frequently available to us. Weinstein and Lachendro (1982) have demonstrated that people's unrealistic optimism regarding future negative life events stems partially from our tendency to give ourselves credit for risk-decreasing factors, while underestimating or overlooking risk-descreasing factors that others have in their favor. This tendency to emphasize differences in risk factors between ourselves and others may be especially strong when we are face-to-face with victims of misfortune. By highlighting dissimilarities between ourselves and the subjects of our research whenever possible, the world remains predictable and makes sense in light of these instances. These individuals did not threaten our view of the world as safe, for our assumption of safety entailed a belief that by taking appropriate (and largely minimal) precautions, or simply by possessing certain physical characteristics, the world would be a secure, benevolent place in which misfortune could be avoided.

It was those instances that seemed to occur with absolutely no assumption of risk, and those that happened in spite of apparent caution, that were extremely disturbing. Examples were the woman who was raped while asleep in her locked house, the woman with breast cancer who had no family history of the disease and yet had a mastectomy in her early 30s, and the paralysis victim who was a passenger in a car going the speed limit when another car jumped the center divider and smashed into his automobile. Those people were not careless but were careful and reasonable, and yet they were victimized. Interestingly, in a recent study of rape victims, Scheppele and Bart (1983) found that raped women suffering the greatest psychological disturbances following the rape were those who had been raped in a situation they had assumed was safe; factors such as how well they knew the rapist and time since the rape did not distinguish this group from those who had an easier time coping. Likewise, in reacting to victims, it was those who were victimized when they appeared to be following the "rules" for safety, or who would be considered by experts to be at minimal medical risk, who created the greatest problems for us as observers.

There was an attempt to search for distinguishing characteristics of our research subjects, in order to keep our assumptive world intact. Yet it gradually became clear that the reasons for victimization did not rest with the particular people. As more and more instances of victimization in the face of care and caution were discussed, as more and more individuals were interviewed who appeared similar to us in terms of character or behavior, our implicit assumptions came under increasing scrutiny. We had operated under a type of fundamental attribution error (Ross, 1977) in accounting for victimization by using person-centered explanations. There had to be something about these specific people that caused or contributed to the misfortune, or why would it have happened to them and not others. Quite obviously, such assumptions served our own needs for a perception of invulnerability, a perception that we ordinarily have no need to question, particularly not in light of the isolated misfortunes that we hear about every now and then.

As the similarity between the victims and ourselves became increasingly undeniable, we found ourselves truly beginning to take our own assumptions to task. In the social psychological literature, Shaver (1970) developed a theory of "defensive attribution," which he believed operates particularly when the observer and victim are perceived as similar. Shaver defined two types of similarity: personal and situational. The former refers to the belief that one is like the victim, whereas situational similarity refers to the belief that there is a possibility the observer will one day find him or herself in the same position as the victim. According to Shaver, if one feels similar to the victim in these ways, the negative outcome is likely to be attributed to chance rather than blamed on the victim. We choose not to blame the victim, in Shaver's (1970) analysis, because we wish to protect ourselves from being blamed should we be in the same situation. We found that the issue of similarity was important in our assessments; in fact, it was a willingness to recognize that these individuals were similar to us, and that we could have been the victims, that slowly but surely led us to question aspects of our assumptive world. Our avoidance of blaming the victim at this point, however, did not appear to reflect a desire to avoid blame if in a similar situation. The shift in attribution away from the victim and toward chance (i.e., unpredictability and randomness) was not self-protective, for psychologically the stress and anxiety that accompanied these responses were enormously distressing. Not only were our old assumptions no longer viable, but our new assumptions were anxiety provoking in and of themselves. The problem was that we could no longer believe that the world was meaningful and predictable in terms of how it "distributed" misfortune; we could no longer believe that we were invulnerable.

We had tried to maintain our old assumptions by engaging in attributions (i.e., blaming the victim) that would enable us to validate our expectations. As Marris (1975) points out, we are conservative in our tendencies to attempt to preserve conceptual systems. Nevertheless, the constant presentation of new evidence that simply could not fit and could not be ignored forced a reexamination of old theories and an embrace of new assumptions. The process was gradual, but the end result was a metamorphosis in our beliefs and theories regarding the world and our place in it. Prior to investigating victimization, the world in our eyes was not a place in which randomness truly played a role. But the misfortunes of the victims we were seeing could not be explained by virtue of our old theories regarding just desserts and controllability; these did not enable us to make sense of the events. We were forced to forfeit our conception of the world as predictable. It was not that personal deeds and actions were irrelevent to outcomes; carelessness and lack of caution could certainly increase the probabilities of negative outcomes. Yet, caution and concern were no longer sure guarantees against misfortune. At any moment disaster could strike—and it could strike us.

The changes in our self- and world theories were not solely a consequence of the realization that "It could happen to us," for in addition we developed a newfound perception that victimization is relatively common—certainly more common than we had thought it to be. This belief in the prevalence of misfortune probably arose in connection with a cognitive bias identified by Tversky and Kahneman (1974), the availability heuristic. When people use the availability heuristic, they estimate the frequency of a class or the probability of an event by the ease with which instances or occurrences of the event can be imagined or remembered. "For example, one may assess the risk of heart attack among middle-aged people by recalling such occurrences amone one's acquaintances"

(Tversky & Kahneman, 1974, p. 1127). According to the availability hypothesis, if occurences of a specific misfortune among one's family, friends, or acquaintances are easily recalled or imagined, people may overestimate the probability of experiencing the misfortune. The availability hypothesis also implies that judgments about the probability of suffering any type of victimization depend partly on the extent to which vivid images of that victimization are available when people think about it.

An example of how perceptions of vulnerability to misfortune can be biased through use of the availability heuristic is provided by the phenomenon of "medical student's disease." Mechanic (1972) points out that medical students frequently experience physical symptoms that they ascribe to some pathologic process. Students notice in themselves an innocuous physiological dysfunction and attach to this an incorrect causal attribution "of a fearful kind," which is usually modeled after a patient recently observed, a clinical anecdote casually overheard, or a family member who has been ill. The medical student's exposure to specific knowledge about disease offers a new framework for perceiving, identifying, and giving meaning to previously neglected bodily feelings.

It is easy to see how the mechanism of availability would alter one's perceptions of personal vulnerability during the research process of conducting interviews with victims. Our own perceived likelihood of suffering a negative event increased greatly within the periods that we were initially exposed to repeated instances of victimizations. Furthermore, because our interviews with victims were often quite lengthy and sometimes contained highly emotional content, we were afforded vivid images of detailed accounts of victimizing incidents, from the time preceding the misfortunes through their aftermath. As a result, we came to believe that the frequency of negative outcomes is much higher than we formerly had believed it to be and thus felt more vulnerable to the possibility of experiencing misfortune ourselves.

A cognitive bias related to the availability heuristic concerns the potency of individual case history information over statistical information in making probabilistic judgments. As noted by a number of researchers (e.g., Nisbett & Borgida, 1975; Nisbett & Ross, 1980), it appears that people's inferences and behaviors are much more affected by vivid, concrete information than by pallid and abstract propositions of substantially greater probative and evidential value. This is partially because vivid information—information that is emotionally interesting, imagery provoking, and proximate in a sensory, temporal, or spatial way—is more likely to be stored and remembered and so is more available. Therefore, even though statistical information is objectively better for estimating one's personal vulnerability to negative events, tangible case history information is more likely to influence such estimates. Thus, although we were informed before we began to actually interview victims that, for example, one out of 11 women gets breast cancer (American Cancer Society, 1981), it was not until we were able to communicate directly with victims that we fully appreciated how common this type of victimization is. Our opportunities to share in the experiences of victims encouraged a new awareness that victimization is by no means a rare or unusual event.

It is certainly conceivable that we actually overestimated the frequency of misfortunes. Nevertheless, not only were our self-theories about personal invulnerability shattered, but the world itself became a far more malevolent place. Misfortune was not distributed wholly on the basis of people's efforts or goodness, but rather randomness and unpredictability also played an important role. In addition, not only was the process of "distribution" unpredictable, but the "amount" of misfortune distributed was greater than we had assumed. Our anxiety about existence dramatically increased. Our beliefs were expressed by Wortman, Abbey, Holland, Silver, and Janoff–Bulman (1980) when they wrote:

> However, our experience has forced us to realize that outcomes, like permanent paralysis or life-threatening illness, can happen to anyone at any time, and this realization has been accompanied by a great deal of anxiety and distress. Especially at the initial stages of our work, we were in a perpetual state of concern that disaster might strike at any moment. If we experienced the most minor ache, we were sure it was bone cancer, if not multiple sclerosis; if we spotted an oncoming car or truck, we expected the worst and prepared for impact; if a man approached us at any time, for any reason, we saw him as a potential rapist. Interestingly, we have since learned that patients and victims themselves share many of these same fears. (p. 211)

Unlike the victims, however, we had not directly experienced the victimization; it was by coming into contact and working with victims in our research that we went through personal change. Our interactions with the victims forced us to examine our own theories of the world, and these theories came up wanting. It is certainly the case, as mentioned by Wortman et al. (1980), that the stress and anxiety experienced were far worse at the beginning of our work with victims than now. We have incorporated our new beliefs into a new assumptive world, and as each day passes and disaster does not strike, the malevolence of the world seems less marked. There is still a belief in unpredictability, randomness, and personal vulnerability, but the passage of time makes instances of misfortune less vivid and salient. Certainly, on each occasion a new study is undertaken, the same issues rearise as central, due to repeated interactions with innocent victims. Yet each time it is a little easier, for despite the fact that meaninglessness, unpredictability and vulnerability become important issues, one's assumptive world has already incorporated and integrated these beliefs, and thus one is no longer confronting anomalies; the distress associated with an inadequate assumptive world is absent.

THE BRIGHTER SIDE: THE PSYCHOLOGICAL
STRENGTH OF VICTIMS

One might wonder why, in the face of anxiety, distress, and confusion, researchers would choose to continue to work with victims. It is thus important to point out that there is a very positive, bright side to the research as well. This bright side derives from the incredible psychological strength that is so readily visible in the victims with whom one is working. Researchers in the area no doubt share a common belief that if we can understand how people react to extremely negative events, we can get a bit closer to understanding the human condition. Not only do we learn about those assumptions we take for granted in day-to-day living, but we learn about the flexibility, viability, and ingenuity of the human being. We have been particularly struck by the outstanding abilities of people to cope with unquestionably powerful negative events. It is as if our more pessimistic view of the world has been balanced by our more positive view of people; the world is less predictable and more malevolent than previously believed, but humans are far stronger and more admirable than previously recognized as well.

Whereas the apparent meaninglessness of events forced a reexamination of old assumptions and a shift to new, more adequate theories of the world and one's role in it, the new beliefs about people did not create a confrontation with old beliefs; it is as if assumptions about the coping abilities of humans were simply not a part of one's assumptive world, or at least not major postulates in the conceptual system. No doubt our newly formed conceptions, resulting from our research experiences, have since been incorporated into our assumptive world. Now they are presumably an important aspect of our network of theories regarding vulnerability, for our positive discoveries in this area appeared to compensate in many ways for negative discoveries regarding the distribution of misfortune in the world.

The remarkable ability of victims to cope well with serious misfortune is immediately apparent to the researcher. Certainly, there is a minority of people, perhaps even a large minority, that does not substantially recover from personal tragedies (see Silver & Wortman, 1980). And no doubt these are the same people we are least likely to see in our research, which involves voluntary participation and therefore self-selected populations. Nevertheless, as Taylor (1983) states, "Despite serious setbacks such as personal illness or death of a family member, the majority of people facing such blows achieves a quality of life or level of happiness equivalent to or even exceeding their prior level of satisfaction" (p. 1161). In some of our own work we found, for example, that the psychological adjustment of women who on the average were nine months postmastectomy (and never more than two years) was excellent, as indicated by depression, self-esteem, and other coping measures (Timko & Janoff–Bulman, 1984). In an earlier study involving data from the Bulman and Wortman (1977) interviews with paraplegics and quadraplegics, it was found that the self-reported happiness of these accident victims (who were no more than one year postaccident) was not significantly different (using the same measures) from that reported by lottery winners of substantial sums (Brickman, Coates, & Janoff–Bulman, 1978). Through various modes of adaptation (see Silver & Wortman, 1980; Taylor, Wood, & Lichtman, 1983), individuals seem to readjust their lives and their assumptive worlds so as to cope effectively with traumatic, negative life events.

For us, one of the most remarkable aspects of this coping process was the ability of victims to reevaluate their misfortune in a positive light, to see and stress the optimistic side of their victimization. In the study with accident victims (Bulman & Wortman, 1977), we found that approximately 20% of the sample managed to reevaluate the accident and even the resulting disability (i.e., paralysis) positively. Sample responses were:

> Since the accident I've learned an awful lot about myself and other people. You meet different people in a hard-up situation that I never would have met. I was leading a sheltered life, I suppose, compared to what it is now. Now I'm just in a situation which I enjoy. (p. 359)

> I see the accident as the best thing that could have happened because I was forced to decide my faith, whereas there would have been a possibility that I would have lived and never made a decision—been lost the rest of my life. (p. 359).

> I was moving too fast at the time and I think this was the best way to slow me down . . . I think it was the best thing—maybe I'll live a little longer. (p. 359).

In a recent paper reporting the results of a multidimensional scale of meaning, Thompson and Morasch (1982) used the "Why me?" responses of the Bulman and Wortman study and found that reevaluating the accident as positive (vs. no reevaluation) was one of two primary dimensions of victims' perceptions of meaning. Reevaluating the victimization as positive (e.g., emphasizing benefits accrued) was positively related to good coping in the sample of paralyzed individuals.

In research with breast cancer patients this reevaluation is even more apparent. For example, Taylor, Wood, and Lichtman (1983; also see Taylor, 1983) in their work with a sample of mastectomy patients, reported that the women they interviewed found benefits in the victimizing event of cancer. In our own work, fully 60% of a sample of mastectomy patients said that breast cancer had fostered a greater appreciation for life and other people. The women frequently suggested that they now could truly enjoy life and not take it for granted, as they had so readily done before. Consistent with such a perspective was that of women who said this new appreciation led them to live one day at a time, and in this way life became far more meaningful. For many of these respondents, having cancer had led to a reordering of priorities, such that they now devote more time to what's really important (e.g., their loved ones) and far less to insignificant tasks (e.g., cleaning the house). There was also a sizeable group of women (30%) who felt they were now better people as a result of their bout with cancer. Some said that they were now more tolerant and compassionate towards others, whereas some stressed their belief that they were now psychologically stronger than before. Overall, the reevaluation of the event of cancer as positive seemed to follow one of two general courses: (1) a newfound appreciation of life and what is important, resulting primarily from having confronted one's own mortality, and (2) a more positive conception of oneself and one's own possibilities and strengths.

The latter perspective, involving a change in self-conception, was particularly striking in the case of the rape victims we interviewed. In this sample, there were few women who expressed a new appreciation of life; rather, they were more apt to express a new appreciation for their own strengths, as is evident in the following statements:

> I feel different now, like I went through a door. I feel much stronger now, even though I feel vulnerable to being raped in this culture. Part of that rape was to dominate and humiliate me and he didn't succeed at that. I came through with my integrity—I got through those months of hell.

> An event like rape separates you from the mainstream. It forces you to develop a personal philosophy; you have to do some thinking and searching. I've separated myself and the world. The world is more dangerous to me now, but I am less vulnerable. I am stronger, able to handle anything. Life is a vulnerable situation—I could die tomorrow. But I have a certain pride in my own invulnerability; internally, I feel much stronger. I hold myself in higher esteem, and I'm also more sensitive to the feelings of others.

The latter statement parallels a reaction that we, as observers, experienced as a result of working with victims. Our assumptive worlds could not be stretched so as to incorporate the "evidence" before us; our theories therefore shifted, and we began to perceive the world as a far more unpredictable and malevolent place. And yet the impact of the research was not solely of this disturbing nature, for our view of the world was balanced by a new view of people and their possibilities. We perceived ourselves as far more vulnerable, yet, personally, we could still maintain a belief in our psychological invulnerability. In other words, although bad things could now happen to us, as they had happened to the victims we studied, our discoveries about the remarkable psychological strengths of humans enabled us to believe that we too would be able to cope and adjust so as to effectively handle these negative events. The similarities between ourselves and victims represented serious threats to our assumptions of predictability and control but also provided reassurance that we would be able to adapt to misfortune should we have to. This compensatory view of people has in many ways softened the impact of our more pessimistic, although perhaps realistic, view of the world. We remain both more anxious and wary than we were prior to conducting research with victims, but we are also in far greater awe of the human spirit and its capabilities.

EXPECTED DIFFICULTIES IN CONDUCTING RESEARCH WITH VICTIMS

Prior to conducting research with victimized populations, we had assumed that the interpersonal aspects of the face-to-face interview situations would be uncomfortable. This discomfort was expected on the basis of two separate beliefs: (1) that we would not know how to react appropriately to the respondents, and (2) that we were imposing on the respondents by conducting our research. As it turned out, these issues were quickly and favorably resolved, but they did cause concern at the very early stages of research.

It has been fairly well documented that individuals are not entirely comfortable in the presence of victimized populations (Wortman & Dunkel–Schetter, 1979; see Silver & Wortman, 1980, for a review). Most adults feel somewhat ambivalent in the presence of the physically handicapped, for example, attempting to verbalize attitudes that are very favorable, while simultaneously feeling quite rejecting (e.g., Goffman, 1963; Wright, 1960; see also Coates & Wortman, 1980). Kleck and his colleagues (Kleck, 1969; Kleck, Ono, & Hastorf, 1966) conducted several well-controlled studies that demonstrated this ambivalence. Respondents evaluated a disabled confederate more positively than a "normal" one and tried to agree more with his opinions; they also, however, exhibited more motoric inhibition and ended the interaction with the disabled sooner than with the "normal." In general, interactions between the nondisabled and the disabled are often marked by ambiguities. The nondisabled appear uncertain as to how they should behave and may as a result vacillate between attempts to completely ignore the disability (which is actually uppermost in awareness) and attempts to treat the disabled as total invalids (Schur, 1980; see also Davis, 1964).

Although one sample of our respondents was visibly physically disabled (Bulman & Wortman 1977; all subjects were paralyzed), the majority of victims we have studied (e.g., victims of disease such as cancer or violent assault such as rape) have not been physically handicapped. Nevertheless, the same discomfort was expected to arise, for these were individuals who had been through a trying psychological ordeal, one that singled them out as "victims." We wondered, how is one to act with these individuals? As Wortman and Dunkel–Schetter (1979) point out in the case of cancer victims, people often seem to operate on the assumption that it's best for these patients to feel cheerful, and thus there is a tendency to avoid all negative affect and express only positive affect. Although we felt (inappropriately) that such a position might be the "easiest," we also knew that we would be asking questions that were almost certain to arouse negative affect. The question of how to act appropriately was one that concerned us, for it was clear that we had little experience learning what is, in fact, appropriate behavior, and what would be most comfortable for the victims. There was a fear that we might slip and say the wrong thing, that we might not be sensitive enough to the respondents' needs, and that we might give the awful, mistaken impression that we regarded them as oddities. Overall, there was a concern about being able to conduct the interview in such a manner as to properly acknowledge the respondent's past victimization and yet not overly exaggerate its impact on the face-to-face interaction.

The discomfort with the interpersonal aspects of the interview stemmed not simply from the prospect of dealing with victimized populations with which we were generally unfamiliar, but also from dealing with these populations in the context of a research setting. We were uneasy with the possibility of being too intrusive, of asking questions the respondents did not want to discuss, and of forcing our way into the private lives of individuals who might prefer to keep matters to themselves. Further, we suffered from an intense embarrassment, prior to the research studies, of "imposing" our scaled items on individuals who would find such quantification trivializing and demeaning. We felt that we would be optimally comfortable asking a long series of open-ended items, in which respondents would describe what happened, their reactions, others' reactions, and the like. However, our research was comprised of both open-ended questions and scaled items. We were concerned about respondents' reactions to the use of Likert-type scales in our attempts to obtain quantifiable data regarding questions of coping, recovery, attributions, and so on. It was expected that individuals would state that it was not possible to use such simplified schemes for measurement, that choosing a number was impossible in the light of the complexity of their responses.

Needless to say at this point, our concerns were misplaced. Perhaps they did make us more sensitive to the interaction and in that sense were helpful. Yet, we found quite early on that the interactions flowed very smoothly; yes, the first paralysis victim, the first rape victim, and the first cancer patient witnessed somewhat more discomfort on our part than subsequent respondents. However, armed with an interview schedule for moral support, it soon became very obvious that these people were no different from you or me. They had experienced incredible ordeals, at least as perceived from our perspective, but their similarity to us was greater than their dissimilarity, and they appeared as concerned about our comfort as we felt about theirs. We did not feel like intruders, but rather as though we were students attempting to learn from a situation. Although the samples were self-selected, in that they agreed to the interviews, we were pleased to find that extremely small numbers of potential respondents were unwilling to participate in our research. The victims we interviewed appeared eager for the opportunity to talk and vent their feelings (see Silver & Wortman, 1980) and also appreciated the possibility that their participation would somehow benefit others in circumstances similar to their own. The interviews were frequently far longer than expected; although all interview items were covered, respondents generally brought up new issues of concern or interest to them, and we felt we actually got to know the respondents fairly well in those limited hours. Never were we confronted with displeasure at the sight or use of scaled items; never were we made to feel that the research enterprise was trivializing the victims' catastrophic life experiences. It did not take long to realize that the face-to-face interactions were very comfortable and very gratifying, certainly for the researchers, and hopefully for the respondents.

FINAL NOTES: EMPATHIC OBSERVATION

Our research with victims has involved (and continues to involve) intensive interviews with individuals who have experienced extremely negative life events. It is not easy to ascertain the extent to which the interview method or our willingness to deal with the victims' emotional reactions was responsible for the great impact the research had on us. Others working with victims have reported similar responses regarding their increased anxiety and feelings of vulnerability (Wortmen et al., 1980). Certainly, it is possible to conduct research with victims that would not have any marked psychological effects on the researchers; for example, questionnaires could be mailed and all data collected without face-to-face interactions. Perhaps even face-to-face interactions could be conducted in a way that would minimize the study's impact on the researcher; in these cases a questionnaire could be given to the victim for completion in one's presence. There would be face-to-face contact, but little direct verbal communication, save for clarification of questionnaire items and the like. Such techniques would no doubt be regarded as methodologically clean, for they would be untainted by the emotional responses of the researcher. The general conception of truly scientific studies involves an implicit belief that personal feeings must not enter into sound inquiries.

From our own perspective, detachment is not always a benefit in the research enterprise. Detachment and distance certainly protect researchers from experiencing any unsettling changes in their own assumptive worlds and theories of reality. Yet it is questionable whether such methods maximize the probability of collecting the most meaningful, valid, and reliable data; one can be so objective that one misses one's subject matter (Dalton, 1964). Affective involvement need not be blinding; rather, as Schwartz and Schwartz (1967) note, an observer's empathic relationship with the observed can facilitate an understanding of their inner life and social world, and can, consequently, actually increase the validity and meaningfulness of observations. We have found that establishing a relationship that includes the sharing of feelings and sentiments fosters a deeper understanding of the experiences of our victim–respondents and a personal validation of the data we collect through both scaled measures and open-ended questions. We agree with Glazer (in press) when he writes:

> Rather than celebrate the requirement of distance, it seems advisable to highlight another reality which characterizes many fieldwork relationships. *Compassionate analysis* suggests the desirability of researchers becoming closely attuned to the feelings and world views of those they are studying, of identifying with these and of attempting to experience the emotional vibrations and the intellectual perspectives associated with them. Concurrently, in accordance with the mission of the scientific observer, it is also necessary to analyze the content and derivation of these perspectives. It is a trying but reachable goal. (pp. 39–40).

For purposes of understanding the experiences of victims, "compassionate analysis" strikes us as essential; one must get to know each respondent in order to understand his or her reaction to victimization. An unexpected consequence of our involvement with the victim populations we have studied was the tremendous psychological impact that their victimization in turn had on us. We no longer view the world or ourselves as we had prior to the research; in many ways we are sadder but wiser.

REFERENCES

American Cancer Society. (1981). *Cancer facts and figures.* New York: American Cancer Society.

Bard, M., & Sangrey, D. (1979). *The crime victim's book.* New York: Basic Books.

Bowlby, J. (1969). *Attachment and loss* (Vol. 1): Attachment. London: Hogarth.

Brickman, P., Coates, D., & Janoff–Bulman, R. (1978). Lottery winners and accident victims: Is happiness relative? *Journal of Personality and Social Psychology, 36,* 917–927.

Bulman, R. J., & Wortman, C. B. (1977). Attributions of blame and coping in the "real world": Severe accident victims react to their lot. *Journal of Personality and Social Psychology, 35,* 351–363.

Coates, D., & Wortman, C. B. (1980). Depression maintenance and interpersonal control. In A. Baum & J. Singer (Eds.), *Advances in environmental psychology* (Vol. 2). Hillsdale, NJ: Lawrence Erlbaum Associates.

Dalton, M. (1964). Preconceptions and methods in "Men who manage." In P. E. Hammond (Ed.), *Sociologists at work: Essays on the craft of social research.* New York: Basic Books.

Davis, F. (1964). Deviance disavowal: The management of strained interaction by the visibly handicapped. In H. S. Becker (Ed.), *The other side: Perspectives on deviance.* New York: Free Press.

Epstein, S. (1973). The self-concept revisited, or a theory of a theory. *American Psychologist, 28,* 404–416.

Epstein, S. (1979). The ecological study of emotions in humans. In P. Pliner, K. R. Blanstein, & I. M. Spigel (Eds.), *Advances in the study of communication and affect* (Vol. 5): Perception of emotions in self and others. New York: Plenum.

Epstein, S. (1980). The self-concept: A review and the proposal of an integrated theory of personality. In E. Staub (Ed.), *Personality: Basic issues and current research.* Englewood Cliffs, NJ: Prentice–Hall.

Glazer, M. (in press) The threat of the stranger: Vulnerability, reciprocity, and field work. In J. Sieber (Ed.), *Ethical decision making in social science research.*

Goffman, E. (1963). *Stigma.* Englewood Cliffs, NJ: Prentice–Hall.

Horowitz, M. J. (1979). Psychological response to serious life events. In V. Hamilton and D. M. Warburton (Eds.), *Human Stress and cognition.* New York: Wiley.

Janoff-Bulman, R., & Frieze, I. H. (1983). A theoretical perspective for understanding reactions to victimization. *Journal of Social Issues, 39,* 1–17.

Janoff–Bulman, R., & Lang–Gunn, L. (in press) Coping with disease and accidents: The role of self-blame atributions. In L. Y. Abramson (Ed.), *Social-personal inference in clinical psychology.* New York: Guilford.

Janoff–Bulman, R., Madden, M. E., & Timko, C. (1980). *The illusion of invulnerability.* Unpublished manuscript, University of Massachusetts.

Jenkins, H. M., & Ward, W. C. (1965). Judgment of contingency between responses and outcomes. *Psychological Monographs, 79,* (1, whole No. 594).

Kleck, R. (1969). Physical stigma and task oriented instructions. *Human Relations, 22,* 53–60.

Kleck, R., Ono, M., & Hastorf, A. M, (1966). The effects of physical deviance upon face-to-face interaction. *Human Relations, 19,* 425–436.

Kuhn, T. S. (1962). *The structure of scientific revolutions.* Chicago: The University of Chicago Press.

Langer, E. (1975). The illusion of control. *Journal of Personality and Social Psychology, 32,* 311–328.

Lerner, M. J. (1980). *The belief in a just world.* New York: Plenum.

Lifton, R. J., & Olson, E. (1976). Death imprint in Buffalo Creek. In H. J. Parad, H. L. P. Resnik, & L. G. Parad (Eds.), *Emergency and disaster management.* Bowie, MD : Charles Press.

Marris, P. (1975). *Loss and change.* Garden City, NY: Anchor/Doubleday.

Masterman, M. (1970). The nature of a paradigm. In I. Lakatos & A. Musgrave (Eds.), *Criticism and the growth of knowledge.* Cambridge, England: University Press.

Mechanic, D. (1972). Social psychological factors affecting the presentation of bodily complaints. *The New England Journal of Medicine, 286,* 1132–1139.

Nisbett, R. E., & Borgida, E. (1975). Attribution and the psychology of prediction. *Journal of Personality and Social Psychology, 32,* 932–943.

Nisbett, R. E., & Ross, L. (1980). *Human inference: Strategies and shortcomings of social judgment.* Englewood Cliffs, NJ: Prentice–Hall.

Notman, M. T., & Nadelson, C. C. (1976). The rape victim: Psychodynamic considerations. *American Journal of Psychiatry, 133,* 408–413.

Parkes, C. M. (1971). Psycho-social transitions: A field for study. *Social Science and Medicine, 5,* 101–115.

Parkes, C. M. (1975). What becomes of redundant world models? A contribution to the study of adaptation to change, *British Journal of Medical Psychology, 48,* 131–137.

Perloff, L. S. (1983). Perceptions of vulnerability to victimization. *Journal of Social Issues, 39,* 41–61.

Ross, L. (1977). The intuitive psychologist and his shortcomings. In L. Berkowitz (Ed.), *Advances in experimental social psychology* (Vol. 10). New York: Academic Press.

Scheppele, K. L., & Bart, P. B. (1983).Through women's eyes: Defining danger in the wake of sexual assault. *Journal of Social Issues. 39,* 63–80

Schur, E. M. (1980). *The politics of deviance.* Englewood Cliffs, NJ: Prentice–Hall.

Schwartz, M. S., & Schwartz, C. G. (1967). Problems in participant observation. In P. Rose (Ed.), *The study of society: An integrated anthology.* New York: Random House.

Seligman, M. E. P. (1975). *Helplessness: On depression, development, and death.* San Francisco: W. H. Freeman.

Shaver, K. G. (1970). Defensive attribution: Effects of severity and relevance on the responsibilities assigned for an accident. *Journal of Personality and Social Psychology, 6,* 100–110.

Silver, R. L., Boon, C., & Stones, M. H. (1983). Searching for meaning in misfortune: Making sense of incest. *Journal of Social Issues, 39,* 81–101.

Silver, R. L., & Wortman, C. B. (1980). Coping with undesirable life events. In J. Garber & M. E. P. Seligman (Eds.), *Human helplessness: Theory and application.* New York: Academic Press.

Taylor, S. E. (1983). Adjustment to threatening events: A theory of cognitive adaptation. *American Psychologist, 38,* 1161–1173.

Taylor, S. E., Wood, J. V., & Lichtman, R. R. (1983). It could be worse: Selective evaluation as a response to victimization. *Journal of Social Issues. 39,* 19–40.

Thompson, S. C., & Morasch, B. (1982). *Two dimensions of meaning affecting reactions to stressful events.* Submitted for publication.

Timko, C., & Janoff–Bulman, R. *Attributions, vulnerability, and coping: The case of breast cancer.* Manuscript submitted for publication, (1984).

Tverksy, A., & Kahneman, D. (1974). Judgment under uncertainty: Heuristics and biases. *Science, 185,* 1124–1131.

Walster, E. (1966). Assignment of responsibility for an accident. *Journal of Personality and Social Psychology, 3,* 73–79.

Weinstein, N. D. (1980). Unrealistic optimism about future life events. *Journal of Personality and Social Psychology, 39,* 806–820.

Weinstein, N. D., & Lachendro, E. (1982). Egocentrism as a source of unrealistic optimism. *Personality and Social Psychology Bulletin, 8,* 195–200.

Weisman, A. D. (1979). *Coping with cancer.* New York: McGraw–Hill.

Wolfenstein, M. (1957). *Disaster: A psychological essay.* Glencoe, IL: The Free Press.

Wortman, C. B. (1976). Causal attributions and personal control. In J. H. Harvey, W. Ickes, & R. F. Kidd (Eds.), *New directions in attribution research* (Vol. 1). Hillsdale, NJ: Lawrence Erlbaum Associates.

Wortman, C. B., & Dunkel–Schetter, C. (1979). Interpersonal relationships and cancer: A theoretical analysis. *Journal of Social Issues, 35,* 120–155.

Wortman, C. B., Abbey, A., Holland, A. E., Silver, R. L., & Janoff–Bulman, R. (1980). Transitions from the laboratory to the field: Problems and progress. In L. Bickman (Ed.), *Applied social psychology annual* (Vol. 1). Beverly Hills, CA: Sage.

Wright, B. A. (1960). *Physical disability—A psychological approach.* New York: Harper & Row.

4 Simulation and Related Research Methods in Environmental Psychology

Siegfried Streufert
College of Medicine, The Pennsylvania State University—Hershey

Robert W. Swezey
Science Applications Inc.—McLean, VA

Although there are certain commonalities in the approach of the sciences in general to their respective subject matters, each discipline must adapt its methods to the specific phenomena under investigation. To a lesser but nonetheless substantial degree, the same may be said for the diverse branches of individual sciences: It would be preposterous to suggest, for example, that environmental psychology should use exactly the same methods that we know from research in learning theory. Environmental psychology is different: In contrast to at least some of the other "psychologies," the field often deals with human behavior in response to or in interaction with quite *complex* stimulus settings. It is then hardly surprising that the observed human responses to multifaceted environments tend to be multifaceted and complicated as well. Environmental psychology must be able to capture the complexities of the environment as well as the complexities of the resultant human responses. In other words, to have wide predictive validity, at least some of the methods used in environmental psychology should bear considerable relationship to the complexity of the stimulus environment and to the complexity of the associated responses. At least these methods should not depart far enough from that complexity to destroy the potential of what might be termed a *meaningful level of analysis*.

This chapter deals with research methods that attempt to reflect the complexity of the environmental variables to which people are typically exposed when they function in the "real world" surrounding them in many of their day-to-day activities. The methods under consideration represent an effort to obtain both external and internal validity without sacrificing more than minimal reliability and applicability of the obtained data. The focus is on simulation and related research approaches such as computer modeling, role playing, and so forth. The advantages and disadvantages of these approaches to research in environmental psychology are considered. Some examples and suggestions of how these methods may be useful to environmental psychologists and related researchers are provided. While the methods considered in this chapter are certainly not the only research techniques that are important to this field, they are central to at least some of the questions that are a pivotal part of the field of environmental psychology.

THE FUNCTION OF MULTIPLE VARIABLES

The majority of human behavior occurs in complex environmental settings, i.e., people are typically exposed to a number of stimuli simultaneously. This typical complexity of real-world environments was for a time aversive to behavioral scientists: It was assumed that quality science would have to focus on single elemental stimuli and measure single, equally elemental, responses. External validity was sacrificed to obtain internal validity because it was assumed that only one kind of validity could be achieved (e.g., Aronson & Carlsmith, 1968). Objections to such arguments were soon to come. For example, Fromkin and Streufert (1976) suggested that phenomena could not be subjected to reductionism beyond a certain minimal level without loss of their essential characteristics, or, as Streufert and Streufert (1978) have stated, beyond their "minimum common denominator." Obviously, the level of this common denominator often rises with the number of variables under simultaneous consideration, and with the degree to which these variables represent quite disparate phenomena.

As suggested earlier, environmental psychology investigates behavior that often occurs in complex settings where people are simultaneously exposed to a number of stimuli. Considerable research has shown that such complex settings have effects above and beyond the kind brought about in simple settings that are more easily (and more typically) reproduced or created in the laboratory experiments common to a number of other areas of psychology. For example, findings from environmental stress research tend to show that any single stressor has quite limited effects on human responding until that stressor reaches severe levels. Yet several stressors operating simultaneously, even at relatively mild levels, *can* combine to produce increased physiological arousal, dissatisfaction, and serious detriments in social and/or task performance. In other environmental settings, however, the results may be reversed: The simultaneous or subsequent occurrence of a number of stimuli may even have ameliorating effects. For example, would someone who is having a serious disagreement with the boss respond (socially or in terms of physiological arousal) as severely if he or she knows that there will be someone at home in another hour who will be comforting and understanding? Would that response be different if another argument is expected at home? At present, we are only beginning to understand the diverse responses to interactive stimuli and their cognitive representations. We must realize that we cannot avoid studying these interactive characteristics of environmental variables if we wish to accurately predict the effects on complex environments on complex human behaviors. Fortunately, we now have techniques that permit us to engage in such efforts. In some research efforts in environmental psychology, we may wish to measure the effects of several interacting variables across a number of levels; in other cases, we may wish to study some of them as boundary variables and others as independent or dependent variables (cf. Fromkin & Streufert, 1976). In either case, we cannot ignore their individual or interactive contributions to human responding in complex environments. In the following section we take a closer look at some of the methods that were designed to help us study more effectively variables that are inherent in complex environments and their impact.

SIMULATIONS AND OTHER METHODS THAT APPLY TO COMPLEX ENVIRONMENTS

Simulations were first developed in the physical and engineering sciences. Aircraft design engineers, for example, might place an operating model of a future airplane within a wind tunnel to determine the flight characteristics of that aircraft. Such a procedure would allow identification of potential problem areas and would lead to improvement of airframe design. The success of simulation procedures in engineering suggested adaptation of the technique to other fields as well. A number of years ago, Guetzkow and his associates discovered the value of simulation for behavioral, social, political, and organizational sciences (e.g., Guetzkow, 1962). These researchers suggested that an operating model of a social organization should be built and tested in the same fashion in which aircraft engineers test the design of a fuselage or wing structure. With the advent of simulation techniques in the behavioral sciences, the ground was broken and several more or less related methods were developed to measure the effects of relatively complex environmental, task, and individual variables as they interact with each other.

Simulations and their relatives among research methods tend to place participants, either individually or in groups, into more or less realistic task environments. Typically, the task provided to simulation participants is identical to or only marginally abstracted from tasks that people perform in the real world. Participants (subjects) may act as themselves (i.e., they are given some task to complete). In some research, the participants may even be hired to do a job and have no idea that the "company" that hired them represents a research effort. In other cases, the participants may be assigned a task that they themselves normally would not experience; yet the task is often sufficiently interesting and involving so that the feeling of being in an experiment soon gives way to goal orientation and "normal" experience.

Simulations differ from other experimental methods, not only in the complexity of the work (and variable) environment, but also on the time dimension. Simulations have been defined as "construction and manipulation of an operating[1] model" (Dawson, 1962), as an "operating representation of central features of reality" (Geutzkow, 1963). They may potentially take several forms: they may look like games, they may be computerized, they may employ people and computers. In any case, they occupy both space and time (Inbar & Stoll, 1972). To summarize, simulations and related methods *operate* in complex environments *over time*. Participants are exposed, through feedback from their own actions, through preprogrammed environmental events, or some combination of these two, to a continuously modifying environment (cf. Streufert & Suedfeld, 1977). Within the limitations of their resources, the participants are able to perceive, to respond, and to initiate actions. In some forms of simulated environments these perceptual and behavioral options are more restricted, in others, practically no restrictions exist at all (see following). In all the simulation techniques and related research methods, however, the experimenter is able to observe human responding to complex stimuli of interest in a relatively realistic environmental setting. Moreover, these responses are observed as they develop and change over time.

Before proceeding with a description of the specific research methods represented by the simulation family, a word of caution is in order. Researchers in psychology, including environmental psychology, have recently misused the term *simulation* in a large number of publications. While definitions of concepts can change, a modification of the meaning of simulation is not advisable, because psychologists, in changing the meaning of the term, would sharply differ from the rest of the scientific community. As discussed later, simulation represents an *ongoing* process in which persons interact continually with an active complex environment. Responding to paper and pencil questions on how one would respond to some environmental change, how one would vote if selected for a jury, and so forth *does* represent experimentation. It does *not*, however, represent simulation research. Several of the required components of the simulation method, in particular the ongoing interactive environment over time, are missing (cf., Streufert & Suedfeld, 1977).

Free Simulations

Fromkin and Streufert (1976) have termed the simulation techniques developed by Guetzkow and associates (e.g., Guetzkow, 1959; Guetzkow, Alger, Brody, Noel, & Snyder, 1963) *free* simulations. In free simulations, participants are free

---

[1]Obviously an "operating model" is not static: It must *continue* on the *time* dimension. How variables are treated over time is, as is explained later, a major parting point for diverse kinds of simulation techniques.

to choose their own courses of action (within the constraints of their resources and the limitation of given rules). More importantly, they also are free to modify the environment through their action over time. The result of such activity is a simulated system in which the individuals, groups, teams, or organizations that operate as participants in the simulation produce *changes in their environment over time*. Obviously, their subsequent responses to those changed environments will differ from participant to participant because they must be based on the diverse stimulus configurations that have developed.

Free simulations have been used for a large number of purposes (cf., Inbar & Stoll, 1972; Shubik, 1960). To Guetzkow and his associates and to many other researchers associated with this particular point of view, the free simulation represents a model or *theory* of some behavior under analysis (e.g., Guetzkow, Kotler, & Schultz, 1972; Inbar & Stoll, 1972). The goal of a free simulation is most often the prediction of real-world events that might defy understanding by the human mind because of their inherent complexity. For example, if some event is determined by an interaction of 50 or so variables, the human brain lacks the capacity to understand it. We cannot, for example, cognitively conceptualize 50-way interactions. Nonetheless, the proponents of free simulations would argue that we might *replicate* such complex historical events and learn to anticipate future events if these events will naturally occur in a simulated setting that contains all essential variables. Because of its postulated capacity to predict future events, the free simulation (often computerized, i.e., players are replaced by parameters[2]) may be considered a theory.

As an attempt at successive approximations toward a better and better theory (with repeated improvements of parameters), the free simulation lacks the needed ingredients to be widely useful for experimental research on the relationship among specific variables. Because the participants in free simulations are able to modify their environments, groups of subjects in one simulation would produce and, consequently, experience quite divergent environmental stressors (after some time) than any other group placed into the same simulation. Experimental comparisons among groups of participants in free simulations are consequently limited to the interpretation of outcomes as a function of common (or planned diverse) starting points.

Nonetheless, some researchers have utilized free simulation techniques for experimental purposes. One of the earliest efforts in this direction was reported by Driver (1962), who studied the behavior of simulated nations within Guetzkow's (1963) Internation Simulation (INS) system. An environment was devised within which two large powers with allies of various sizes interacted economically, politically, and militarily. Because of the changes that different groups of subjects produced as they operated as national decision makers in the simulation, Driver was only able to study the effects of different initial condi-

---

[2]See the section on computer simulations, following.

tions in the simulated environment. Nonetheless, he obtained quite interesting results. For example, his data point toward the possibility that a moderate-size power with nuclear arms capacity in a political environment dominated by two large powers that are in political conflict might fire a nuclear rocket at the major powers, hoping that they will exhaust each other in a subsequent war, leaving the moderate-size power to take control.

Experimental Simulations

To obtain experimental control over independent variables across time, Streufert, Clardy, Driver, Karlins, Schroder, and Seudfeld (1965), and Drabeck and Haas (1969), in separate efforts, developed experimental simulation techniques.

Experimental simulations contain the same environmental complexity to which we have become accustomed from free simulation techniques. Participants in this form of simulation are led to believe that they are interacting with an ongoing environment, and that their actions, behaviors, and decisions affect that environment in turn. Participants in experimental simulations believe that the outcomes to which they will be exposed in the future are in some part direct consequences of their own previous activities. In fact, however, experimental simulations utilize an environment that is controlled by the experimenter. The experimenter may select one or more independent variables and manipulate these variables over time according to the research design. Other variables are held constant or randomized. The events to which participants are exposed thus actually reflect the operations of independent variable manipulations, rather than the effects of previous participant behavior. In well-designed experimental simulations, the participant does not realize that behavior is without direct effect on future outcomes.

Obviously, such a research technique has great advantages for experimenters who wish to measure effects of multiple controlled variables in complex, real-world environments. The technique has proven valuable in environmental and organizational experimentation within a variety of settings and has produced useful data both for theoretical and for applied purposes. However, experimental simulations tend to be restricted to research efforts and theory testing. Because of experimenter control over potentially all environmental variables, the experimental simulation technique per se can generally not be considered to be a theory or a model. Some examples of experimental simulation methodology may be useful. In one of the earlier efforts with this technique, Drabeck and Haas (1969) simulated the environment of a police dispatcher. By using police dispatchers operating as simulation participants at their usual work stations, these researchers obtained a high degree of external validity. To obtain performance measures under environmental (input overload) stress, Drabeck increased the load on the dispatcher by introducing specific numbers of calls to the dispatch operation in addition to the incoming "normal" calls. Similar methods were also used by

Streufert and Schroder (1965) and Streufert and Driver (1965) in an earlier simulation of tactical decision making. In the latter case, all inputs to decision-making teams were preprogrammed and precisely controlled in number (from 2 to 40 per 30-minute period) and in their degree of complexity (each input consisted of a simple subject–predicate–object statement from which only a single informative statement could be obtained). Research of this nature has been exceptionally productive because a number of different dependent variables (e.g., diverse measures of performance, perceptual characteristics, attitudes, satisfaction, group-oriented behavior, and many more) can be measured in response to the same carefully controlled, but *complex,* environmental setting. Moreover, the effects of variable levels introduced sequentially over time can be obtained, increasing the wealth of data even more (see following for cautions on the interpretation on multiple data sets obtained from single sets of participant groups). Experimental simulation research has, for example, repeatedly demonstrated that complex strategic behavior occurs at its highest levels during intermediate load conditions (i.e., when an item of information is presented approximately once every 3 minutes), while simple responsive behavior rises with increasing environmental stimulation until the maximum response capacity of the human responder (or group) is reached.

Quasiexperimental Simulation Procedures

Streufert and Swezey (1980) have suggested that it is possible to design a quasiexperimental simulation that combines the desirable effects of free simulations with those of experimental simulation techniques. Basically, such a method could provide participants with direct feedback based upon previous actions. At the same time, it could also allow retention of experimenter control over relevant experimental variables. Such a technique borrows control of independent variable manipulation over time from experimental simulation methodology but applies that control *only* to variables that are of specific interest to an experimenter. Other variables that may be held constant or randomized in an experimental simulation can be freed to vary "realistically" as a function of the actions of participants and potentially of established parameters.

The conceptualizations upon which quasiexperimental simulation technology is based are quite similar to the thoughts on which Campbell and Stanley (1963) based their quasiexperimental research design paradigms. If an environment of interest to the researcher is too complex to fit within the rather rigid and restrictive requirements of standard experimental technology, quasiexperimental methods may be used to allow the setting to remain "natural" yet to gain the necessary control over *important* components of that environment and thus allow inference of causality in predicting dependent variable data from independent variable events or manipulations. Quasiexperimentation is a necessary compromise between the limitations imposed by working with real-world phenomena and the desire to obtain meaningful and reliable data.

The experimenter using quasiexperimental simulation technology can, of course, select those variables to be manipulated, as well as those that are left to vary freely with the actions of participant subjects. Obviously, independent variable(s) of interest to the research *must* remain under experimenter control. Variables that are likely to interact with the independent variable(s) should also be controlled. To the degree to which control can be extended further to cover other environmental and event characteristics in the simulation, the advantages of experimental simulation methodology are approached and the problems associated with free simulations are reduced. To the degree to which control is relaxed, realism may be increased further, but the potential confounding problems found in free simulation technology may emerge. To make best possible use of the quasiexperimental "compromise," the research design that most closely approximates the experimental simulation paradigm within the given circumstances should be selected.

An example of a specific quasiexperimental simulation might be useful here. Among other simulated environments, Streufert and associates developed the Tactical and Negotiations Game (Streufert, Kliger, Castore, & Driver, 1967), where participant subjects make decisions about the economic, military, intelligence, and negotiation components of a small internation conflict. The participants arrive at the lab and are presented with a manual that informs them in detail about history, current conditions, and their task in a country called "Shamba." They are to resolve the Shamba conflict, a limited international conflict situation with some similarity to several real-world problems in recent history. Via the manual and some video presentations, the participants spend about 3 hours in which they receive the necessary pretraining and the persuasive communications that reliably lead them to "believe in" the cause they are representing.

As the simulation begins, they believe that they are faced by an opposing decision-making group. They may interact with the other group in written form (i.e., at a distance) as long as they do so within the resources they have according to the manual. It appears to them that the events that occur with time are the direct effects of their own decisions as they interact with the decisions of their opponents. In other words, they learn to believe that they can and do have a direct effect on their own future. That effect, however, is only partial. The supposed opposing group's actions (if any other group is present at all) have no effect at all on the outcomes of the participant's decisions. Some outcomes of participants' actions are determined via predetermined parameters (relationships among variables). For example, a greater investment of money into an environmental clean-up fund may actually produce a cleaner environment *as long as that outcome does not interfere with variables of interest to the experimenters.* If, for example, success levels of information received were of interest (or might confound some other important variable) or if the experimenters wanted to investigate the effects of environmental pollution on the actions of their decision makers, then the parameter relationship would be replaced with a preprogrammed fixed outcome.

Although the experimenters may allow some variables (that are not of experimental interest and are not likely to confound) to vary with the actions of the participants in the quasiexperimental simulation, they would maintain strict outcome control over those independent variables that are of interest in the research design. If, for example, the interest would be in information load (amount of information coming from the environment per unit time), then only a limited number of information statements from the environment would be permitted (spaced as appropriate for the research design). Further, because we know that failure information tends to increase effective load levels, participants in a research design measuring the effects of environmental load would have to be exposed to failure levels held constant at a zero or some other interesting level to eliminate potential confounds.[3] Other characteristics of the information to be received by the participants could, however, be responsive to the previous actions of the participants. For example, in a research effort studying the effects of environmental load, the *content* of the information messages would be of lesser importance and could well vary with previous decisions made by participants. If the decision had been made to invest funds in the construction of a refinery, an informative statement that the requested amount had been deposited in the appropriate account would be reasonable. It would be equally reasonable for the participants to receive a message stating that the construction of the plant had been started as long as the message would not increase the load level beyond that planned for the manipulation.

Games

Games are research techniques where rules are provided and players usually have few alternatives in responding to the moves (actions) of opposing players. More likely than not, games are of zero-sum nature, i.e., a win for one player represents a loss for the opponent. Games (parallel to simulations) may be "free," "experimental," or "quasiexperimental" in nature. Thus, the players may operate either against a fixed predetermined program or may play against a partially or fully responsive program/opponent. Although playing an experimental game could certainly be surrounded with extensive information about underlying environmental conditions, about preceding events and so forth, such complexity has typically been avoided by the researchers employing this medium of data collection.

Using games for measuring human responding to environmental stimuli reflects the underlying assumption that a simplification of environmental condi-

---

[3]See later for problems generated by unknown confounding variables.

tions and environmental stimuli (by reduction in number or in levels of occurrence and levels of potential responsivity) does not violate relationships between the independent and dependent variables of interest. Considerable gaming research, based on the well-known prisoner's dilemma and related paradigms (cf., Deutsch, 1958; Deutsch & Krauss, 1960, 1962) and later developed toward considerable levels of sophistication (e.g., Rapoport, 1963, 1966, 1968, 1969, 1970, 1974b) has been claimed (at times by authors, at times by reviewers) to have wide-ranging implications for environments as complex as the internation system of politics (cf. Rapoport, 1974a). Certainly, such assumptions can be met with considerable doubt. Nonetheless, games may be useful if we know with some certainty that variable relationships of interest are indeed likely to be simple and unaffected by extraneous variables that cannot be included in simple game settings.

Role Playing

In the typical role-playing task, a person or group of persons imagine themselves in the role of another (or in some cases in a future situation they, themselves, could experience). They try to report how they would behave in the imaginary environment or report (or act out) how they believe another person would behave.

Some writers have suggested role playing as an alternative to simulation and/or laboratory experimentation or have not clearly distinguished between role playing and simulations (or games) as a basis for research design (e.g., Crano & Brewer, 1972). Certainly role playing has seductive qualities. As a technique, it requires little preparation and effort, no props, and usually little or no equipment. More importantly, there is absolutely no deception of subjects involved (cf. Kelman, 1967). In other words, for those who would trust that people's role-playing responses would be identical or similar to their responses to a "real" environment, this research method has many advantages.

Can one trust the accuracy of these predictions? Early investigations of role playing (comparisons between role playing and other research techniques and a few comparisons between role playing and real-world events) have shown that role playing *can* reproduce main effects that are observed both in experimental simulations and in post hoc analysis of real-world events (e.g., Freedman, 1969). However, role-playing techniques can rarely, if ever, demonstrate the complex interactive effects that other research techniques or real-world-based observations can produce (e.g., Freedman, 1969; Fromkin & Streufert, 1976; Willis & Willis, 1970). Meaningful role-playing analysis must consequently be limited to the kind of simple settings that occur more rarely in the field of environmental psychology.

Role playing has (probably for good reason) not been a method of choice in environmental psychology. Nonetheless, it could have been employed albeit with limited success. Let us take, for example, the work of Nogami (1976), who varied both space available and number of persons present to measure the effects of density on various dependent variables. Certainly, this researcher could have asked subjects whether they *would* feel crowded in specified (e.g., photographically presented) smaller and larger spaces. Possibly the subjects might have been able to report with some accuracy what size space might have begun to be perceived as uncomfortably crowded. Similarly, pictures of the number of persons present in a specified size space could have been shown to the subjects. Again, some accuracy of prediction might have been obtained. However, most likely the role-playing subject would have been hopelessly lost in predicting the joint and interactive effects of number of persons and size of space on his or her perceptions and behavior in an actual crowded setting.

Computer Simulation (Computer Modeling)

Psychologists of various theoretical and content orientation (e.g., Abelson, 1968, Guetzkow et al., 1972) have embraced computer simulations as their method of choice. Early computer simulations developed from free simulation methodology. As the typical behavior of persons, groups, or other acting systems introduced into the simulation could be identified and mathematically specified, the human acting system became potentially unnecessary and could be replaced by a parameter statement, i.e., a precise statement of the relationship and/or interaction among the relevant variables of interest. As knowledge increased (or was thought to increase), more and more of these variable relationships could be mathematically described, more and more eliminating the need for persons as part of the simulation system. Naturally, as soon as all relationships among all variables that are part of a system of interest can be precisely and reliably specified, the entire system can be mathematically summarized in terms of parameter relationships.

Even before we know all relationships among relevant variables, we can make assumptions about those relationships that we do not yet know or understand. In the latter case, the mathematically described system could no longer be an accurate representation of reality, but rather a "theory" or model of reality. This "theory" can then be tested against real-world events: With the introduction of some specified level of environmental variation in the real world *and* in the computer simulation, will the same outcomes occur? If not, then either some parameter statement needs to be corrected or not all the complexities of the real world (variables and variable interaction parameters) are as yet represented in the computer simulation system. To state that characteristic of computer simulations somewhat differently: Such models are attempts at mathematical successive approximations of reality. Obviously, the approximation (the implied theory of reality) is limited by the degree of accuracy of the stated parameters. The accuracy of the parameters, in turn, is at least partly a reflection of our degree of reliable knowledge of variable effects and variable interactions in a relevant field of study. Environmental psychology as a relatively new field has so far obtained only limited knowledge of variables, their effects, and interactions. As a consequence, the use of computer simulations in this field is likely premature.

A second use of computers is as a part of an overall man–machine system simulation. Here the computer merely fulfills a part of the systemic requirements; for example, it may operate as a source of input to simulation participants. While some parameter assumptions or environmental input specifications are typically involved in determining computer responses, the computer's role is basically an auxiliary one. In this form, computer assistance may in fact be desirable for research designs in environmental psychology. The use of computers in such situations, however, does not introduce any major changes into the basic research design characteristics. For example, the feedback to participants in experimental and/or quasiexperimental simulations can be handled with computer assistance.

EVALUATION OF THE AVAILABLE RESEARCH METHODS FOR COMPLEX RESEARCH IN ENVIRONMENTAL PSYCHOLOGY

From the preceding discussion, it is evident that methods such as role playing and gaming represent environments that are probably too simple to be relevant to many of the research concerns of environmental psychologists. It is probably equally evident that the time for computer simulations has not yet arrived. Much too much has yet to be learned about variables and their complex interactions to establish meaningful relationships among environmental variables in extensive parameter form. (This is not to argue that those who wish to approach environmental psychology from a purely mathematical modeling point of view should not be encouraged.)

What remains then, aside from approaches discussed in other chapters of this volume, are the various forms of simulation. Let us assume that we wish to test theory in environmental psychology. Or, let us assume that we merely want to operate on the principal of "I wonder what would happen if . . . .," based on an apparently reasonable hunch. What would be the advantages and the disadvantages of employing simulation in general and the different forms of simulation in particular?

ADVANTAGES AND PROBLEMS OF SIMULATION DESIGNS

Simulations are compromises and, as such, display both the advantages and disadvantages that compromises tend to have. As scientists, we wish to obtain data with considerable precision. As human beings with an interest in the world in which we live, we want to obtain data and develop theory that is directly applicable to that "real world." Years ago, many of us argued for precise laboratory manipulations of smaller and smaller segments of variables, reducing events to minimum observable phenomena. We did obtain reliable data by this method, and we were able to increase the experimental validity of our efforts (e.g., the discussions of Aronson & Carlsmith, 1968). Others among us sat in "armchairs" and philosophized about the state of our environment. Some misguided environmental "philosophers" even provided grounds for some societies' arguments that war was the justified means to gain needed living space. Obviously, neither of these approaches can provide solutions that are defensible to those of us who wish to build a bridge from the experimental to the applied, i.e., those of us who want to make use of externally valid scientific information to understand and improve the environment in which we must survive.

Simulation techniques can provide us with some assistance toward this goal. They contain the internal validity sought after by those who were once so enamored with infinite regress. They also contain external validity favored by those who are looking for an applied science of environmental psychology. Yet, as stated previously, simulations are compromises losing some degree of both external and internal validity in the attempt to obtain both. Some "experimental validity" is lost because of the introduction of the larger number of variables that are simultaneously operative. On the other side, some of the "external validity" is lost because the researcher is not likely to recognize and, consequently, may not introduce *all* the variables that are important to some "real-world" environment. Moreover, the researcher may well be forced to consider some variables he or she recognizes as important to be boundary variables; for example, the researcher may find it necessary to treat some variables as constant at one level *or* to vary them at only a few levels or over a rather restricted range. As a result, some external and some internal validity may be lost.

Nonetheless, simulations have considerable advantages over other research methods when we are interested in predicting human behavior in complex environments. While there are some restrictions on internal and external validity, simulations are probably the most effective method to produce maximal amounts of both kinds of validity simultaneously within the same research design. Obviously, the selection of a particular simulation type will increase either one or the other of the validity levels, and the choice should be based on the intents of the researcher.

Another primary advantage of simulation techniques is the high level of involvement that these methodologies *can* produce *if* they are well designed. If a simulation is interesting *and* appears realistic to the participants, it tends to produce the same level of involvement (and consequently equivalent resultant behavior) as is produced by the task and environment that the simulation represents. Because of this high level of involvement and because of the ability to manipulate variables "realistically," the experimenters can often select variables that could not be manipulated or even measured in the "real world" due to technical or ethical considerations.

Advantages and Problems of Free Simulations

Because free simulations do not permit an experimenter to control events over time, the experimenter is limited to introduction of the independent variable(s) at the time the simulation activities are initiated. Divergent environment starting points, various instructions, different resources, etc. are means for making (between-group) comparisons of resultant behaviors in different groups of participant subjects. Such comparisons must be evaluated in terms of simulation outcomes. Either a cut-off point in time may be selected to compare the effects of different starting points on different sets of groups, or the experimenter may wait until an end product has been achieved. He or she may then measure the time it took to complete the task, the quality of task performance, the number of errors committed during the process of task completion, etc. Assuming all relevant environmental and task variables have been introduced into the simulation at appropriate levels, the observed and measured outcome is likely to be based on a natural and consequently realistic process, yielding considerable external validity, at least for the prediction of how any *one* group of participants could behave in a number of parallel situations. Unfortunately that external validity does not necessarily extend from one group of participants to the next.

Because different groups of participants behave differently, they are subsequently exposed to diverse environmental elements over time.[4] These diverse environmental characteristics may have unique effects that may alter, modify, or even completely change subsequent participant behaviors. (Of course, it is possible to argue that such aspects of free simulations are in fact advantageous, because results that are repeatedly obtained from free simulation techniques are probably quite robust, having survived the interference of numerous confounding influences.) In other words, free simulations may well have applied value, but they tend to be too insensitive for purposes of general controlled experimentation or theory testing.

The major shortcomings of free simulation are the inability to: (1) measure *planned* effects of independent variables *over time,* and (2) introduce independent variable levels sequentially. For example, if we wished to investigate the effects of sudden bursts of environmental information or of required activities after a previous lull in information or activity, we could not obtain such data

---

[4]This problem may be less severe when the independent variables cannot be influenced by the behavior of the participants; for example, when such environmental conditions as temperature, uncontrollable noise, etc. are externally induced. Nonetheless, some effect of participant's actions might even exist here *if* the perception of or response to uncontrollable externally induced events is modified by events or situations that are the outcome of previous participant behaviors.

from a free simulation paradigm. In free simulation, no control exists over independent variable manipulations across time.

These shortcomings, at least from the standpoint of experimentation, seem to suggest that some form of a more experimental simulation paradigm is often preferable for purposes involving many complex environmental research designs.

Advantages and Problems of Experimental Simulations

Organizational psychologists have been concerned with simulation methods for some time. Such early writers on methodology in organizational psychology, as Kennedy (1962) and Weick (1965), have pointed out that simulations can become quite unrealistic, if not well designed, thereby destroying desired effects upon participants. Weick was criticizing free simulations, because experimental simulation methods had not yet been extensively developed. However, the cited problem could be even worse for experimental simulation techniques, because the programming of information that reaches experimental simulation participants makes it even more of a challenge to maintain credibility. Subsequent work, however, (cf. Fromkin & Streufert, 1976) has shown that it is possible (with some effort and considerable pretesting) to design experimental simulations that do not suffer from these defects. Simulations in environmental psychology are no exception to this rule.

A second potential problem for experimental simulations is their necessarily restricted nature. Due to the manipulation of controlled independent variables, experimental simulations are not typically as large as free simulations (i.e., uncontrolled fluctuations of events that may arise from the potential richness of many free simulation environments must be restricted in experimental techniques to enable realistic and complete control of experimental variables). This presents no major problem when a system of naturally limited size is being simulated; however, it may become an issue when the intent is to simulate a very large system with many interactive components.

Third, experimental simulations do not serve as well for early ''I wonder what would happen if . . .'' aspects of theory development. The spontaneous emergence of relationships among events (which an experimenter may not expect) are much less likely to occur in experimental than in free simulations, because the feedback loop from participant action-to environment reaction-to participant action is eliminated.

Despite those limitations, experimental simulations can be of great value when a realistic scenario and a realistic environmental input sequence can be designed *and* when the responses of individuals, groups, or organizations to specific environmental systems or to changes in environmental conditions over time are of value. Obviously, more effort has to go into creating a realistic experimental simulation than any other form of simulation. On the other hand, the data obtained are likely to produce even greater experimental validity than data gathered in other simulation methodologies.

Advantages and Problems of Quasiexperimental Simulations

So far we have been concerned with the advantages and the problems a researcher in environmental psychology is likely to encounter in the use of free and experimental simulation methodologies. Because quasiexperimental simulation methods occupy a midpoint between the latter two techniques, one may reasonably ask the question about the extent to which such problems "survive" in a quasiexperimental simulation environment. One basic problem of free simulations, that of time effect discrepancies among participant groups, is reduced in the quasiexperimental paradigm, because those variables that are of interest to the experimenter are maintained under experimenter control across time. Nevertheless, other problems may remain. Because an effect involving participant actions on events outside the manipulated independent variable(s) remains, discrepancies between outcomes that one group of participants might experience in comparison to another group might also continue to exist. While such discrepancies will probably not have a major effect on the relationship between preselected independent and dependent variables, they could exert variable effects across participant groups on the dependent measures obtained. As a consequence, otherwise significant relationships between independent and dependent variables might be diminished. Similarly, marginal relationships between independent and dependent variables that might have been uncovered using pure experimental simulations may not reach required significance levels in a quasiexperimental situation. Thus, research that utilizes a quasiexperimental simulation for theory-testing purposes may permit causal inference but may nevertheless be limited in its ability to discover more marginal relationships among variables. The degree to which such problems might occur would, of course, depend on the number of variables of interest that are maintained under experimental control (i.e., the degree to which such a simulation approaches either free or experimental simulation methodology).

SELECTING A RESEARCH METHOD FOR A RESEARCH EFFORT IN ENVIRONMENTAL PSYCHOLOGY

It should be stated again that this chapter is concerned with research methods that are applicable to complex problems, i.e., research questions where a multifaceted environment is likely to produce a multifaceted response in an exposed person, group, or organization. This chapter is not an argument against experimentation in the laboratory where all but one variable are held constant: The knowledge obtained in that kind of research can certainly provide us with useful questions for investigations in more complex settings. This chapter is also not an argument against the brainstorming that occurs in the armchairs of more or less wise men. Again, their conclusions can provide the basis for conceptualizations or hypotheses that the applied researcher might utilize to design relevant experiments.

This chapter has argued that we do have some methods that provide us with reasonably good data when we wish to study the effects of complex environments on human behavior. The chapter has attempted to point out the shortcomings and the advantages of these methods. It is hoped that research will be carried out at a *number* of different levels: in the restricted lab, in the simulation environment, and by observation in the real world whenever that is possible. To the degree to which the data obtained in these quite different settings do overlap or show degrees of identity, we can be more sure that we understand and know how to predict the phenomena in which we are interested.

Selecting an appropriate research method from those available must, of course, depend on the research question, on the variables of interest, on the ability to control and manipulate variables, and on the conditions under which observations are to be obtained. If the researcher wishes to utilize simulations or related methods, he or she may well start with a free simulation technique unless considerable data for at least some of the variables of interest have been collected previously. If conclusions are to be drawn from observed events and if relationships that are potentially important are, at present, purely hypothetical, then the researcher may learn much more by watching uncontrolled processes and interactions between environmental variables and the participating human beings. Once variables can be clearly defined, once predictions or, at least, guesses about relationships among variables can be stated, then quasiexperimental simulation designs or, if possible, experimental simulation designs tend to have greater advantages: more precision, more variable control, greater certainty about causal relationships, and finally more information about event sequences. However, the researcher must be aware that simulations become more difficult to design and that it is more difficult to achieve realism as we move from the more free to the more experimental methodologies.

One final note may be required. As Fromkin and Streufert (1976) have pointed out, simulations are *very* expensive to design and operate. Part of the high initial costs are due to the expense of "realism," others are due to the time requirements: Participants must be paid for several hours of participation in the simulation environment. On the other hand, the amount of data that can be collected in simulation runs is very large[5] and can cross modalities (e.g., data

---

[5]The collection of multiple data from a limited number of groups in specific experimental conditions can be criticized because constant errors due to nonrandom selection (error) might be evident in all sets of (within) data, producing potentially misleading results. As Fromkin and Streufert (1976) have pointed out, this problem can be diminished by partial replication (overlapping designs) of variable relationships (for more information, see Fromkin & Streufert).

may in part be based on behavioral activity, in part on scale responses, in part on observer ratings, and so forth). As a result, although the cost of the simulation as a whole may be relatively high, unit data obtained from simulation methodolgoies tend to be inexpensive.

REFERENCES

Abelson, R. P. (1968). Simulation of social behavior. In G. Lindzey & E. Aronson (Eds.), *Handbook of social psychology*, (2nd Ed. Vol. 2, pp. 274–356). Reading, MA: Addison–Wesley.

Aronson, E., & Carlsmith, J. M. (1968). Experimentation in social psychology. In G. Lindzey & E. Aronson (Eds.), *The handbook of social psychology*. Reading, MA: Addison–Wesley.

Campbell, D. T., & Stanley, J. (1963). *Experimental and quasi-experimental designs in research*. Chicago: Rand McNally.

Crano, W. D., & Brewer, M. P. (1972). *Principles of research in social psychology*. New York: McGraw–Hill.

Dawson, R. E. (1962). Simulation in the social sciences. In H. Guetzkow (Ed.), *Simulation in social science: Readings*. Englewood Cliffs, NJ: Prentice–Hall.

Deutsch, M. (1958). Trust and suspicion. *Journal of Conflict Resolution, 2,* 265–279.

Deutsch, M., & Krauss, R. M. (1960). The effect of threat on interpersonal bargaining. *Journal of Abnormal Social Psychology, 61,* 181–189.

Deutsch, M., & Krauss, R. M. (1962). Studies of interpersonal bargaining. *Journal of Conflict Resolution, 6,* 52–76.

Drabeck, T. E., & Haas, J. E. (1969). Laboratory simulation of organizational stress. *American Sociological Review, 34,* 224–238.

Driver, M. J. (1962). *Conceptual structure and group processes in an internation simulation.* (Part 1): *The perception of simulated nations.* Princeton University and Educational Testing Service (ONR Technical Report #9, NR 171–055 and AF Technical Report AF 49(638)-742, and Research Report NIMH Grant M 4186), Princeton, NJ.

Freedman, J. L. (1969). Role playing: Psychology by consensus. *Journal of Personality and Social Psychology, 13,* 107–114.

Fromkin, H. L., & Streufert, S. (1976). Laboratory experimentation. In M. Dunnette (Ed.), *Handbook of organizational and industrial psychology*. Chicago: Rand McNally.

Guetzkow, H. (1959). A use of simulation in the study of international relations. *Behavioral Science, 4,* 183–191.

Guetzkow, H. (Ed.). (1962). *Simulation in social science: Readings*. Englewood Cliffs, NJ: Prentice–Hall.

Guetzkow, H. (1963). A use of simulation in the study of inter-nation-relations. In H. Guetzkow, C. F. Alger, R. A. Brody, R. C. Noel, & R. C. Snyder (Eds.), *Simulation in international relations*. Englewood Cliffs, NJ: Prentice–Hall.

Guetzkow, H., Alger, C. F., Brody, R. A., Noel, R. C., & Snyder, R. C. (1963). *Simulation in international relations: Developments for research and teaching*. Englewood Cliffs, NJ: Prentice–Hall.

Guetzkow, H., Kotler, P., & Schultz, R. L. (1972). *Simulation in social and administrative science*. Englewood Cliffs, NJ: Prentice–Hall.

Inbar, M., & Stoll, C. S. (1972). *Simulation and gaming in social science*. New York: Free Press.

Kelman, H. C. (1967). Human use of human subjects: The problem of deception in social psychological experiments. *Psychological Bulletin, 67,* 1–11.

Kennedy, J. L. (1962, February). The system approach: Organizational development. *Human Factors, 25–52.*

Nogami, G. Y. (1976). Crowding: Effects of group size, room size or density. *Journal of Applied Social Psychology, 6,* 105–125.

Rapoport, A. (1963). Formal games as probing tools for investigating behavior motivated by trust and suspicion. *Journal of Conflict Resolution, 7,* 520–579.

Rapoport, A. (1966). *Two-person game theory.* Ann Arbor: The University of Michigan Press.

Rapoport, A. (1968). Prospects for experimental games. *Journal of Conflict Resolution, 12,* 461–470.

Rapoport, A. (1969). Games as tools of psychological research. In I. R. Buchler & H. G. Nutini (Eds.) *Game theory in the behavioral sciences.* Pittsburgh: University of Pittsburgh Press.

Rapoport, A. (1970). *N-person game theory.* Ann Arbor: The University of Michigan Press.

Rapoport, A. (Ed.). (1974a).*Game theory as a theory of conflict resolution.* Dordrecht, Holland and Boston: D. Reidel Publishing Company.

Rapoport, A. (1974b). Prisoner's dilemma - recollections and observations. In A. Rapoport (Ed.), *Game theory as a theory of conflict resolution.* Dordrecht, Holland: D. Reidel Publishing Company.

Shubik, M. (1960, December). Bibliography on simulation, gaming, artificial intelligence and allied topics. *Journal of the American Statistical Association,* 736–751.

Streufert, S., Clardy, M. A., Driver, M. J., Karlins, N., Schroder, H. M., & Suedfeld, P. (1965). A tactical game for the analysis of complex decision making in individuals and groups. *Psychological Reports, 17,* 723–729.

Streufert, S., & Driver, M. J. (1965). Conceptual structure, information load and perceptual complexity. *Psychonomic Science, 3,* 249–250.

Streufert, S., Kliger, S. C., Castore, C. H., & Driver, M. J. (1967). A tactical and negotiations game for analysis of decision integration across decision areas. *Psychological Reports, 20,* 155–157.

Streufert, S., & Schroder, H. M. (1965). Conceptual structure, environmental complexity and task performance. *Journal of Experimental Research in Personality, 1,* 132–137.

Streufert, S., & Streufert, S. C. (1978). *Behavior in the complex environment.* Washington, D.C.: V. H. Winston and John Wiley.

Streufert, S., & Suedfeld, P. (1977). Simulation as a research method: A problem in communication. *Journal of Applied Social Psychology, 7,* 281–285.

Streufert, S., & Swezey, R. W. (1980). *Organizational simulation: Theoretical aspects of test bed design.* McLean, Virginia: SAI Report No. SAI 80-101-178.

Weick, K. (1965). Laboratory experimentation with organizations. In J. G. March (Ed.), *Handbook of Organizations.* Chicago: Rand McNally.

Willis, R. H., & Willis, Y. A. (1970). Role playing vs. deception: An experimental comparison. *Journal of Personality and Social Psychology, 16,* 472–477.

5

Environmental Exposure and Disease: An Epidemiological Perspective on Some Methodological Issues in Health Psychology and Behavioral Medicine

Stanislav V. Kasl
Department of Epidemiology and Public Health
Yale University School of Medicine

INTRODUCTION

A lengthy title generally suggests that the author finds it difficult to characterize the intent and the scope of his invited contribution. *In this chapter I discuss a number of methodological issues that I believe are salient in current etiological research that attempts to link psychosocial factors to health status changes.* The vantage point from which I carry on my discussion is one that derives from epidemiology but is by no means synonymous with it. My intent is to utilize current relevant research in order to work inductively toward a more general statement of methodological problems and issues; epidemiology—its concepts and methods—come in merely as a framework within which to organize and structure these methodological points. I specifically avoid using the discipline of epidemiology in a deductive fashion; that is, lay out, in abstract, the prescribed attributes of good epidemiologic designs and methods and then deduce from these the desirable methodological characteristics of studies in health psychology or behavioral medicine.

There are a couple of reasons why epidemiology does not lend itself easily to such a deductive translation of textbook principles into practical guidelines for behavioral and social scientists investigating psychosocial risk factors for illness. One is that epidemiology cannot (should not) claim unique methods and unique solutions to persistent problems with which other disciplines have struggled as well. For example, the problems of using a sequence of cross-sectional surveys ("synthetic cohorts") to infer both the effects of aging of individuals and of intergenerational experiences (secular trends), as well as the interaction of the two, have been approached by other disciplines such as demography and gerontology, and epidemiology has no basis for claiming superior solutions. It is true that certain approaches, such as the case-control design, have been analyzed, clarified, and refined primarily by epidemiology (e.g., Ibrahim, 1979; Schlesselman, 1982); however, it is not clear whether such advances represent universal solutions cutting across disciplines or only more limited answers to practical problems that epidemiologists frequently encounter.

The last point leads into the second reason for doubting the a priori, across-the-board validity and usefulness of epidemiologic methods for health psychology and behavioral medicine. Epidemiology has only a limited and recent history of dealing with psychosocial risk factors. The methodology that has evolved is based primarily on working with biological risk factors and biomedical models of disease. Thus it is far from self-evident that the body of methodological dicta that has evolved out of this cumulative research experience (i.e., "epidemiologic methods") is sufficiently cognizant of and sensitive to the additional methodological problems encountered by investigators working with psychosocial risk factors, biosocial models of disease, and mechanisms of causation that go beyond purely biological parameters.

A small example may serve to illustrate the preceding two interrelated points. Matching is a bread-and-butter procedure that is of fundamental importance to the refined case-control methodology developed by epidemiology. On the other hand, among some social scientists (viz. Cook & Campbell, 1976 and 1979), matching is viewed with considerably more suspicion and potential problems related to biased selection and statistical regression are more prominently discussed. Who should be borrowing from whom here? Or is it possible that each discipline has arrived at a suitable set of methodological guidelines regarding matching, useful for its own research domain, but not to be exported across disciplinary boundaries.

The previous comments are meant to create a realistic set of expectations regarding the methodological contribution of epidemiology to health psychology and behavioral medicine. Also implied is the admission that occasionally excessive claims have been made for epidemiology and its ability to come to the rescue with research design solutions and methodological innovations not yet discovered by other disciplines (viz. the somewhat presumptuous title *Epidemiology as a Fundamental Science,* chosen by White & Henderson, 1976, for their edited volume on applications to health services research).

A SUITABLE BACKGROUND FOR READING THIS CHAPTER

This chapter builds upon two sets of writings: (1) the epidemiological literature, both methodological as well as substantive, particularly the psychosocial content area, and (2) the "stress & disease" literature, a shorthand notation for etiological research on psychosocial factors in physical illness found in medical sociology, psychosomatic medicine, psychosocial epidemiology, health psychology, and behavioral medicine. Because many readers are likely to be unfamiliar with some of this literature, I provide references that are intended to facilitate accessing this body of writings. However, this chapter does not presuppose more than a very rudimentary knowledge of epidemiology and some broad familiarity with health research.

Epidemiology is conventionally defined by Last (1983) as "the study of the distribution and determinants of health-related states and events in populations, and the application of this study to control of health problems" (pp. 32-33). It is commonplace, furthermore, to make a distinction between descriptive and analytic epidemiology, with the latter referring to specific hypothesis-testing efforts. The boundaries of epidemiology, particularly analytic epidemiology, would be most difficult to define. A number of useful textbooks are available for perusal for those who are curious to learn if knowing about epidemiologic methods would help them with their research (e.g., Alderson, 1976; Fox, Hall, & Elveback, 1970; Friedman, 1980; Kleinbaum, Kupper, & Morgenstern, 1982; Lilienfeld & Lilienfeld, 1979; MacMahon & Pugh, 1970; Mausner & Bahn, 1974; Morris, 1975). In addition to the general textbooks, one can also find volumes designed to deal with applications of epidemiologic methods, such as to the medical care setting (e.g., Barker & Rose, 1979; Knox, 1979; White & Henderson, 1976). Last's (1983) *A dictionary of epidemiology* may also be a useful reference for the social scientist, because in many instances the ideas are the same but only the terminology is different.

Epidemiology has a long tradition of emphasizing the ecologic triad of agent-host-environment, and this makes it highly suitable for application to the study of psychosocial risk factors (Susser, 1975). The domain of psychosocial epidemiology is not particularly well defined and most of the relevant writings (e.g., Cassel, 1974, 1975; Graham, 1974; Graham & Reeder, 1979; Hinkle, Dohrenwend, Elinson, Kasl, McDowell, Mechanic, & Syme, 1976; Kasl, 1977a; Sexton, 1979; Syme, 1974) have been fragmentary and illustrative rather than systematic and comprehensive. However, it is not difficult to extend the general definition of epidemiology and define psychosocial epidemiology as that part of epidemiology that is concerned with psychosocial determinants of "health-related states." A somewhat similar-sounding term, psychiatric epidemiology, has conventionally referred to that part of epidemiology that is defined by a specific subset of health states with which it is concerned, psychiatric outcomes (e.g., Weissman & Klerman, 1978). However, definitions count for very little in an emerging field of amorphous boundaries. To some investigators, the term *social epidemiology* has also meant a broadening of "health-related states" to include such health-linked behaviors as smoking and drug abuse. And a recent set of publications by Prodist, entitled "Monographs in Psychosocial Epidemiology," has dealt with such diverse topics as help-seeking behavior (Mechanic, 1982) and stressful life events (Dohrenwend & Dohrenwend, 1981).

The second set of writings upon which this chapter builds, the "stress & disease" area, is likely to be more familiar to the typical reader of this chapter. This should be particularly true for recently edited volumes, such as *Health Psychology* (Stone, Cohen, & Adler, 1979), the several volumes of *Handbook of Psychology and Health* (Baum & Singer, 1982; Gatchel, Baum, & Singer, 1982; Krantz, Baum, & Singer, 1983), the volume on *Environmental Stress* (Evans, 1982), The *Handbook of Stress* (Goldberger & Breznitz, 1982), and the *Perspectives on Behavioral Medicine* (Weiss, Herd, & Fox, 1981). Journals such as *Health Psychology* and *Journal of Behavioral Medicine* are also likely to be quite familiar. Less familiar may be recent volumes and journal reviews that represent other disciplines, particularly medical sociology, psychosomatic medicine, and psychosocial epidemiology (e.g., Cox & McKay, 1982; Elliott & Eisdorfer, 1982; Hamburg, Elliott, & Parron, 1982; Henry, 1982; Jenkins, 1982; McQueen & Siegrist, 1982; Mechanic, 1983; Steptoe & Mathews, 1984; Sterling & Eyer, 1981; Weiner, 1977). In addition, it would be useful to examine the major journals in these areas, such as *Journal of Health and Social Behavior, Social Science and Medicine, Psychosomatic Medicine, American Journal of Epidemiology, International Journal of Epidemiology,* and *Journal of Chronic Diseases.*

The methodological discussion that follows is based on my familiarity with reasonably diverse areas of research. Implicitly, I draw upon some of the following reviews in presenting my methodological evaluation of the "stress & disease" area (these reviews are listed here because in this chapter I cannot deal with both the substantive content areas as well as the methodological issues): retirement (Kasl, 1980), migration (Kasl & Berkman, 1983), work environment (Kasl, 1978; Kasl & Cobb, 1983), economic instability (Kasl, 1982), residential environment (Kasl, 1977b; Kasl & Rosenfield, 1980), social support (Kasl & Wells, 1985), stressful life events (Kasl, 1983a), health of the elderly (Kasl & Berkman, 1981), course of disease (Kasl, 1983b), and general reviews of stress (Kasl, 1977a, 1984a,b).

CROSS-SECTIONAL AND RETROSPECTIVE DESIGNS

The etiological process of interest in the "stress & disease" association can be reduced to the following schema (Elliott & Eisdorfer, 1982; Pearlin, Lieberman, Menaghan, & Mullan, 1981): environmental exposure (psychosocial risk) → biological and/or psychosocial reaction → health status change. The fundamental issue that is the subject of this chapter is the ability of our research design and data analysis methodology to reconstruct unambiguously and comprehensively as much of this etiological process as is possible.

In this section I comment on designs that represent data collection efforts at one point in time. In epidemiology, the primary designs that fall in here are the cross-sectional survey and the case-control study. These designs are a good starting point for discussion because they permit one to develop a particularly convincing list of methodological issues and weaknesses. Subsequent sections elaborate on some of these points and discuss potentially stronger research designs. The analytic strategy that I follow is the one so well developed and formalized by Campbell and colleagues (Campbell & Stanley, 1966; Cook & Campbell, 1976, 1979): to propose and to examine alternative hypotheses (threats to validity) that undermine our confidence in the initial interpretation that a particular etiological process is being described.

In the cross-sectional survey one examines the relationship between a disease (or some health-relevant characteristic) and selected variables, as they exist in a defined population and at one point in time. In the case-control design, there is a targetted selection both of persons with the disease (or some other characteristic) and of some suitable comparison subjects (controls). Because the cases and controls are, in principle, no more than a very specific subset of all the subjects eligible for the cross-sectional survey (unless, of course, one is trying to generalize to different populations, such as treated vs. untreated cases), there is presumably no scientific advantage to the case-control design over the cross-sectional survey. Its advantages are primarily those of economy of effort and these could be considerable. The disadvantages of the case-control design inhere in the targetted selection of subjects. Some of the consequences may be: (1) inability to make population estimates of disease prevalence or of population rates of risk factors; (2) inability to generalize results to the desired population because selection processes for obtaining cases and controls are complex and biases are unknown, particularly those associated with the process of coming to be diagnosed or treated; (3) inability to detect true risk-factor differences or detecting spurious differences, because of matching procedures or failure to match. The methodology of case-control designs is discussed by Schlesselman (1982) and the epidemiologic texts listed earlier.

The major methodological issues of concern to health psychology and behavioral medicine inhere in the cross-sectional nature of the data, and it is not really necessary to offer separate discussions for the cross-sectional survey and case-control designs. The major point is this: The cross-sectional data may reveal an association (or fail to reveal one), but this does not reproduce the true dynamic, longitudinal nature of the underlying etiological process. The results can be misleading in at least three major ways: (1) the current status of the risk factors is different from what they were before the disease developed; (2) data collection efforts to assess the current or earlier status of the risk factors (''retrospection'') are biased; (3) there has been a selective attrition of subjects, primarily via mortality or institutionalization of persons with the disease, from some earlier time and thus the data are based upon an incomplete ascertainment of relevant subjects.

Clearly, the major concern in interpreting cross-sectional information on psychosocial risk factors for a disease is that the presence of the disease (or of some health-relevant condition) has actually altered the presumptively antecedent risk factor or has influenced its assessment, or both. The notion of "presence of disease" could refer to somewhat different processes: (1) the effects of the distress and pain of having the condition, (2) the effects associated with the process of detection (diagnosis) and treatment, and (3) the effects of knowledge and beliefs about the condition (e.g., it causes or its prognosis). Similarly, the effects could be somewhat different: (1) primarily affective, such as anxiety and depression, or (2) cognitive, such as causal reattribution as one looks back at the prodromal period, or (3) functional, such as social interaction with friends and relatives.

(The aforementioned are "true" effects of the disease itself, with no reference to misclassification regarding the presence of a disease or some condition. However, if assessment of disease presence is biased with respect to some factor that also influences the assessment of risk factors, then we have a methodological effect of the "presence of disease." This receives a separate discussion later.)

It is not difficult to provide some concrete illustrations of the preceding points. Reviews of the literature on coronary heart disease (e.g., Jenkins, 1976, 1982) reveal that higher levels of anxiety and distress are a consequence of myocardial infarction (MI) but are not its antecedents. (Such a conclusion, naturally enough, can only be based on longitudinal studies of initially healthy subjects.) It follows that the many case-control studies (and some cross-sectional surveys) that have revealed higher levels of anxiety and distress among the MI patients are detecting a spurious "risk factor," one that was altered by the disease. The evidence further suggests that these are truly higher levels of anxiety and would be detected by other, more objective measurement procedures. However, it is certainly possible that the MI has had, in addition, some influence on the measurement process itself, when this is based on self-reports. There is also evidence from studies of public beliefs about causes of heart attacks (Marmot, 1982; Shekelle & Lin, 1978), which reveals that "stress, worry, nervous tension, pressure" is the most frequently stated cause, even ahead of the accepted biological risk factors. Thus retrospective accounts of heart attack victims about their premorbid life circumstances are likely to be influenced by a "search for meaning," an attribution process that increases the tendency to report stress or pressure or overwork for the period before the hear attack. This is presumably the explanation for an otherwise puzzling finding that male MI patients reported more "nervous stress" during the previous 10 years, even as the controls (without disease) were the ones more likely to be found in work settings where the work pace was hectic, as determined by objective methods (Maschewsky, 1982).

The best practitioners of the art of raising alternative hypotheses in order to analyze etiological interpretations believe that it is important to raise plausible alternatives, not just a catalogue of problems irrespective of their plausibility. However, it is often easier to detect flaws in abstract than it is to assess their plausibility and relevance. The previous discussion has raised, for cross-sectional data, the alternative hypothesis of the effects of presence of disease on detecting risk factors. But it is not clear how damaging, in specific instances, those alternative hypotheses are. Among cases of MI, one would presumably be suspicious of measures that can be influenced by anxiety and distress, or by subjective ratings of environmental stress. Thus everything we know about the various related instruments for assessing stressful life events (Dohrenwend & Dohrenwend, 1981; Kasl, 1983a, 1984c) would suggest that additional retrospective studies of stressful events by cases of MI and controls are quite unnecessary unless they can deal more effectively than heretofore with this bias. However, how bad is the retrospective bias in such measures as marital satisfaction or life satisfaction? At this moment we just don't know. One must also remember that plausibility is no substitute for actual data. Thus the evidence reviewed by Jenkins (1976, 1982) clearly shows that elevated levels of anxiety are a prospective risk factor for angina pectoris. If we had only case-control data on angina, the elevated levels of anxiety among angina patients—in view of the extensive MI evidence—would most plausibly be seen as another effect of the disease even though this is not the correct interpretation.

Retrospective case-control studies of cancer represent a particularly problematic design when searching for psychosocial risk factors, because of the overwhelming plausibility of the effects of the disease, especially anxiety, distress, and the search for meaning. One particularly poignant illustration of the likely bias in such designs comes from a study of children with cancer (mostly leukemia) and controls (Jacobs & Charles, 1980); only 32% of mothers of cases, compared to 90% of mothers of controls, described the original pregnancy as "planned." Surely this represents a desperate effort to cope with a dreaded disease in a small child; its status as a biologically plausible risk factor is close to nil. The stress and cancer literature has been subjected to searching methodological reviews (e.g., Fox, 1978; Morrison & Paffenbarger, 1981), and clearly the status of psychosocial risk factors detected in case-control studies is extremely shaky.

In concluding this section, note that I have dealt with the issue of cross-sectional data in a highly selective way, emphasizing the influence of the disease itself and the difficulty of reconstructing the predisease levels of putative risk factors. This I feel is appropriate, given the whole orientation of this chapter. I have obviously ignored the large literature on multivariate analysis and the strategies of pinning down the role of the generic third variable in order to understand a cross-sectional association between the first two variables. Later sections elaborate on additional methodological issues, some of which are raised in the context of supposedly more powerful designs, such as those involving longitudinal data. It is a fair bet that many such limitations are applicable to cross-sectional designs as well—though there are some obvious exceptions, such as the effects of repeated testing.

SOME EFFORTS TO STRENGTHEN CROSS-SECTIONAL DATA

Once one has set up the best design along traditional textbook guidelines (e.g., optimal control group(s) in the case-control design), are there additional strategies that reduce the vulnerability of the cross-sectional or retrospective data to the alternative hypotheses discussed previously? In principle, it follows from the earlier discussion that such strategies should either reduce the impact of the disease or make the measurement process more impervious to the possible biasing influences of the presence of disease.

Certainly one suitable strategy is to seek other sources of data, those that go beyond the self-reports of the subjects studied. For example, "verifying" environmental exposures, such as a high level of job demands, with various types of institutional data might be a very satisfactory solution. Using other respondents may or may not be helpful, depending on what data they are asked to supply and how they themselves might be affected by the presence of the disease in the focal respondent. The wife of a man with an MI may go through the same causal attribution process regarding prodromal stresses in the life of her husband as he would himself, and her reports may thus be equally suspect. If the instrument is the Holmes and Rahe (1967) social readjustment rating scale, then the amount of agreement between the reports of life events by the man with MI and by the wife may reflect a much more complex process than just "verifying" that certain events did take place. If they both report "trouble with boss," it could only mean that he complains about his work situation to his wife, but such agreement does not necessarily establish the reality of the actual work situation. Conversely, if she fails to report the same event that he reported, it could mean that he failed to confide in his wife. In short, a measure of agreement intended to verify environmental exposure may in fact be a measure of adequacy of sharing and communication in the marriage. Outside the marriage, other respondents acting as "significant others" also may or may not provide the strengthening of self-reports one is seeking. For example, a recent study of social support in the work setting (Karasek, Triantis, & Chaudhry, 1982) reported a strong positive correlation between instrumental support from supervisor and perceptions of him as demanding–authoritarian; apparently, task-relevant help from the supervisor is difficult to deliver in an unambiguously positive way. One can certainly imagine that supervisor's reports of his own behavior might not be suitable to "verify" the focal subject's reports of either supportiveness or job demands.

Depending on what the specific alternative hypothesis is with which one is concerned, other strategies may become useful. For example, if the concern is that the painful and disabling aspects of a disease are influencing self-reports, then a statistical control for disease severity (or a specific analysis of patients who are in remission) may adequately handle this alternative possibility. Thus, for example, the absence of an association between severity of the disease, rheumatoid arthritis, and the amount of anger–irritation among female cases with the disease was seen as suggesting that disease alone was not producing the higher case levels of anger–irritation in the case-control comparisons (Kasl & Cobb, 1969). Of course, this strategy does require a wide variation in severity of diseases, including enough cases that are in remission. It might also be noted that if the concern is regarding the impact of an unfavorable life prognosis associated with the disease itself (particularly cancer), and if temporary remission of disease does not alter (objectively or subjectively) the prognosis, then, of course, controlling on severity of disease does nothing to help us reject such an alternative explanation.

Subgroup analyses may be another strategy of dealing with alternative hypotheses, though generally one needs to introduce additional assumptions upon which to build an interpretive case. For example, Orth–Gomer (1979) carried out a case-control study of men in New York and Stockholm with and without ischemic heart disease. The Swedish men ascribed stress mainly to the job situation, whereas American men reported stress caused by family conflict, but there were no differences in overall quantity of stress. A second study (Siegrist, Dittman, Rittner, & Weber, 1982) obtained similar differences comparing German and American male cases with heart disease and controls. If one makes the additional assumption that the effects of disease, such as the reattribution process or reporting of specific stressors, do not differ across countries, then the preceding findings would appear to provide etiological clues about stress specificity and heart disease. However, it is rather likely that the attribution process does systematically differ across countries or social strata; note, for example, the social class differences in lay explanations of the etiology of arthritis (Elder, 1973).

The strategy of collecting data on biological or biomedical parameters in one's cross-sectional study of psychosocial risk factors and disease must always be viewed as potentially very valuable. This potential translates into actuality to the extent that (1) the biological parameters themselves are not compromised by the cross-sectional design, and (2) they help us identify a biologically more plausible mechanism linking the psychosocial data and the disease. For example, a couple of studies (Crown & Crown, 1973; Rimon, 1973) have used serological data to subclassify cases of rheumatoid disease into seropositive and seronegative. The findings of higher levels of anxiety and resentment–suspicion among the seronegative cases suggests a differential etiology in the two groups of patients, provided the serological data are unobtrusive, that is, uncorrelated with overt clinical manifestations of disease and provided that the diagnosis of rheumatoid disease is made equally securely in both groups. A similar strategy applied to patients with low back pain (Leavitt, Garron, & Bielauskas, 1979) may not be equally successful, because the distinction between presence versus absence of definite organic disease may have different implications: Those without organic disease may qualify for the diagnosis partly because of strong tendencies to complain, which could also influence the measurement of the psychosocial risk factors, particularly those assessing stressors or distress. Finally, utilizing bilogical data may sometimes only falsely increase one's confidence in a dubious etiological interpretation. One study (Orth–Gomer & Ahlbom, 1980) showed that patients with ischemic heart disease reported more stress (dissatisfactions, conflicts, major changes) for the 5 years prior to onset, even after adjusting for standard risk factors. However, such adjustments in no way reduce the plausibility of the hypothesis that having the disease alters the reporting and/or perception of stress; if anything, one might suppose that patients with average levels of biological risk would be propelled even more strongly toward interpreting their disease in stress terms. One might also note that the standard risk factors are not uninfluenced by the disease itself and the subsequent treatment.

One particularly interesting strategy is the design of studying an undifferentiated group of patients awaiting biopsy results and trying to predict for whom later biopsy results will reveal malignancy (e.g., Greer & Morris, 1978; Horne & Picard, 1979; Schmale & Iker, 1966, 1971; Wirsching, Stierlin, Hoffmann, Weber, & Wirsching, 1982). The presumption is that the distinction between presence versus absence of malignancy determined by biopsy is silent and unobtrusive, that is, not differentially associated with any clinical manifestations, and that, therefore, any effects of illness (e.g., anticipatory fears) are equal in both groups. Thus any obtained differences in psychosocial variables in the two groups are thought to point to etiological processes linked to tumor initiation and/or preclinical tumor progression. In point of fact, it would be nice to verify the preceding presumptions. For example, there is much clinical lore suggesting that the physician can anticipate with some accuracy the biopsy results; if such expectations are communicated to the patient, verbally or nonverbally, we no longer have as clean a design as we think. Nevertheless, this remains a valuable strategy worth pursuing, even though it may not be equally applicable to other diseases. Thus, awaiting the results of angiography, which will reveal the severity of coronary artery occlusion, may not be the same kind of a situation because presenting symptoms and degree of occlusion may be associated, though apparently not in any simple way (Jenkins, Stanton, Klein, Savageau, & Harken, 1983).

THE NECESSARY BUT INSUFFICIENT VIRTUES OF LONGITUDINAL DESIGNS

If one were to administer to investigators in health psychology and behavioral medicine a semantic differential for rating designs, "cross-sectional" would surely score near the "bad" anchor point and "longitudinal" would score near the "good" anchor point. Epidemiologists would probably do the same, but very likely they would grumble first, claiming that there are several different longitudinal designs and that, therefore, the referent is rather ambiguous. Indeed. It is the purpose of this section to probe critically the notion (which in its slight oversimplification asserts) that whatever is wrong with cross-sectional data can be remedied by a longitudinal design.

The bread-and-butter design in epidemiology is the prospective study in which a sample of persons (often referred to as a cohort), who are initially free of the target disease, are assessed for various (potential) risk factors and then followed up for the development of the disease. Careful monitoring of outcome is needed so that all incident events (deaths, hospitalizations, untreated episodes, "silent" events) can be ascertained. Because such careful monitoring generally requires face-to-face contact with the research team, the follow-up data collection may include repeated assessments of the risk factors. However, data analysis aimed at identifying the relevant risk factors is most often based on the initial assessment, and later values of the risk factors (or risk factor change) are less frequently utilized in analysis. The preceding design characterizes well the prospective studies of coronary heart disease (Pooling Project Research Group, 1978), and these have made a major contribution to clinical medicine.

From the perspective of philosophy of science and anlysis of causation, the previous schema really addresses only one issue: the temporal ordering of cause and effect. In practical terms, however, the prospective design is associated with a substantial increase in one's faith that causal agents, or indicators of causal agents, have been identified, compared to the cross-sectional or case-control designs. The major limitations of this prospective design are generally twofold: (1) it may not explain much about actual (biological) mechanisms involved, and (2) it still does not provide the kind of evidence that comes from controlled clinical trials altering the risk factor(s) or experimental assignment to risk factor status (a rather uncommon enterprise in epidemiology). This can be stated another way: We can seldom distinguish between causal agents and indicators of cause, nor can we tell how distal the indicator might be from the actual cause (underlying mechanism).

In specifically psychosocial epidemiologic studies, the fundamentals of the preceding prospective design *may* remain unaltered; what may differ only is the enlarged scope of initial data collection to include a variety of psychosocial variables. This characterizes the well-known Framingham Heart Study, although not from the start (e.g., Haynes, Eaker, & Feinleib, 1983; Haynes & Feinleib, 1982; Haynes, Feinleib, & Kannel, 1980) and the equally well-known Western Collaborative Group Study (WCGS), investigating Behavior Type A as a risk factor for coronary heart disease (e.g., Brand, Rosenman, Sholtz, & Friedman, 1976; Rosenman, Brand, Jenkins, Friedman, Straus, & Wurm, 1975).

It is worth noting that a certain implicit consensus has developed regarding the way the psychosocial and biological data ought to be jointly analyzed. In general, one develops a multiple logistic model, utilizing the established biomedical risk factors. Then one introduces the behavioral or psychosocial variable in order to see if that variable adds significantly to the prediction of disease. This characterizes the analysis of the data from Framingham, WCGS, and other well-known studies, such as the Israeli Ischemic Heart Disease project (Goldbourt, Medalie, & Neufeld, 1975; Medalie & Goldbourt, 1976; Medalie, Papier, Goldbourt, & Herman, 1975). Unfortunately, this approach is driven primarily by a statistical model, not a conceptual one; it assumes that we are not interested in the psychosocial variable, unless its contribution is additive to what is already accounted for by as complete a set of biological predictors as possible. This assumption is appropriate in such situations as when investigating the contributory role of subjective evaluations of one's health status to mortality (Kaplan & Camacho, 1983; Mossey & Shapiro, 1982); unless there is a thorough control for the confounding effects of "actual" health status, the contribution of the subjective variable is likely to be interpreted either in a trivial or misleading fashion. On the other hand, when the psychosocial variable represents an early influence in a "developmental sequence" (Alker, 1965), which later operates via some of the biological variables, then an adjustment on statistical grounds for the prior contribution of such biological variables will prematurely consign such a psychosocial variable into irrelevance—when, in fact, from an ecological-public health perspective we ought to remain interested in it. This is not quite a plea to investigators in psychosocial epidemiology and behavioral medicine to resist the reductionist premises of the purely biomedical community; rather, it is only a plea for the development of conceptual models, rather than purely statistical ones, in guiding our multivariate analyses.

The classical prospective design in epidemiology is simplicity itself—partly because some of its implications and complexities are not well drawn out in epidemiologic textbooks. One neglected issue derives from the distinction between *predisposing* and *precipitating* factors. It follows that the prospective design is more likely to detect those disease risk factors that are either relatively stable predisposing factors or precipitating factors indexed by relatively stable environmental conditions (such as severe deadline pressures that come up periodically in a particular work setting). Less likely to be identified are precipitating factors that are part of acute dynamics that take place shortly before disease onset. For example, prospective studies of gout have clearly identified stably high levels of serum uric acid as a primary predisposing factor (Cobb, 1971), but precipitating factors have been difficult to pin down among those previously free of the disease.

When the model of disease is one where precipitating factors play a major role, then the skeleton of the prospective epidemiologic design (collect risk factor data on healthy subjects and then sit tight and wait till cases of disease develop) must be fleshed out with interim monitoring of the cohort. For example, when we are studying the development of infectious mononucleosis (IM), we must pay attention both to: (1) a stable predisposing factor, absence of antibody to Epstein–Barr virus of the IgG type, at the start of the study, and (2) a necessary (but not sufficient) precipitating factor, becoming infected (seroconversion) during the study (Evans, 1978). If we assess our subjects only at the start of the study, we will only be able to predict from the predisposing factor who will *not* get IM; among susceptibles, lack of data on the precipitating factor will prevent us from making any further predictions.

In the stress and disease area it is rather common to have a model of disease that is similar to infectious mononucleosis: It takes a precipitating factor (exposure to a stressor) to ''activate'' predisposing risk factors into disease outcomes. For example, Brown and Harris (1978) have proposed a model for onset of depression (among women) in which vulnerability factors (such as loss of mother before age 11 or lack of a confiding relationship with husband or boyfriend) do not translate into risk for depression unless there are also provoking agents (i.g., stressors such as stressful life experiences) present. The question is: If precipitating factors are important, how do we need to alter the classical prospective epidemiologic design so that we don't miss out on detecting promising psychosocial risk factors because they are of the precipitating variety?

One solution is to collect data on precipitating factors retrospectively, that is, at the time of follow-up contact when cases who have developed the disease are being identified. This is not a happy solution because we may run into the kinds of methodological problems of retrospective data that have been already discussed. In addition, we would need some assurance that the dating of exposure and of onset of disease can be done accurately and without bias from retrospective data (or other data available to the study). In the 4-year follow-up of a sample of Chicago residents (Pearlin et al., 1981), data were collected on disruptions in work life (fired, laid off, downgraded, left work because of illness) for the interim 4-year interval; a complex analysis of the results led to the interpretation that such disruptions contributed to diminished self-concept (self-esteem, mastery) and higher depression. However, it does not seem likely that even a highly sophisticated statistical treatment of initial values of self-esteem or depression (covariates) can satisfactorily dispose of the alternate hypothesis that (unmeasured) adverse changes in self-esteem or depression preceded many of the disruptions in work life.

An alternate solution is to schedule additional monitoring of the cohort so that data on exposure (precipitating events) can be collected more often. This will lead to more instances when such data on exposure will be obtained prospectively with respect to disease onset; it will also shorten the period of recall and may reduce bias and/or inaccuracy, especially with respect to dating onset. Unfortunately, such increased monitoring can become very expensive. And whether or not it will do the job may depend on the phenomenon we are examining. Consider the following example: In a study of blood pressure among male prisoners (D'Atri, Fitzgerald, Kasl, & Ostfeld, 1981), monthly data collections were carried out. One hypothesis that was tested (Kasl, D'Atri, Ostfeld, & Fitzgerald, 1983) was that the experience of solitary confinement would be associated with an increase in blood pressure levels. Prisoners with this experience were identified from records and the two monthly blood pressure values bracketing this experience were examined. No significant before–after effects were observed. A more refined analysis, however, determined that when the confinement took place closer in time to the first data collection, the prisoners showed a decline in blood pressure, whereas when the confinement took place closer in time to the second data collection, they did show an increase. This pattern of results suggests a model of blood pressure reactivity (for this particular setting and experience) in which the impact is relatively short-lived and where "anticipatory" effects are present (either in the sense of a true anticipatory reaction, or as a result of misdating the onset of the total disruptive experience that ended rather than began with the confinement).

Such a model of reactivity of an outcome variable (obviously a reversible one) in relation to an exposure of a difficult-to-date onset may be rather common in health psychology and behavioral medicine. The usual data analysis strategy— examine differential changes in a variable collected in two waves of data collection for those who did versus those who did not experience an event during that time—may not be sensitive enough to identify the actual impact, as noted previously. And the optimal scheduling of additional data collection contacts also may be difficult to determine and costly. This may be the occasion to consider the suitability of a "natural experiment" as a design paradigm: Subjects are selected because they are about to go through a particular experience (job redesign, plant closing, divorce, retirement, migration, bereavement, etc.), and data collection is scheduled in relation to some presumptive stages of adaptation to that experience. The merits of such an alternative (discussed elsewhere, e.g., Kasl, 1983a; Kasl, Gore, & Cobb, 1975) are highly idiosyncratic and more dependent on the opportunity that presents itself to the investigator and less on his or her ability to sculpt the design according to a priori intentions and considerations. At its best the "natural experiment" is a design that reduces self-selection factors, permits collection of "before exposure" data (but seldom true base line prior to awareness of impending exposure), and allows one to keep track of selective attrition. However, a suitable and equivalent comparison group of persons not going through the experience is seldom part of the package and they may be somewhat difficult to identify.

Another neglected issue in textbook discussions of the classical prospective design in epidemiology is the fact that "prospective" means, explicitly, only that healthy subjects, free of target disease, are sampled, assessed for possible risk factors, and followed for onset of the disease. However, implicitly, other notions may lurk in the shadows as well. The most important one, I believe, is that the cohort has been picked up at the optimal point (developmental stage, environmental circumstances) for: (1) detecting the dynamics of the transition from risk factors to overt disease, and (2) describing the most "representative" characteristics of the etiological process of disease development. A few examples may be necessary to clarify these statements. If one studied the incidence of coronary heart disease (CHD) in a cohort of adolescent males free of CHD, the only risk factor detected for this quite rare outcome would probably be extremely high levels of serum cholesterol that would, in turn, have a strong genetic component. A similar prospective study of healthy men ages 70+ would probably identify high blood pressure as the major risk factor, with cigarette smoking playing no role (selective survival?), and total cholesterol contributing very little (though one lipoprotein fraction, HDL, remains a predictor; viz. Kannel & Gordon, 1980). The information from prospective studies of men in the broad age range of 35 to 55 (Pooling Project Research Group, 1978), of course, tells us that all three factors—blood pressure, cholesterol, and cigarette smoking—are risks of sufficient magnitude (relative risks of 2.0 or more).

Another example can further clarify the preceding statements. Under some conditions we do not preselect our subjects to be free of a target disease. This is particularly so when we are interested in nonspecific health outcomes (mortality, hospitalizations) and when our subjects are mature adults or the elderly; it would be, of course, awkward to select such subjects to be free of all major diseases. Here then, we have a longitudinal follow-up that is not "prospective" with respect to anything in particular. It is a "slice of life" longitudinal follow-up study that only detects *de novo* health status changes during the specific follow-up period, incremental to the status of health at the start of follow-up. Thus, if we are looking at the effects of health habits, social networks, and subjectively rated health on mortality (Berkman & Breslow, 1983; Kaplan & Camacho, 1983; Mossey & Shapiro, 1982), we need to adjust first for initial health status. However, such an adjustment means that all the effects of these variables of interest on health status that took place prior to the start of the study are removed; of course, any effects that took place after the follow-up ended are missed as well.

Of late, we have seen in social and psychiatric epidemiology a good number of "slice of life" longitudinal follow-up studies (e.g., Billings & Moos, 1982a; Eaton, Regier, Locke, & Taube, 1981; McFarlane, Norman, Streiner, & Roy, 1983; Myers, Lindenthal, & Pepper, 1974; Pearlin et al., 1981; Thoits, 1982; Williams, Ware, & Donald, 1981). The advantages of such a design, compared to cross-section studies, are amply appreciated (if not somewhat exaggerated). However, it is not clear that their limitations are equally appreciated. In terms of the previous discussion, the relevant limitation is that the cohort may not have been picked up at the *optimal* point for detecting the causal dynamics of a specific disease process and its most characteristic features. This is to say, the total study design is a very diluted way of studying many specific age–sex–social stratum subcohorts exposed to different environmental conditions and followed for different health outcomes. It is not optimal for any one purpose; it is suboptimal for many purposes. The cohort is not picked up because something extraordinary has happened to them or is expected to happen. In such a steady state situation (for most of them), rigorous analysis of change on health status variables (that is, some adjustment for initial levels) will leave little more than error of measurement with which to play around. This would seem to explain, for example, why longitudinal studies of stressful life events and symptoms of ill health have shown few effects of such events in the face of careful statistical adjustments for necessary covariates (e.g., Billings & Moos, 1982b; Gersten, Langner, Eisenberg, & Simcha–Fagan, 1977; Goldberg & Comstock, 1976; Kobasa, Maddi, & Courington, 1981; McFarlane et al., 1983; Rundall, 1978; Williams et al., 1981), even as earlier reviews and compilations of the literature, based on cross-sectional designs or inadequately analyzed longitudinal data, suggested consistently broad effects (e.g., Dohrenwend & Dohrenwend, 1974; Gunderson & Rahe, 1974; Haney, 1980; Rahe & Arthur, 1978; Theorell, 1982). Of course, an additional problem here are the inadequacies of the instruments for measuring exposure to stressful life events (Dohrenwend & Dohrenwend, 1981; Kasl, 1983a, 1984c).

One final example illustrates the importance of optimal timing that converts an insensitive "slice of life" longitudinal design into a sensitive prospective design. Much evidence has accumulated regarding the fact that blue-collar workers on machine-paced jobs describe their work as boring, simple, and demanding little attention; however, their level of job satisfaction is not very different from that of other blue-collar workers and adverse mental health impact has been difficult to document (e.g., Caplan, Cobb, French, Van Harrison, & Pinneau, 1975; Kasl, 1973; Kornhauser, 1965). How should one study the mental health impact of a dull and monotonous blue-collar job? It is easy to imagine that taking a large sample of blue-collar workers, 35 years and older, and following them for 10 years, may miss the phenomenon altogether. The casualties of inadequate adaptation may have disappeared from observation already and the remainder may have adapted "successfully"—that is, by giving up on expecting work to be a meaningful human activity in order to avoid constant frustration—but the costs of such a "successful" adaptation can no longer be reconstructed through the belated follow-up because the causal dynamics between environmental exposure and outcome may have already played themselves out.

MEASURING EXPOSURE AND OUTCOMES: THE POSSIBILITIES FOR CONFOUNDING

It is useful to characterize, first, an *idealized* research design situation so that we may think through the difficulties that we are likely to encounter as a consequence of the inevitable limitations of the *actual* design that we are forced to adopt (or into which we stumble because we don't know any better).

The strongest design here would have the following characteristics: (1) the total cohort of subjects is picked up before anyone is exposed; (2) proximate preexposure status is nonreactive (no anticipatory effects or selective preexposure attrition); (3) the environmental condition (exposure) is objectively defined and measured; (4) self-selection factors, which determine exposure status for some and absence of exposure for others, are minimal or negligible; (5) surveillance for target health outcomes is complete (no attrition) and of sufficient duration; (6) health outcomes are measured "objectively."

In this section I consider primarily measurement issues: those limitations of the measurement of exposure and/or outcome that give rise to alternative interpretations of results or distort cause–effect relationships. In the preceding listing of strong design characteristics, not all the points represent issues of measurement; however, weaknesses in measurement are frequently aggravated or exaggerated by other design limitations. Thus it is good to keep in mind the overall design context when considering limitations of measurement.

A very common measurement variation on the previous ideal schema involves the use of subjective measures of exposure. There is, of course, a powerful tradition in psychology, both social (e.g., Lewin) and clinical (e.g., Lazarus), that encourages the use of subjective indicators, of perceptions and evaluations, of exposure. Many theoretical formulations, particularly in the stress area, are subjectivistic. Subjective perceptions are considered crucial in studying intervening processes, underlying mechanisms, and individual differences in vulnerability. And, of course, the subjective measures are frequently more easily obtained.

Unfortunately, subjective measures also tend to create problems for the investigator. Three salient problems that may be thereby precipitated are: (1) we may not know to what objective environmental conditions, if any, the subjective perceptions can be linked; (2) we may not know what other variables influence the perceptions (particularly stable characteristics of the individual); (3) we may not know what conceptual and methodological overlap there exists between the subjective exposure variable and our outcome. An obtained association between reports that "my husband does not understand me" and the wife's high scores on a depression scale may be viewed as prototypic of all three problems.

It is necessary to examine the overall design methodology before making an assessment of the limitations of the subjective measure of exposure. For example, when the outcome is a biological parameter or a diagnostic category based on biomedical criteria, then the third concern listed earlier (conceptual and methodological overlap between measures of independent and dependent variables) may be viewed as minimal. Thus, reporting a certain cluster of symptoms—sleep disturbance, feeling tired on awakening or exhausted at the end of the day, inability to relax—has been related prospectively to incidence of myocardial infarction (Jenkins, 1976, 1982). We do not know to what objective environmental conditions, such as a demanding job, such symptoms can be linked, or even whether the symptoms represent any kind of a reaction to an environmental situation, as opposed to an expression of a stable trait with no concurrent environmental determinants. However, the independent or separable methodology for assessing the risk factor and the outcome argues that we are dealing with a nontrivial association. If the evidence were based only on retrospective designs, the association would remain nontrivial, but the direction of causality would become considerably more ambiguous. When the diagnosis is based on characteristic symptoms, but not on observable signs or laboratory results, as in the case of angina pectoris, then the situation is less clear. Thus the prospective association between reports of problems with supervisors (such as "being hurt" or "not being appreciated" by them) and later development of angina (Medalie & Goldbourt, 1976) may be inflated by some general, stable trait of complaining, maladjustment, neuroticism. Note that if this is viewed as a stable trait, then the prospective design does not rule out or diminish the confounding influence of such a trait on the assessment of both the "independent" and the "dependent" variable. A somewhat different problem arises when the diagnosis is based on observable signs and laboratory data, but it is based on individuals who have sought medical care. The distinction between illness and illness behavior is now a well-established and well-analyzed one (e.g., Mechanic, 1982, 1983), and the role of distress in seeking medical attention is well recognized. Thus the underlying variable of distress can create a confounding influence both on the measurement of subjective exposure and (apparently) "objective" outcome.

The preceding comments about objective and subjective measures of exposure are, in some sense, a heuristic simplification of the issues, because the distinction between the two may often be a difficult one to make—conceptually, operationally, practically. Consider, for example, the type of measures based on lists of "stressful life events," such as the Social Readjustment Rating Scale (Holmes & Rahe, 1967). As has been discussed elsewhere (e.g., Dohrenwend & Dohrenwend, 1981; Kasl, 1983a, 1984c), the list of life events encompasses a mixed bag of objective exposures with minimal self-selection (e.g., death of a close relative), objective exposures with likely strong self-selection (e.g., change in residence), objective events that are environmental exposures closely linked to "outcome" behaviors (e.g., fired at work), subjective exposures (e.g., change in arguments with spouse), and "events" that are best seen as subjectively assessed behavioral outcomes (e.g., sex difficulties). It might be noted that some recent developments in this area, such as the "daily hassles" scale (DeLongis, Coyne, Dakof, Folkman, & Lazarus, 1982; Kanner, Coyne, Schaefer, & Lazarus, 1981), represent a considerable aggravation of the confounding problem being discussed. Because the scale contains many more items that are subjectively assessed behavioral or affective outcomes, it represents a dual retrenchment: away from objective exposures toward subjective ones, and away from indicating an independent variable and toward reflecting an outcome.

Objective measures of exposure are not necessarily free of confounding with health status outcomes. However, the mechanism of confounding is not via assessment but rather via self-selection. For example, the recent emphasis in health psychology and behavioral medicine on control (or sense of control) has led to an interest in studying the health impact of involuntary versus voluntary exposures, such as in retirement or institutionalization. However, the evidence (e.g., Kasl, 1980; Kasl & Rosenfield, 1980) strongly suggests that such involuntary exposures are associated with poorer health status before exposure. Thus one needs a stronger design in order to detect the initial health status differences and then adjust for such confounding.

The possibility of confounding via self-selection of those with poorer health into a particular exposure category is an unremitting nuisance in health research. For example, the observation of lower mortality among those with higher church attendance and/or greater religiousness (Comstock & Partridge, 1972) had to be reinterpreted as spurious when controls for differences in education and functional status were introduced into analysis (Comstock & Tonascia, 1977). Of course, often the confounding may be relatively subtle and is suspected rather than demonstrated. For example, Linn, Ware, and Greenfield (1980) reported that relief from chest pain following emergency care was greater for patients who shared the decision to seek care with spouse or relative and were accompanied to the emergency room by them. This is a relatively objective operationalization of presence of social support; however, if patients without social support delay seeking care until their condition is considerably worse, then the finding represents self-selection rather than the effects of social support on recovery.

There is no doubt that when our study design includes both objective and subjective measures of environmental exposure, we are in a better position to interpret our findings. Whether we actually do a better job of interpretation may depend on the pattern of findings, our awareness of possible pitfalls, and our skills in operationalizing the specific measures of objective and subjective exposure that are to be strung together into a causal chain. Consider the results of a British study of behavioral and mental health effects of aircraft noise (Jenkins, Tarnapolsky, & Hand, 1981; Tarnapolsky, Watkins, & Hand, 1980; Watkins, Tarnapolsky, & Jenkins, 1981). The pattern of results is somewhat of a puzzle: (1) there was a substantial association (gamma = .50) between objectively measured noise (NNI, The Noise and Number Index) and the level of being bothered and annoyed, the primary subjective measure of exposure; (2) being bothered and annoyed was associated with levels of various symptoms, with use of (any) drugs, and with use of psychotropic drugs (only); (3) however, the objective indicator of noise, NNI, was not related to these same outcomes; (4) within each level of annoyance, higher symptom levels and higher use of drugs were observed in the *lower* NNI areas. The study examined many other variables, such as psychiatric hospital admissions and outpatient visits to general practitioners, but none showed a significant impact of the objective noise levels. The results of another study of airport noise and community symptom levels (Graeven, 1974) obtained findings consistent with the British data. The puzzle in these results is that the subjective measure of exposure appears to be an intervening variable—in a nonexistent overall relationship between objective noise and indicators of impact! The following appears to be a defensible interpretation: The subjective measure of exposure, level of annoyance, is causally heterogeneous and is influenced by two sources, the objective noise and some preexisting (stable) personality characteristic, which can be designated "adjustment" or "neuroticism" or "propensity for distress." The second of the two is, of course, related to the various indicators of impact, such as level of symptoms. Objective noise does not have an impact and, thus, that part of the annoyance measure that is determined by objective noise would also be unrelated to the various outcomes (if we could partition it out). Within objectively lower levels of noise, higher proportion of the annoyance level is more purely a reflection of the personality characteristic and thus the symptom levels are higher.

The important lesson to be drawn from this example is that we need to keep close attention to all three relationships: objective exposure with outcome, objective exposure with subjective exposure, and subjective exposure with outcome. Only if the objective measure is confirmed as a risk factor for disease outcome and the subjective measure is associated with both the objective measure and the disease outcome (and the latter two associations are stronger than the first) do we have strong suggestion of a disease effect of exposure, operating substantially through the intervening process of subjective perception or reaction.

However, there are two other patterns of associations that may falsely encourage investigators to pursue the subjective variable as an indicator of the intervening process. One is the pattern obtained in the aforementioned British study of aircraft noise: The absence of an overall association between the objective measure of exposure and the outcome variable strongly suggests that whatever influence the subjective measure has on the outcome, it is an independent one and does not originate in the environmental exposure itself. An investigator who only paid attention to the fact that the objective and subjective measures are associated, and from there on worked only with the subjective indicator (on the mistaken grounds that its role as an intervening variable had been demonstrated), would be in serious danger of eventually misinterpreting his findings and the role of actual environmental exposure. Of course, the influence of the subjective measure on the outcome variable may still be eminently worth pursuing, but its antecedents in objective exposure must be seriously questioned.

The other pattern of associations that calls for the investigator's caution is the altogether rather common situation (particularly in the occupational stress literature; viz. Kasl, 1978; Payne & Pugh, 1976) in which the objective and subjective measures are not correlated with each other, and only the subjective measure is related to a disease outcome. Such a pattern could arise because: (1) we have not identified properly the actual environmental exposure, but the subjective measure does in fact represent an intervening process; (2) the subjective measure has its antecedents, not in actual environmental exposure, but in some characteristic of the person, possibly reflecting the impact of earlier experiences; (3) the presence of disease (in retrospective designs) has biased the subjective measure. Here again it can be seen that embarking on a further program of research that drops the objective measures of exposure and concentrates on the subjective ones only, will cut the investigator off from any reasonable possibility of resolving later crucial ambiguities in the future findings.

The preceding comments may be construed as a strong endorsement of the strategy of including, above all and first of all, objective measures of environmental exposure in our research designs. However, as already noted, the distinction between objective and subjective measures is entirely an uncomfortable one. Furthermore, the previous comments do not really adequately reflect the range and complexity of environmental exposures one may wish to study. For example, the recent formulations involving the Person–Environment Fit model (e.g., Caplan, 1983; French, Caplan, & Van Harrison, 1982) have become so rich and so complex that a heavy reliance on subjective measures appears to be a reasonable temporizing strategy.

It also needs to be made explicit that the emphasis on objective measurement of exposure does not mean at all an emphasis on physicalistic definitions of what constitutes exposure. Consider the example of a chemical in the work setting, not perceptible by the senses but considered carcinogenic. Physical measurements of the concentrations of the chemical represent a physicalistic definition of exposure. However, we may wish to study the mental health consequences of "awareness of exposure," even if the chemical is completely benign. Thus it is our measure of awareness that needs to be objective, e.g., distribution of a report from the industrial hygienist to the workers in one factory versus absence of any such report in another factory because the presence of the chemical is not even suspected. If, instead, we ask an unselected sample of workers: "Do you think your work exposes you to dangerous chemicals?," then any associations with mental health variables (particularly phobic anxiety or paranoia) could be easily viewed as the influence of prior mental health status on perceptions of dangerousness.

Concrete findings can illustrate this point. In a study of the impact of the accident at the Three Mile Island on nuclear workers (Kasl, Chisholm, & Eskenazi, 1981) the independent variable, "Threat of exposure to radiation," was operationalized objectively by the contrast of workers at TMI with workers at a comparison nuclear plant some 40 miles away. A subjective measure was also utilized: "Did your job ever expose you to radiation during . . ." Workers at TMI showed higher levels of demoralization and of psychophysiological symptoms and scored higher on the subjective measure, than the workers at the comparison plant. However, the associations between the subjective measure and the two scales of impact were nearly identical: .25 for both correlations at TMI and .26 for both correlations at the comparison plant. Thus the effect of the accident appeared superimposed upon a preexisting association (with its own, unknown causal dynamics, possibly largely autistic) between the subjective measure and the outcomes; it changed the levels of the indicators but not the slope of associations between them. Without the objective measure it would not have been possible to disentangle these separate processes.

SUMMARY

This chapter is not an attempt to introduce investigators in health psychology and behavioral medicine to some distillation of epidemiologic methods and concepts. Rather, the chapter represents my effort to utilize epidemiology in order to provide a consistent framework and a perspective to my discussion of what I believe are important methodological issues in health psychology and behavioral medicine. Needless to say, the choice of specific issues for this discussion may be idiosyncratic and does not necessarily represent the views of other epidemiologists; it is based on my reading and reviews of the various segments of this large domain of "social science and medicine" literature.

The chapter is primarily concerned with three issues: (1) dealing with methodological problems that arise out of cross-sectional data collection strategies; above all, these involve the influence of the outcome state (disease) on risk factors (their status and their assessment), and difficulties in recapturing an earlier (predisease) state of the risk factors; attempts to strengthen cross-sectional data are also discussed; (2) achieving a fuller understanding of longitudinal and prospective data collection strategies; this includes a discussion of the difference between "merely" longitudinal versus prospective designs, an analysis of the question "prospective with respect to what?", and a consideration of the distinction between predisposing and precipitating factors and its influence on design; (3) avoiding confounding problems in the measurement of exposure (risk factors) and of disease outcomes; above all, this includes a discussion of the importance of a design paradigm in which "objective" data on exposure are collected and a critique of the practice of relying solely on "subjective" exposure data, however that may appear justifiable on grounds of a psychological theory.

REFERENCES

Alderson, M. (1976). *An introduction to epidemiology*. London: Macmillan.

Alker, H. R., Jr. (1965). *Mathematics and politics*. New York: Macmillan.

Barker, D. J. P., & Rose, G. (1979). *Epidemiology in medical practice* (2nd ed.) Edinburgh: Churchill Livingstone.

Baum, A., & Singer, J. E. (Eds.). (1982). *Handbook of psychology and health* (Vol. 2). Hillsdale, NJ: Lawrence Erlbaum Associates.

Berkman, L. F., & Breslow, L. (1983). *Health and ways of living*. New York: Oxford University Press.

Billings, A. G., & Moos, R. H. (1982a). Social support and functioning among community and clinical groups: A panel mode. *Journal of Behavioral Medicine, 5,* 295–311.

Billings, A. G., & Moos, R. H. (1982b). Stressful life events and symptoms: A longitudinal model. *Health Psychology, 1,* 99–117.

Brand, R. J., Rosenman, R. H., Sholtz, R. I., & Friedman, M. (1976). Multivariate prediction of coronary heart disease in the Western Collaborative Group Study compared to the findings of the Framingham Study. *Circulation, 53,* 348–355.

Brown, G., & Harris, T. (1978). *The social origins of depression: A study of psychiatric disorder in women.* London: Tavistock.

Campbell, D. T., & Stanley, J. C. (1966). *Experimental and quasi-experimental designs for research.* Chicago: Rand McNally.

Caplan, R. D. (1983). Person–environment fit: Past, present, and future. In C. L. Cooper (Ed.), *Stress research: Issues for the eighties.* Chichester: Wiley.

Caplan, R. D., Cobb, S., French, J. R. P., Jr., Van Harrison, R., & Pinneau, S. R., Jr. (1975). *Job demands and worker health.* Washington, DC: HEW Publication No. (NIOSH) 75–160.

Cassel, J. (1974). An epidemiological perspective of psychosocial factors in disease etiology. *American Journal of Public Health, 64,* 1040–1043.

Cassel, J. (1975). Social science in epidemiology: Psychosocial processes and "stress" theoretical formulation. In E. L. Struening & M. Guttentag (Eds.), *Handbook of evaluation research* (Vol. 1). Beverly Hills, CA: Sage.

Cobb, S. (1971). *The frequency of rheumatic diseases.* Cambridge: Harvard University Press.

Comstock, G. W., & Partridge, K. B. (1972). Church attendance and health. *Journal of Chronic Diseases, 25,* 665–672.

Comstock, G. W., & Tonascia, J. A. (1977). Education and mortality in Washington County, Maryland. *Journal of Health and Social Behavior, 18,* 54–61.

Cook, T. D., & Campbell, D. T. (1976). The design and conduct of quasi-experiments and true experiments in field settings. In M. D. Dunnette (Ed.), *Handbook of industrial and organizational psychology.* Chicago: Rand McNally.

Cook, T. D., & Campbell, D. T. (1979). *Quasi-experimentation: Design & analysis issues for field settings.* Chicago: Rand McNally.

Cox, T., & McKay, C. (1982). Psychosocial factors and psychophysiological mechanisms in the aetiology and development of cancers. *Social Science and Medicine, 16,* 381–396.

Crown, J. M., & Crown, S. (1973). The relationship between personality and the presence of rheumatoid factor in early rheumatoid disease. *Scandinavian Journal of Rheumatology, 2,* 123–126.

D'Atri, D. A., Fitzgerald, E. F., Kasl, S. V., & Ostfeld, A. M. (1981). Crowding in prison: The relationship between changes in housing mode and blood pressure. *Psychosomatic Medicine, 43,* 95–105.

DeLongis, A., Coyne, J. C., Dakof, G., Folkman, S., & Lazarus, R. S. (1982). Relationship of daily hassles, uplifts, and major life events to health status. *Health Psychology, 1,* 119–136.

Dohrenwend, B. S., & Dohrenwend, B. P. (eds.). (1974). *Stressful life events: Their nature and effects.* New York: Wiley.

Dohrenwend, B. S., & Dohrenwend, B. P. (Eds.). (1981). *Stressful life events and their contexts.* New York: Prodist.

Eaton, W. W., Regier, D. A., Locke, B. Z., & Taube, C. A. (1981). The epidemiologic catchment area program of the National Institute of Mental Health. *Public Health Reports, 96,* 319–325.

Elder, R. G. (1973). Social class and lay explanations of the etiology of arthritis. *Journal of Health and Social Behavior, 14,* 28–38.

Elliott, G. R., & Eisdorfer, C. (Eds.). (1982). *Stress and human health.* New York: Springer.

Evans, A. S. (1978). Infectious mononucleosis and related syndromes. *American Journal of Medical Sciences, 276,* 325–329.

Evans, G. W. (Ed.). (1982). *Environmental stress.* New York: Cambridge University Press.

Fox, B. H. (1978). Premorbid psychological factors as related to cancer incidence. *Journal of Behavioral Medicine, 1,* 45–133.

Fox, J. P., Hall, C. E., & Elveback, L. R. (1970). *Epidemiology, man and disease.* New York: Macmillan.

French, J. R. P., Jr., Caplan, R. D., & Van Harrison, R. (1982). *The mechanisms of job stress and strain.* Chichester: Wiley.

Friedman, G. D. (1980). *Primer of epidemiology* (2nd ed.) New York: McGraw–Hill.

Gatchel, R. J., Baum, A., & Singer, J. E. (Eds.). (1982). *Handbook of psychology and health,* (Vol. 1). Hillsdale NJ: Lawrence Erlbaum Associates.

Gersten, J. C., Langner, T. S., Eisenberg, J. G., & Simcha–Fagan, O. (1977). An evaluation of the etiologic role of stressful life-change events in psychological disorders. *Journal of Health and Social Behavior, 18,* 228–244.

Goldberg, E. L., & Comstock, G. W. (1976). Life events and subsequent illness. *American Journal of Epidemiology, 104,* 146–158.

Goldberger, L., & Breznitz, S. (Eds.). (1982). *Handbook of stress.* New York: Free Press.

Goldbourt, U., Medalie, J. H., & Neufeld, H. N. (1975). Clinical myocardial infarction over a five-year period—III. A multivariate analysis of incidence, the Israeli Ischemic Heart Disease Study. *Journal of Chronic Diseases, 28,* 217–237.

Graeven, D. G. (1974). The effects of airplane noise on health: an examination of three hypotheses. *Journal of Health and Social Behavior, 15,* 336–343.

Graham, S. (1974). The sociological approach to epidemiology. *American Journal of Public Health, 64,* 1046–1049.

Graham, S., & Reeder, L. G. (1979). Social epidemiology of chronic diseases. In H. E. Freeman, S. Levine, & L. G. Reeder (Eds.), *Handbook of medical sociology* (3rd ed.), Englewood Cliffs, NJ: Prentice–Hall.

Greer, S., & Morris, T. (1978). The study of psychological factors in breast cancer: Problems of method. *Social Science and Medicine, 12A,* 129–134.

Gunderson, E. K. E., & Rahe, R. H. (Eds.). (1974). *Life stress and illness.* Springfield, IL: Thomas.

Hamburg, D. A., Elliott, G. R., & Parron, D. L. (Eds.). (1982). *Health and behavior: Frontiers of research in biobehavioral sciences.* Washington, DC: National Academy Press.

Haney, C. A. (1980). Life events as precursors of coronary heart disease. *Social Science and Medicine, 14A,* 119–126.

Haynes, S. G., Eaker, E. D., & Feinleib, M. (1983). Spouse behavior and coronary heart disease in men: Prospective results from the Framingham Heart Study. I. Concordance of risk factors and the relationship of psychosocial status to coronary incidence. *American Journal of Epidemiology, 118,* 1–22.

Haynes, S. G., & Feinleib, M. (1982). Type A behavior and incidence of coronary heart disease in the Framingham Heart Study. *Advances in Cardiology, 29,* 85–95.

Haynes, S. G., Feinleib, M., & Kannel, W. B. (1980). The relationship of psychosocial factors to coronary heart disease in the Framingham Study: III. Eight-year incidence of coronary heart disease. *American Journal of Epidemiology, 111,* 37–58.

Henry, J. P. (1982). The relation of social to biological processes in disease. *Social Science and Medicine, 16,* 369–380.

Hinkle, L. E., Jr., Dohrenwend, B., Elinson, J., Kasl, S. V., McDowell, A., Mechanic, D., & Syme, S. G. (1976). Social determinants of human health. In *Preventive medicine USA.* New York: Prodist.

Holmes, T. H., & Rahe, R. H. (1967). The social readjustment rating scale. *Journal of Psychosomatic Research, 11,* 213–218.

Horne, R. L., & Picard, R. S. (1979). Psychosocial risk factors for lung cancer. *Psychosomatic Medicine, 41,* 503–514.

Ibrahim, M. A. (Ed.). (1979). The case control study: Concensus and controversy. *Journal of Chronic Diseases, 32,* 1–144.

Jacobs, T., & Charles, E. (1980). Life events and the occurrence of cancer in children. *Psychosomatic Research, 42,* 11–24.

Jenkins, C. D. (1976). Recent evidence supporting psychologic and social risk factors for coronary disease. *New England Journal of Medicine, 294,* 987–994 and 1033–1038.

Jenkins, C. D. (1982). Psychosocial risk factors for coronary heart disease. *Acta Medica Scandinavica Supplement 660,* 123–136.

Jenkins, C. D., Stanton, B.-A., Klein, M. D., Savageau, J. A., & Harken, D. E. (1983). Correlates of angina pectoris among men awaiting coronary by-pass surgery. *Psychosomatic Medicine, 45,* 141–153.

Jenkins, L., Tarnapolsky, A., & Hand, D. (1981). Psychiatric admissions and aircraft noise from London airport: Four-year three-hospitals' study. *Psychological Medicine, 11,* 765–782.

Kannel, W. B., & Gordon, T. (1980). Cardiovascular risk factors in the aged: The Framingham study. In S. G. Haynes & M. Feinleib (Eds.), *Second Conference on the Epidemiology of Aging.* Washington, DC (NIH Publication No. 80-969).

Kanner, A. D., Coyne, J. C., Schaefer, C., & Lazarus, R. S. (1981). Comparison of two modes of stress measurement: Daily hassles and uplifts versus major life events. *Journal of Behavioral Medicine, 4,* 1–39.

Kaplan, G. A., & Camacho, T. (1983). Perceived health and mortality: A nine-year follow-up of the Human Population Laboratory cohort. *American Journal of Epidemiology, 117,* 291–304.

Karasek, R. A., Triantis, K. P., & Chaudhry, S. S. (1982). Coworker and supervisor support as moderators of associations between task characteristics and mental strain. *Journal of Occupational Behaviour, 3,* 181–200.

Kasl, S. V. (1973). Mental health and the work environment: An examination of the evidence. *Journal of Occupational Medicine, 15,* 509–518.

Kasl, S. V. (1977a). Contributions of social epidemiology to studies in psychosomatic medicine. In S. V. Kasl & F. Reichsman (Eds.), *Advances in psychosomatic medicine* (Vol. 9). *Epidemiologic studies in psychosomatic medicine.* Basel: Karger.

Kasl, S. V. (1977b). The effects of the residential environment on health and behavior: A review. In L. E. Hinkle, Jr., & W. C. Loring (Eds.), *The effect of the manmade environment on health and behavior.* Washington, DC (DHEW Publication No. CDC 77–8318).

Kasl, S. V. (1978). Stress at work: Epidemiological contributions to the study of work stress. In C. L. Cooper & R. Payne (Eds.), *Stress at work.* Chichester: Wiley.

Kasl, S. V. (1980). The impact of retirement. In C. L. Cooper & R. Payne (Eds.), *Current concerns in occupational stress.* Chichester: Wiley.

Kasl, S. V. (1982). Strategies of research on economic instability and health. *Psychological Medicine, 12,* 637–649.

Kasl, S. V. (1983a). Pursuing the link between stressful life experiences and disease: A time for reappraisal. In C. L. Cooper (Ed.), *Stress research: Issues for the eighties.* Chichester: Wiley.

Kasl, S. V. (1983b). Social and psychological factors affecting the course of disease: An epidemiological perspective. In D. Mechanic (Ed.), *Handbook of health, health care, and the health professions.* New York: The Free Press.

Kasl, S. V. (1984a). Chronic life stress and health. In A. Steptoe & A. Mathews (Eds.), *Health care and human behaviour.* London: Academic Press.

Kasl, S. V. (1984b). Stress and health. *Annual Review of Public Health, 5,* 319–341.

Kasl, S. V. (1984c). When to welcome a new measure (editorial). *American Journal of Public Health, 74,* 106–108.

Kasl, S. V., & Berkman, L. F. (1981). Some psychosocial influences on the health status of the elderly: The perspective of social epidemiology. In J. L. McGaugh & S. B. Kiesler (Eds.), *Aging: Biology and behavior.* New York: Academic Press.

Kasl, S. V., & Berkman, L. F. (1983). Health consequences of the experience of migration. *Annual Review of Public Health, 4,* 67–88.

Kasl, S. V., Chisholm, R. F., & Eskenazi, B. (1981). The impact of the accident at the Three Mile Island on the behavior and well-being of nuclear workers. *American Journal of Public Health, 71,* 472–483 & 484–495.

Kasl, S. V., & Cobb, S. (1969). The intrafamilial transmission of rheumatoid arthritis-V. Differences between rheumatoid arthritics and controls on selected personality variables. *Journal of Chronic Diseases, 22,* 239–258.

Kasl, S. V., & Cobb, S. (1983). Psychological and social stresses in the workplace. In B. S. Levy & D. H. Wegman (Eds., *Occupational health: Recognizing and preventing work-related disease.* Boston: Little, Brown.

Kasl, S. V., D'Atri, D. A., Ostfeld, A. M., & Fitzgerald, E. F. (1983). Determinants of blood pressure changes among male prisoners (abstract). *Psychosomatic Medicine, 45,* 84–85.

Kasl, S. V., Gore, S., & Cobb, S. (1975). The experience of losing a job: Reported changes in health, symptoms, and illness behavior. *Psychosomatic Medicine, 37,* 106–122.

Kasl, S. V., & Rosenfield, S. (1980). The residential environment and its impact on the mental health of the aged. In J. E. Birren & R. B. Sloane (Eds.), *Handbook of mental health and aging.* Englewood Cliffs, NJ: Prentice–Hall.

Kasl, S. V., & Wells, J. A. (1985). Social support and health in the middle years: Work and the family. In S. Cohen & S. L. Syme (Eds.), *Social support and health.* New York: Academic Press.

Kleinbaum, D. G., Kupper, L. L., & Morgenstern, H. (1982). *Epidemiology: Principles and quantitative methods.* Belmont: Lifetime Learning Publications.

Knox, E. G. (Ed.). (1979). *Epidemiology in health care planning.* London: Oxford University Press.

Kobasa, S. C., Maddi, S. R., & Courington, S. (1981). Personality and constitution as mediators in the stress-illness relationship. *Journal of Health and Social Behavior, 22,* 368–378.

Kornhauser, A. (1965). *Mental health of the industrial worker.* New York: Wiley.

Krantz, D. S., Baum, A., & Singer, J. E. (Eds.). (1983). *Handbook of psychology and health,* (Vol. 3). Hillsdale, NJ: Lawrence Erlbaum Associates.

Last, J. M. (Ed.). (1983). *A dictionary of epidemiology.* New York: Oxford University Press.

Leavitt, F., Garron, D. C., & Bielauskas, L. A. (1979). Stressing life events and the experience of low back pain. *Journal of Psychosomatic Research, 23,* 49–55.

Lilienfeld, A. M., & Lilienfeld, D. (1979). *Foundations of epidemiology* (2nd ed.). New York: Oxford University Press.

Linn, L. S., Ware, J. E., & Greenfield, S. (1980). Factors associated with relief from chest pain following emergency care. *Medical Care, 18,* 624–634.

McFarlane, A. H., Norman, G. R., Streiner, D. L., & Roy, R. G. (1983). The process of social stress: Stable, reciprocal, and mediatin relationships. *Journal of Health and Social Behavior, 24,* 160–173.

MacMahon, B., & Pugh, T. F. (1970). *Epidemiology: Principles and methods.* Boston: Little, Brown.

McQueen, D. V., & Siegrist, J. (1982). Social factors in the etiology of chronic disease: An overview. *Social Science and Medicine, 16,* 353–367.

Marmot, M. G. (1982). Hypothesis-testing and the study of psychosocial factors. *Advances in Cardiology, 29,* 3–9.

Maschewsky, W. (1982). The relation between stress and myocardial infarction: A general analysis. *Social Science and Medicine, 16,* 455–462.

Mausner, J. S., & Bahn, A. K. (1974). *Epidemiology.* Philadelphia: Saunders.

Mechanic, D. (Ed.). (1982). Symptoms, Illness Behavior, and Help-Seeking. New York: Prodist.

Mechanic, D. (Ed.). (1983). *Handbook of health, health care and the health professions.* New York: Free Press.

Medalie, J. H., & Goldbourt, U. (1976). Angina pectoris among 10,000 men. II. Psychosocial and other risk factors as evidenced by a multivariate analysis of a five-year incidence study. *The American Journal of Medicine, 60,* 910–921.

Medalie, J. H., Papier, C. M., Goldbourt, U., & Herman, J. B. (1975). Major factors in the development of diabetes mellitus in 10,000 men. *Archives of Internal Medicine, 135,* 811–817.

Morris, J. N. (1975). *Uses of epidemiology.* London: Churchill Livingstone.

Morrison, F. R., Paffenbarger, R. A., Jr. (1981). Epidemiological aspects of biobehavior in the etiology of cancer: A critical review. In S. M. Weiss, J. A. Herd, & B. H. Fox (Eds.), *Perspectives on behavioral medicine.* New York: Academic Press.

Mossey, J. M., & Shapiro, E. (1982). Self-rated health: A predictor of mortality among the elderly. *American Journal of Public Health, 72,* 800–808.

Myers, J., Lindenthal, J. J., & Pepper, M. (1974). Social class, life events, and psychiatric symptoms. A longitudinal study. In B. S. Dohrenwend & B. P. Dohrenwend (Eds.), *Stressful life events: Their nature and effects.* New York: Wiley.

Orth–Gomer, K. (1979). Ischemic heart disease and psychological stress in Stockholm and New York. *Journal of Psychosomatic Research, 23,* 165–173.

Orth–Gomer, K., & Ahlbom, A. (1980). Impact of psychological stress on ischemic heart disease when controlling for conventional risk indicators. *Journal of Human Stress, 6*(1), 7–15.

Payne, R., & Pugh, D. S. (1976). Organizational structure and climate. In M. D. Dunnette (Ed.), *Handbook of industrial and organizational psychology.* Chicago: Rand McNally.

Pearlin, L. I., Lieberman, M. A., Menaghan, E. G., & Mullan, J. T. (1981). The stress process. *Journal of Health and Social Behavior, 22,* 337–356.

Pooling Project Research Group. (1978). Relationship of blood pressure, serum cholesterol, smoking habit, relative weight and ECG abnormalities to incidence of major coronary events. Final report of the pooling project. *Journal of Chronic Diseases, 31,* 201–306.

Rahe, R. H., & Arthur, R. J. (1978). Life change and illness studies: Past history and future directions. *Journal of Human Stress, 4*(1), 3–15.

Rimón, R. (1973). Rheumatoid factor and aggression dynamics in female patients with rheumatoid arthritis. *Scandinavian Journal of Rheumatology, 2,* 119–122.

Rosenman, R. H., Brand, R. J., Jenkins, C. D., Friedman, M., Straus, R., & Wurm, M. (1975). Coronary heart disease in the Western Collaborative Group Study: Final follow-up experience of 8 1/-2 years. *Journal of the American Medical Association, 233,* 872–877.

Rundall, T. G. (1978). Life change and recovery from surgery. *Journal of Health and Social Behavior, 19,* 418–427.

Schlesselman, J. J. (1982). *Case-control studies: Design, conduct, analysis.* New York: Oxford University Press.

Schmale, A. H., & Iker, H. P. (1966). The affect of hopelessness and the development of cancer. *Psychosomatic Medicine, 28,* 714–721.

Schmale, A. H., & Iker, H. P. (1971). Hopelessness as a predictor of cervical cancer. *Social Science and Medicine, 5,* 95–100.

Sexton, M. M. (1979). Behavioral epidemiology. In O. F. Pomerleau & J. P. Brady (Eds.), *Behavioral medicine: Theory and practice.* Baltimore: Williams & Wilkins.

Shekelle, R. B., & Lin, S. C. (1978). Public beliefs about causes and prevention of heart attacks. *Journal of the American Medical Association, 240,* 756–758.

Siegrist, J., Dittmann, K., Rittner, K., & Weber, J. (1982). The social context of active distress in patients with early myocardial infarction. *Social Science and Medicine, 16,* 443–453.

Steptoe, A., & Mathews, A. (Eds.). (1984). *Health care and human behaviour.* London: Academic Press.

Sterling, P., & Eyer, J. (1981). Biological basis of stress-related mortality. *Social Science and Medicine, 15E,* 3–42.

Stone, G. C., Cohen, F., & Adler, N. E. (Eds.). (1979). *Health psychology.* San Francisco: Jossey–Bass.

Susser, M. (1975). Epidemiological models. In E. L. Struening & M. Guttentag (Eds.), *Handbook of evaluation research* (Vol. 1). Beverly Hills, CA: Sage.

Syme, S. L. (1974). Behavioral factors associated with the etiology of physical disease: A social epidemiological approach. *American Journal of Public Health, 64,* 1043–1045.

Tarnapolsky, A., Watkins, G., & Hand, D. J. (1980). Aircraft noise and mental health. I. Prevalence of individual symptoms. *Psychological Medicine, 10,* 683–698.

Theorell, T. G. T. (1982). Review of research on life events and cardiovascular illness. *Advances in Cardiology, 29,* 140–147.

Thoits, P. A. (1982). Life stress, social support, and psychological vulnerability: Epidemiological considerations. *Journal of Community Psychology, 10,* 341–362.

Watkins, G., Tarnapolsky, A., & Jenkins, L. M. (1981). Aircraft noise and mental health. II. Use of medicines and health care services. *Psychological Medicine, 11,* 155–168.

Weiner, H. (1977). *Psychobiology and human disease.* New York: Elsevier.

Weiss, S. M., Herd, J. A., & Fox, B. H. (Eds.). (1981). *Perspective on behavioral medicine.* New York: Academic Press.

Weissman, M. M., & Klerman, G. L. (1978). Epidemiology of mental disorders. *Archives of General Psychiatry, 35,* 705–712.

White, K. L. & Henderson, M. (Eds.). (1976). *Epidemiology as a fundamental science.* New York: Oxford University Press.

Williams, A. W., Ware, J. E., Jr., & Donald, C. A. (1981). A model of mental health life events, and social supports applicable to general populations. *Journal of Health and Social Behavior, 22,* 324–336.

Wirsching, M., Stierlin, H., Hoffmann, F., Weber, G., & Wirsching, B. (1982). Psychological identification of breast cancer patients before biopsy. *Journal of Psychosomatic Research, 26,* 1–10.

6 Survey Research Methods in Environmental Psychology

Judith M. Tanur
State University of New York at Stony Brook

Survey methodology finds many applications in environmental psychology. Aspects of the environment, human exposure to these aspects, the response of human beings to such exposure, and people's attitudes towards aspects of the environment all can be, and have been, studied through the use of sample surveys.

Aspects of the environment are often studied using a process in which sites are chosen on a sampling basis (using probability sampling or some other kind). Then technicians measure the relevant aspect of the environment, for example, the level of some pollutant or the quality of the air, directly at the site, using sophisticated measuring instruments and methods developed in the physical and biological sciences. No human respondent/informant is involved. Whereas such surveys provide useful data for environmental psychology and often use sampling techniques also used in surveys of human populations, we restrict our attention in this chapter to surveys in which a measurement is taken on, or information is supplied by, a human being other than the surveyor. Such surveys of human beings have the special problems of nonresponse and response errors that—together with ways and means of dealing with such problems—are the substance of this chapter.

Let us look at some examples of such surveys. To monitor physical effects of pesticides, the EPA maintains a Human Monitoring Program measuring the incidences of pesticide residues in the general U.S. population. The program includes The National Human Adipose Tissue Survey, which receives tissue samples from pathologists and medical examiners at randomly selected hospitals. It also includes the Health and Nutrition Survey, carried out by the National Center for Health Statistics, which analyzes blood and urine specimens obtained from a national sample of the general population. EPA has done pilot testing for a national household survey of pesticide usage.

The Fish and Wildlife Service is determining the quality of the nation's water by selecting a probability sample of sections of rivers and then contacting (by mail with phone follow-up) a local informant (usually a fishery biologist) to supply data on each such section.

Reactions to environmental conditions can be exemplified by a survey conducted of a sample of members of the German Airline Pilots Association. The survey found agreement on the dangers of windshear, the need for its measurement on-board airliners, and hints for the design of such instrumentation. (*European Scientific Notes,* 1983).

Public attitudes towards nuclear energy and its environmental effects have been the subject of numerous surveys (e.g., Cole & Fiorentine, 1983; Melber, Nealy, Hammersla, & Rankin, 1977). Changes in those attitudes brought about by TV and radio advertising campaign focusing on information about radiation and nuclear waste disposal were measured by survey techniques in an experiment in Grand Rapids, Michigan (Cambridge Reports, Inc., 1982). Surveys have also been used to assess aesthetic attributes of planned water resources projects— with respondents being shown photos or drawings of proposed projects and asked to render judgments or state preferences (Panel on Aesthetic Attributes in Water Resources Projects, 1982). A major survey that can be construed as measuring the effects of the man-made environment on individuals is the National Crime Survey (NCS). Conducted by the Census Bureau for the Bureau of Justice Statistics, NCS collects data on victimizations of individuals and families—these data complement, and are considered more reliable than, data on crimes reported to the police.

In addition to agencies of the federal government such as the Census Bureau and the Environmental Protection Agency, surveys as we have seen are carried out by commercial polling firms, organizations specializing in market research, university-based research institutes, and state and local governments.

These ubiquitous surveys, broadly construed, are the focal point of our discussion. Let us briefly explore this broad construction that is being placed on surveys for purposes of this chapter.

Surveys can be classified by whether they are cross sectional, involving only one interview, or longitudinal, repeatedly interviewing the same respondents. Longitudinal surveys have major advantages over one-time surveys in their ability to follow individual changes over time and thus illuminate the social processes that are at work. Thus the Panel Study of Income Dynamics (Morgan, 1977) can describe those Americans who are persistently poor (that is, below the poverty line year after year) and contrast them with families who dip below the poverty line only once in a decade of interviewing.

Surveys can also be classified as to whether they are seeking information about a system "as it stands," perhaps in order to establish a base line against which to measure the effect of a change, or about the impact of a change after it has been implemented, either in full or on an experimental basis. The Current Population Survey, carried out each month by the Census Bureau to measure, among other things, the amount of employment and unemployment, is an example of a survey measuring a current condition. Surveys designed to measure the impact of a change are usually embedded in social experiments (e.g., The Negative Income Tax Experiments) or quasi experiments (e.g., evaluations of Head Start Programs).

Surveys in their various forms are one of the tools that Herbert Simon refers to in the centennial issue of *Science* as providing a growing body of data that constitute an important part of the history of the social sciences in the past hundred years. But Simon (1980) goes on to say:

> It is perhaps not important that we have more information than our ancestors; it is vitally important that we have better information. A major part of the effort of trained social scientists has gone into improving our techniques for making the kinds of measurements that I have just enumerated [essentailly survey data]. (p. 72)

Two key aspects of proper surveys in which advances make possible the gathering of better information are sampling and standardization. A survey is used to obtain information, not from every member of the population, but only from a sample selected using probability methods. If the sample is drawn in a properly random manner (and not haphazardly, for example, or by the use of volunteers or those conveniently at hand), then the results of the survey can be generalized to the population from which the sample was drawn. The second key attribute of a proper survey is that its procedures are standardized—it uses prescribed forms of questions and standardized methods of asking them.

In one way or another, sampling and standardization to obtain valid measurement are the themes of this chapter. What are the methods that social scientists and statisticians have devised for making surveys yield better information? Probability sampling methods have a long history of theoretical development, but recently methodological attention has turned to those factors that can destory the value of information from surveys even when probability samples are employed—problems of nonresponse and mistaken responses. Peeling away the variability originating from these extraneous sources purifies our information, giving us more confidence in its validity.

What are the effects of differing decisions about the standardized procedures for a particular survey? Does it matter whether the interviewing is done in person or on the telephone? Does the form, context, or ordering of questions make a difference in the estimates prepared from the surveys? As research is done to answer these and related questions, we learn more about the validity and generalizability of the information given us by surveys and are more able to improve them.

This chapter discusses some of the methods that have been and are being developed to reduce the fuzziness of the knowledge gained from large-scale surveys. Ideally we should like to go out into the world with a coherent theory of human behavior and a fool-proof machine for measuring the effects brought about by our precisely specified causes. But usually our theories are stated only in broad and general terms. We often have only approximate ideas about causality. Our ability to measure effects is limited by the extraneous variability in our measurements brought about not only by the process of sampling but also by the standardization decisions made in any particular case. Our ability to measure effects is also limited by people's insistence on acting like human beings— refusing sometimes to answer our questions, insisting sometimes on their own interpretations of meanings rather than the ones we have in mind, and so on. It is to the separation of these extraneous sources of variability from the actual measurement of the phenomena of interest that we turn as we examine the concept of total survey variability.

TOTAL SURVEY VARIABILITY

Although surveys are conducted using samples of individuals, their purpose as we have seen is to learn more about the broader population from which the sample is taken. That information may range from the answers to such relatively simple questions as "What proportion of the population has measurable residues of PCB's in their tissues?" through more difficult or sensitive ones such as "What is the average annual expenditure for medical care for members of the population?" on up to such conceptually complicated ones as "What would be the effect on attitudes towards nuclear power among the members of this population if they were given firm information on the risks involved?" In all cases, it is correct answers to these questions *for the population* that are of interest, not answers that are correct only for the people surveyed, nor answers that are incorrect even for the people surveyed and hence, of course, incorrect for the population.

As the results of surveys become more important for research and for society, it becomes more and more important to make these results as accurate as possible. Efforts to improve the accuracy of surveys (and other data collection methods) focus on the sources of inaccuracies; the underlying assumption is that if such sources can be identified they can eventually be controlled, or at the very least, their effects can be taken into account in the interpretation of results.

To address sources of inaccuracy many investigators use the concept of total survey error, and several models have been developed to operationalize the concept (e.g., Lessler, 1979; see Mosteller, 1978 for a simple technical exposition of the Census Bureau Model). We use the blueprints of these models to guide our exploration of the effects of variability in surveys.

Total survey error models partition the total variation in survey responses into several components that can be studied separately. These components include sampling variability response effects, nonresponse effects, and their combinations.[1] The goal is to measure and control the total error by providing a mathematical framework for examining separate sources of error. When a real survey is evaluated using the concept of total survey error, the effect of each component is gauged, and then the separate effects are synthesized to arrive at a statement about the accuracy of the entire survey. In an analogous fashion, we examine in turn the major components of total survey variability: sampling variability, response effects, and nonresponse effects, and then look very briefly at some progress being made in synthesizing these ideas in measuring the accuracy of surveys and thus improving them.

Sampling Variability

The training most social scientists receive in sampling works with the classical notions of a population (the target population) and a frame, which is a list of that population. To the extent that the frame includes everyone in the target population and excludes everyone who is not in the target population, the frame is a good reflection of that population and sampling from it will give results that are not biased. But for many large-scale surveys there is no good frame available. It is difficult, for example, to have a list of all the people in the United States, in a particular state, or even within the area that a particular environmental contaminent from a particular source might reach. There are two sorts of solutions that have been used for dealing with the problem of the lack of frame.

A common solution, when telephone interviewing is contemplated, is to use random digit dialing. A table of random numbers, or a computer random number generator, is used to supply the phone numbers that will be dialed. Often such a sample is stratified by area code, and often it is stratified further in terms of exchange within area code. Because many banks of telephone numbers are not being used by telephone companies at any given time, and because many exchanges are used primarily for nonresidential telephones, unrestricted random digit dialing often gives very few answers to very many dialings. Various strat-

---

[1]Surveys share with other forms of research still another sort of error—what has been termed *conceptual error* in this context and is more generally referred to as "validity." It is difficult to measure attitudes or subjective health in any way that will meet with general agreement as "correct." Even a seemingly more concrete measurement—whether or not an individual is employed—is a focus of considerable conceptual controversy as that measurement is taken in the Current Population Survey. Is someone who has been out of work for 6 months and has given up looking for work on the grounds that none is available, "unemployed" or "out of the labor force"? The Current Population Survey would choose the latter category. Clearly these conceptual decisions influence survey results; they must be scrupulously documented and deserve careful analysis. They are, however, beyond the scope of this chapter.

egies have been proposed to deal with this problem. For example, known working residential numbers can be drawn at random from telephone books, and their last digit or digits randomly or systematically altered. Thus the yield of working numbers is increased, and access is provided to unlisted telephones. (Such a procedure, of course, supposes that appropriate telephone books can be chosen and in some sense serve as a "frame.")

A broader solution to the problem of lack of listings dates back at least to Neyman (1934). This is multistage area probability sampling. Let us consider a nation-wide survey. The map of the United States would be cut up into a variety of primary sampling units (PSU's). The PSU's might constitute standard metropolitan statistical areas, counties, or other sensible geographic locations. These PSU's would be stratified according to criteria relevant to the survey at hand. Size, racial composition, climate, region of the country, etc. would be usual stratification variables. Then one or more primary sampling units would be chosen from each stratum, usually with probability proportional to size. (Typically each of certain large PSU's would form a stratum by itself and be selected into the sample with certainty.) Those PSU's that are chosen are then further cut up into smaller areas—secondary sampling units—which are subjected to probability sampling methods. Eventually the procedure gets down to small areas such as blocks or census tracks. Then, typically, at least in large-scale government surveys, listings are made of these small units. This often involves a worker going to the area and actually making a list of every household location in that unit. Finally, still using probability sampling methods, small clusters of household locations, called ultimate sampling units, are chosen to be interviewed. Thus the necessity of having a list for a frame remains, but the actual listing is carried out only for small areas from which households will be chosen. Careful records of procedures of all stages of the sampling are maintained, and thus the probability that each unit would be included in the sample is known. Then if analysis needs to be done to estimate population characteristics, these selection probabilities (or their inverses) can be used as weights to derive unbiased population estimators.

Sampling variability arises from the very act of sampling. Even if all the procedures carried out to measure the quantity of interest on the members of the sample produced perfect accuracy, the luck of the draw might have given us a different sample. Such a different sample would, of course, include different people and thus would be likely to yield slightly different estimates. Conceptually the measurement of this variation over samples is the measurement of sampling error. Operationally, we estimate the variability associated with sampling errors over all possible samples using the variation in a particular set of sample data and the size of the sample. The usual formulas for estimating standard errors, decreasing with $1/\sqrt{n}$, assume simple random sampling.

But as we have seen, most large-scale surveys use much more complicated sampling designs, rendering the usual formulas for standard errors inappropriate.

Two basic approaches have been used to deal with this complication. For quantities that are estimated in a straightforward manner (e.g., using the sample mean to estimate the population mean), many surveys construct, use, and publish so-called design effects (Kish & Frankel, 1974). These are essentially deflation factors that reduce the sample size achieved by the complicated sampling procedure to the approximately equivalent size of a simple random sample. When estimation procedures are more complicated—for example, when ratio estimation is used with estimated population controls and a weighted average is taken over time for those units continuing in the sample, replication methods are used to estimate standard errors. Essentially the total sample is repeatedly broken in half and the entire estimation procedure is carried out separately on each random half sample. The variability among the resulting estimates provides a useful estimate of the standard error of the estimate. (For a description of how these methods are used in practice, see U.S. Bureau of the Census, 1978; much of the basic research is due to Keyfitz, 1957 and McCarthy, 1966, 1969.)

Nonsampling Variability

But all this assumes an ideal world—among other things it assumes that the frame (or the procedure that we use to substitute for a frame) is an accurate representation of the population to which we want to generalize, that everyone chosen for the sample provides the solicited data, that the researcher and the respondent share the same definitions of concepts, that respondents remember correctly and tell the truth, and that nobody makes a mistake in writing down the answer. It is to these nonsampling errors that much interest has recently turned, as results of surveys are taken seriously by the public and policy makers, for in some ways nonsampling errors are harder to understand and control than sampling errors. Some nonsampling errors are essentially random—copying errors, for example—and they will tend to cancel out as the sample size increases, though they will increase the variance of estimates. Other nonsampling errors, such as memory errors and systematic coding errors, will tend to cumulate and cannot be decreased just by increasing the size of the sample; as James A. Davis (1975) has put it, "$\sqrt{n}$ wrongs do not make a right" (p. 42).

Nonsampling variability or errors can be subdivided into nonresponse variability or errors (people are left out of the frame, left out of the sample, or do not answer specific questions) and response or "measurement" variability or effects or errors (answers are obtained, but are in some sense "wrong"). We first consider response errors, a problem that has attracted a good deal of attention in recent years.[2] Indeed, a very recent effort has been made to use the findings and

_____

[2]A glossary of terms used in discussion of nonsampling errors has been prepared, as have several excellent reveiws of the literature and bibliographies in recent years (for example, Bailar, 1976; Bradburn, 1978; Dalenius, 1977; Deighton, Poland, Stubbs, & Tortora, 1978; Kahn & Cannell,

research techniques of the cognitive sciences to understand response errors and other problems of survey methodology (see Jabine, Straf, Tanur & Tourangeau, 1984).

Response Effects

Different types of questions are asked in surveys. There are factual or behavioral questions (How old are you? Have you ever been arrested?) for which there is a "true" answer that can, at least in theory, be ascertained for checking the survey response against. At the other end of a scale of concreteness are attitude questions (Do you feel that this landscape arrangement is more pleasing than that one? Would you install insulation in your home if fuel oil prices tripled?) for which there is no external source of a "true" answer. There are continuing debates about whether the concept of "true" answer is even applicable in such cases, and an extensive literature on the match—or lack of match—between expressed attitudes and actual behaviors; see e.g., Deutscher, 1973. In addition, there are questions that are indeed behavioral—Have you been the victim of an unreported crime this month?—for which no easy outside verification is possible. For current purposes a distinction between factual and attitudinal questions is helpful. With factual questions we may certainly speak of response "errors" when the answer in the survey does not match a publicly recorded fact, whereas with attitude questions we should speak of response "effects" if two different methods in a survey produce two different answers. That is, if a higher percentage of repondents answer "yes" to the question "Would you be opposed to a nuclear power plant being built in your town?" than answer "no" to the reversed question "Would you be in favor of a nuclear power plant being built in your town?" we have a response effect attributable to question wording.

Three broad classes of response effects can be identified (Sudman & Bradburn, 1974): those originating with characteristics of the respondent, those originating with characteristics of the interviewer (or with the interaction between characteristics of the interviewer and those of the respondent), and those originating in the social situation of the interview. This three-fold division is followed here, although the categories and the variables within them interact. For example, a question form that gives valid data in a face-to-face situation may be inappropriate in a mail survey.

1. *Respondent Effects.*   Differences in respondent characteristics, in general, ought to create real response differences, not ones that might be called *errors*.

1978; Mosteller, 1978; Sudman & Bradburn, 1974), often in connection with continuing programs of research on survey methodology. A special issue of *Sociological Methods and Research* on survey design and analysis concentrating on errors in surveys appeared in November, 1977. Two panels sponsored by the Committee on National Statistics of the National Research Council have published work in the general area.

Thus the whole point of a survey, for example, might be to find out if respondents who differ on whether they live with a spouse or live separately also differ in propensity to be victimized. Respondents may also possess other characteristics that predispose them to give particular sorts of responses, such as a need for approval, a propensity to acquiesce, or a wish to give socially desirable answers. These predispositions, unrelated to the content of the researcher's question, are called *response sets*. Thus, if unmarried heads of households tend to give more socially desirable responses than do married ones, they might deny being victimized and the true relationships between marital status and victimization would be obscured. Measures of such a "response set" are hence often included in questionnaires so that their impact can be controlled. But some recent research indicates (Bradburn et al., 1979) that "response sets" may not be artifacts to be eliminated but real personality traits. People who score high on these measures seem to live in limited social environments. They report low levels of behaviors such as sociability, drinking, intoxication, and marijuana use, not because they "are manipulating the image they present in the interview situation, but because [they] have different life experiences and behave differently from persons with lower scores" (p. 103).[3]

Memory is another respondent variable. In factual questions, a respondent must be able to remember correctly in order to give an accurate answer. Two kinds of memory errors can be distinguished: forgetting, and what has come to be known as the "telescoping" of time. In the latter, events, actions (such as the use of pesticides), or victimizations, are reported as happening more recently than they actually did. (This moving of events to more recent times is the usual meaning of "telescoping"; there is some evidence, however, that telescoping may sometimes move events into the more distant past.)

These phenomena work in opposite directions in producing response errors; forgetting leads to underreporting the number of events in a time period, and telescoping typically leads to overreporting. Forgetting can be minimized by using such memory jogs as "aided recall" (perhaps better called recognition), in which the respondent is read or shown a list of the events that may have happened and asked to indicate with a yes or no answer whether indeed they have, but this may increase telescoping. The encouragement of respondents to take the time to find records (for example, of expenditures on such items as health care or of insurance claims) offers increased accuracy and controls telescoping but is of little use when records are fragmentary or nonexistent.

To control telescoping a technique called "bounded recall" has been useful in panel studies where respondents are interviewed repeatedly, as they are in NCS (Neter & Waksberg, 1964). At the start of the second and subsequent interviews,

---

[3]The Panel on Survey-based Measures of Subjective Phenomena of the Committee on National Statistics has produced a further review of the literature on response sets; see Turner & Martin (1981) and the forthcoming full panel report.

repondents are reminded of what they have previously reported and asked what has occurred since those events. Clearly the interviewer needs as easily available and extensive fund of information on the respondent for this technique to be used conveniently, and in this connection Computer Assisted Telephone Interviewing (CATI—see later) should be of great assistance. As the length of time between interviews increases, the amount forgotten increases, but the amount of telescoping decreases; conversely, as the amount of time between interviews decreases, telescoping increases and forgetting decreases. This relationship suggests that there might be an optimum spacing between interviews so that the effects of the two phenomena tend to cancel out (see Sudman & Bradburn, 1973). It may be, however, that optimum spacing varies with the type of information being sought. For example, Cannell, Miller, and Oksenberg (1981) have shown that a higher percentage of short hospital stays than of longer ones are unreported at each time lag between hospitalization and interview. Similarly, small purchases tend to be forgotten more easily than large ones, and we can perhaps speculate that the spacing that optimizes the accuracy of reporting less salient information is far shorter than that which optimizes the accuracy of reporting experiences more salient to respondents.

Problems with faulty memory can be avoided by asking people to keep diaries of their time use. This approach has been employed in basic research in the Time Use Survey conducted at the University of Michigan (see for example Hill & Juster, 1979; Stafford & Duncan, 1979). Purchase/disposal diaries will be used in the EPA's household pesticide survey and gasoline purchase diaries have been used by the Energy Information Agency to supplement the data gathered from the residential energy consumption survey (Thompson, Carlson, Woteki, & Vagts 1980). But diaries are costly, possibly incomplete, and respondent cooperation is difficult to obtain and often deteriorates with time (Kalton & Schuman, 1980). 1980).

Some of these problems can at least be addressed. For example, incentive payments have increased the completion rates of diaries (Thompson et al., 1980), and tape recording can be effective for groups who may have difficulty writing diaries (Sudman & Ferber, 1971). Another approach is to employ electronic "beepers." One group of researchers gave a sample of adolescents these electronic paging devices through which signals were transmitted at random times (Csikszentmihalyi, Larsen, & Prescott, 1977). The youths were quite cooperative in pausing in their activities to fill out a brief questionnaire about what they were doing, with whom, and how they felt about it. (Most time was passed watching TV, or in conversation with peers; only 18% of the adolescents' time was spent studying or working.) This seems a technique with wider applicability and has also been used by the Michigan Time-Use survey, where it was found to give results comparable to those obtained by more usual diary methods. Personal monitoring for exposure to environmental contaminents might well use such a technique, asking a respondent to read some recording device at each randomly chosen and signaled instant.

2. *Interviewer Effects.*   The second sort of response effects are those due to interviewer characteristics or to the interaction of those characteristics with those of the respondents. The change of the U.S. Census after 1950 to mostly self-reporting came about because analysis showed that enumerator effects, whereas not themselves terribly large, constituted a major part of the total variability of the Census.

A recent review of the literature (Sudman & Bradburn, 1974), however, found evidence of only weak effects in this category. Matches between interviewer and respondent on such characteristics as gender or race tend to affect only those questions that relate directly to the matched variable. Thus blacks tend to give more militant answers to black interviewers than to white ones—raising the question of which answer is closer to the "true" attitude or behavior. When such an interaction is thought to be important, the sample can be split between matched and unmatched interviewer–respondent pairs and any response effects that arise be reported as part of the data.

3. *Interview Effects.*   Far more important than the previous two categories in creating response effects are variables having to do with the task confronting the respondent and interviewer, and with the social situation in which they find themselves.

Comprehension and communication are the first interview variables, for the investigator and the respondent must understand the question and the possible answers the same way. Some startling examples of misunderstanding have been reported (Kalton & Schuman, 1980). Respondents ignored a carefully worded definition of "a room" when reporting on the number of rooms in their home (after all, they know what a room is, and nobody has to tell them how to count). And only one of 246 respondents to a question of "What proportion of your evening viewing time do you spend watching news programs?" could specify how to work out the proportion. (Perhaps someone does have to tell respondents how to do complicated counting.) Fitting question wording to respondents' understanding, asking for clarification, and asking parallel questions with consistency checks move in the direction of improving comprehension and communication.

Mode of presentation is a second interview variable. Although the popular image of a survey taker is probably that of an earnest female interveiwer ringing the doorbell of one of the chosen, in many surveys no interviewer appears at all. Some are conducted by mail, with the respondent filling out the questionnaire alone, and many are conducted by telephone. Mail and telephone surveys are less expensive than those conducted in person, so it becomes important to find out whether they produce differential response effects. No method has been shown to give clearly superior results for all kinds of questions (Sudman & Bradburn, 1974).

There are essentailly no differences between telephone and in-person modes for nonsensitive questions (Groves & Kahn, 1979), nor even on somewhat sensitive ones where external validity checks are possible. For example, whereas 57.1% of the noninstitutionalized U.S. population actually voted in the 1972 Presidential election, overreporting of voting occurred at almost the same level among those interviewed in person and those interviewed by phone in the Groves and Kahn study (66.6 and 69.1% claimed to have voted in the two cases). There is some evidence of greater validity on sensitive questions about such matters as minor lawbreaking in self-reporting mail forms.

Telephone interviews have to give up the visual aids often used in face-to-face interviews; for example when the respondents are handed a card and asked to choose a response category. This procedure allows respondents, for example, to say a letter rather than directly state an income in dollars to the interviewer. But some researchers (Durako & McKenna, 1980) have found it possible to mail out visual aids in advance of an appointment for a phone interview. Only small differences in distributions of answers from the two modes resulting from the lack of visual aids have been found.

Open-ended questions (where the respondents must answer in their own words) are answered differently on the phone than in person; by phone, answers tend to be shorter and there tend to be fewer multiple answers. In an experiment done in connection with the National Crime Survey (NCS), respondents who were interviewed mostly by telephone reported themselves victims of fewer small thefts than those who were more often interviewed in person. The effect was strongest for males and those between 25 and 49 years old. Thus a switch to telephone maximization for NCS would change comparisons between population subgroups (Woltman, Turner, & Bushery, 1980). For reasons of economy, such a switch was made in Febraury, 1980. As was expected, drops in estimated victimization rates were noticed (Paez & Dodge, 1982).

Idiosyncracies of particular interviewers tend to have more effect in phone surveys because each interviewer does more interviews (Groves & Magilavy, 1980). Mail and telephone interviews also sacrifice traditional interviewer skills: recognizing puzzlement from nonverbal cues and giving off reassuring nonverbal messages in return; being able to code the ethnicity and social class of respondents; and being able to report on distracting influences present at the interview that may have response effects (for example, victimization by a member of one's family is unlikely to be reported while that family member is present). Telephone interviewing, at least in single-stage procedures, also sacrifices the ability to match the gender and/or race of the interviewer with those of the respondent, but, as we have seen, lack of such matching produces response effects only on the questions to which such attributes are most salient. A countervailing advantage of telephone interviewing is achieved by its centralized nature. Because interviewers are physically all in the same location, training can be more standardized, supervision more thorough (including random "eavesdropping" on interviews), and retraining more prompt and complete.

One mode of presentation tends to increase anonymity because it never forces respondents to tell whether or not a sensitive question has been answered and hence ought to decrease response effects. The randomized response technique (Warner, 1965) requires a respondent to do some kind of randomization to determine whether the sensitive question or an innocuos one is to be answered. Simple probability calculations then give an estimate of the number in the sample who agreed with the sensitive questions, without revealing which respondents did so. The technique has been found to reduce distorted responses to socially undesirable questions (that one would expect to be underreported), but to be ineffective in reducing distortion to questions dealing with socially desirable behavior (that one would expect to be overreported) (Locander, Sudman, & Bradburn, 1974).[4]

Still another mode of presentation designed in part to increase anonymity and hence increase response accuracy is called network sampling. Individuals, rather than being asked about their own behavior or characteristics are asked about behaviors or characteristics of their friends or relatives (Sirken, 1975; Sudman, Blair, Bradburn, & Stocking, 1977).

In summary, the usual modes of presentation introduce few response effects on nonsensitive questions; with more sensitive questions, however, the more anonymous modes seem to elicit more valid responses. Further, the shortness of telephone interviews may permit respondents to decide that some incidents are too trivial to mention. The 1980 census experimented with telephone rather than in-person follow-up for a sample of those who did not mail back the census forms in order to compare the modes on completeness of data, costs, and interviewer attrition (Bailar & Miskura, 1980); the results of the trial are not yet in.

Even while investigators are attempting to understand the response effects connected with "traditional" modes of interviewing, within the last decade a new mode has been developed, and the response effects that it may introduce must take their place on the research agenda. This new mode, which may turn out to be a major innovation, is Computer Assisted Telephone Interviewing (CATI).

Rather than reading from a printed questionnaire, the interviewer reads questions from the screen attached to a computer terminal and records answers by typing them in on the keyboard of the terminal. Because a computer is involved, CATI offers greatly increased flexibility from beginning to end of the interviewing process. Interviewers can be presented with sample telephone numbers to be called in random order, callbacks can be automatically scheduled, and respondent selection probabilities can be altered as interviewing progresses (Dukta & Frankel, 1980; Roshwalb, Spector, & Madansky, 1979).

---

[4]Some have argued that the technique is confusing to both interviewers and respondents, and it is certainly true that it reduces the sample size by soliciting answers from only a fraction of the respondents. Although the evidence on its efficacy is not conclusive, in 16 studies that compared randomized response with some standard, nine showed a notable reduction in response error (Boruch & Cecil, 1979). An important issue is that, when the percentage of people engaging in the sensitive behavior is small, the technique seems sensitive to reporting errors in the innocuous question (Shimizu & Bonham, 1978).

In a printed questionnaire, instructions to the interviewer about which questions to ask of which respondent can get very complicated very quickly, and it has been common practice to allow no more than four levels of contingency (e.g., ask this question only of males, over 28, with children, and no military service). In CATI, because the computer is programmed to do this "branching," as many as 17 levels of contingency have been used (Lebby, 1980). Contingent questioning can be used to explore successively more sensitive areas, thus providing more information and less nonresponse, with respondents typically dropping off only after supplying at least some information. Information from earlier in the interview can easily be introduced in questions later in the interview, as can material from earlier interviews with the same respondent if study is longitudinal. Question wording can be tailored to the repondent, for example, to the appropriate level of education, thus bringing the meaning of the question as intended by the researcher and as understood by the respondent into closer correspondence than is usually possible with a structured questionnaire.

Most systems for CATI can also do calculations to provide sample statistics as data arrive, and sample sizes can be determined sequentially. Errors are reduced because the operations of data coding and entry are short circuited, and because most systems are programmed to recognize wild or inconsistent values and request correction on the spot.

CATI may well offer the opportunity to test much of the conventional wisdom of professional survey researchers (Freeman, 1980). For example, because question order can be easily, independently, and automatically randomized and records automatically kept of which respondents receive what order, experiments on question ordering can be carried out routinely, as can experiments on the effect of the order in which the interviewer reads the possible responses to questions.

Switching from hard-copy questionnaires to CATI creaste some problems: Flexibility that is needed but not anticipated by the system designer is difficult to achieve; interviewer training differs from what is traditionally done; and currently systems from different installations are incompatible (Groves, Berry, & Mathiowetz, 1980; Shanks, 1980). It is not clear at this time whether these are the early growing pains of a new technology or more permanent faults.

There is speculation that CATI, if used imaginatively, can be more than a change in technology. For example, there has been a tension in the construction of survey instruments between the canons of good measurement (which dictate multiple indicators) and time and respondent patience constraints (which dictate the use of single questions or at most a few indicators). One could conceive of asking a question or two to determine the *approximate* scale location of a respondent (e.g., toward the unfavorable end of the scale) and then using the flexibility of CATI to choose further questions tailored to particular respondents and useful in placing them at more precise scale locations. Screening in telephone interviews on routine demographic and other characteristics will, with some regularity, turn up respondents that are of special interest for policy or other reasons, e.g., who are members of sparse groups (young Chicanos, sufferers from a rare disease). If interviews are on-going under CATI for several studies, it would be possible to program the system to introduce a module of questions pertinent to the research concerns about the "sparse" group into an on-going interview whenever a member of that group is found, thus gradually gathering a sample of sufficient size for generalizing. (But see the discussion following of the response effects due to questionnaire context; such problems may make data gathered in this way less attractive than they seem at first glance.)

Question form—the art of question writing and questionnaire construction—has been described for years in texts, manuals, and word-of-mouth instruction. The scientific study of response effects produced by these variables also has a long history, but the more recent availability of survey archives and the increasing seriousness with which survey results are regarded have inspired a new flowering of research.[5]

It has long been believed that open-ended questions give more accurate information on respondents' attitudes than closed-ended ones. Current opinion is that neither form has a clear superiority overall. Open-ended questions are clearly needed, however, in at least two situations: when salience of an issue to the respondent is being investigated, so that the respondent's words indicate the thought invested in the topic; and in the early stages of questionnaire construction, when the freely chosen wording of pretest respondents is crucial to the construction of response categories to be used in the closed questions for the bulk of the survey.

Long questions are in bad repute for slowing down the pace of the interview and supposedly confusing repondents. Recent studies, however, have experimented in lengthening questions by adding redundant or irrelevant material without complicating them. (For example, instead of "What health problems have you had in the past year?" one might say "The next question asks about health problems during the last year. This is something we ask everyone in the survey. What health problems have you had in the past year?") The result is sometimes a longer answer from the respondent and frequently a more accurate one, in the sense that more events are reported. Longer answers seem to be given for shorter questions when they are mixed in with long ones in a questionnaire (Cannell, 1977). Perhaps the interviewer is both modeling and reinforcing longer answers by asking longer questions.

Cannell and his associates (see Cannell et al., 1981) have been experimenting with further techniques to standardize interviews in an effort to elicit more accurate information. These techniques include specific instructions about the response task; both positive and negative feedback made contingent on the quali-

---

[5]Sudman and Bradburn (1974) provided a detailed review, as do Kalton and Schuman (1980).

ty of the response (rather than less specific feedback—such as the interviewer saying "uh huh"—that pilot studies had shown often occurred after valueless responses); and soliciting specific written committment from the respondent to answer questions accurately and fully. These techniques used in combination seem to increase reporting of material often underreported and decrease reporting of material often overreported.

It has long been believed that although changing the form of a question may change the distribution of respondents over the response categories, the correlation between answers to a question and other variables would not change with the form of the question. This is the notion of "form-independent correlation." Recently, as part of a continuing program of research on question effects, Schuman and Presser (1981) have found that the situation is considerably more complicated than common belief had held. Correlations with background variables (e.g., education) generally did not change with the explicit introduction of a "dont't know" or "middle alternative" option, but such correlations did change—in ways that seem context specific—with more fundamental changes in question form (open vs. closed; balancing by adding counterarguments). Correlations between attitudes seemed more sensitive to the simple introduction of an explicit "don't know" option. Surprisingly, Schuman and Presser found little relation between measures of attitude strength and propensity to be influenced by question form, though they advance this conclusion rather tentatively.

The context in which a question is asked—the ordering of questions, inclusion of other questions, the very arrangement of questionnaire—can produce response effects. The ordering of the questions within a questionnaire may produce effects through several mechanisms (Sudman & Bradburn, 1974): (1) Order may influence the salience of topics (with low-salience topics being most affected because it is easier to increase salience than to reduce it); (2) if there is overlap between questions, respondents may be reluctant to be redundant and repeat details they have given earlier; (3) an urge to consistency might cause answers to earlier questions to influence later ones—respondents express less confidence in institutions when such questions are asked after ones on political alienation than when they are asked before (Turner & Krauss, 1978); (4) later questions in a lengthy questionnaire may be answered in a perfunctory manner because of fatigue. In a variant of this problem, fewer incidents of victimization were reported if the questionnaire was structured so that detailed information for each incident was requested immediately after the incident was mentioned than if the respondent was encouraged to list all incidents of victimization before being asked to describe any one in detail (Biderman, Johnson, McIntyre, & Weir, 1967); (5) the opposite of a fatigue effect may occur, with the rapport between respondent and interviewer growing as the interview proceeds—thus, sensitive or threatening questions are often placed late in an interview when rapport is presumably high.

In particular, questionnaire context may well affect responses to questions that have few everyday implications ("What is your opinion of U.S. nuclear policy?'' vs. "How many children do you plan to have?''), to questions with ambiguous response categories (very happy, pretty happy, vs. one child, two children, etc.), and to questions on somewhat vague or amorphous concepts (attempted assault as opposed to actual assault as forms of victimization; Turner, 1980). Several experiments, across survey organizations but at approximately the same time, are discussed in the forthcoming report of the Panel on Survey-based Measures of Subjective Phenomena of the Committee on National Statistics of the National Academy of Sciences/National Research Council.

The very appearance of a self-report questionnaire may produce response effects, especially inaccuracy. The 1980 Census experimental program sent out variants of the usual Census form that were "people-oriented" in contrast to the standard form that is "computer-oriented" (Bailar & Miskura, 1980). These forms, because of the additional data transcription costs and risks of error they entail, will have to show major advantages over the machine readable questionnaire in mailback rate and data completeness if their use is to be justified.

4. *Nonresponse and Nonparticipation Effects.*   We know that those who do not answer some or all questions in a survey, or who are never home to an interviewer, are different from those who answer or are at home at least in terms of refusing to answer or being away from home. It is likely that they are different in other ways as well. And if these ways include differences in the variable(s) the study is trying to measure (say, income or political opinion), then the results of the survey will be biased.

It is useful to distinguish between "unit" nonresponse and "item" nonresponse. In unit nonresponse, entire sets of data are missing for potential respondents because they were missed in the field (e.g., were never at home), were missed in the frame (e.g., for data being collected by telephone surveys, did not have telephones), or refused to participate. Item nonresponse occurs when an individual's answers to some parts of a survey instrument are missing or are inconsistent (e.g., wage income plus interest income plus income from other sources is greater than total income) and so are edited out in the data-cleaning process and must be replaced by a more consistent set of answers.

There is reason to believe that both item and unit nonresponse are high and getting higher, even in surveys under government sponsorship. Refusal rates for the Current Population Survey (CPS) have risen from 1.8% in 1968 to 2.5% in 1976; for the Health Interview Survey (HIS) from 1.2 to 2.1% in the same period (Panel on Privacy and Confidentiality as Factors in Survey Response, 1979). These numbers are particularly worthy of concern when we take into account that both these surveys are conducted by the U.S. government, that extensive and increasing efforts are mounted to reach respondents initially not found at home, and that each 1% of the American population represents over 2 million individuals. The problem is not confined to the United States, however. Results of the Swedish government Labor Force Survey show refusals have risen from 1.2% in 1970 to 3.9% in 1977 (Dalenius, 1979).

Even the U.S. Census, to which responding is required by law, is not immune. In the 1970 U.S. Census, data had to be imputed (filled in) for such items as age (4.5% of the respondents) and total family income (for 20.7% of families, though many of these families reported most of the components of income; Bailar & Bailar, 1979). It is estimated that the 1970 Census undercounted by 2½% (or about 5 million people) even after adding people to the count whenever there was a shred of evidence to do so. (Housing and Post Office checks by the Census Bureau on a sample basis showed that there were some occupied buildings for which no residents were counted. This made it possible to add some 5 million people who had not filled in Census forms before that estimate of the undercount was calculated.) The problem of undercounting or nonresponse in the 1980 Census has been a major source of legal challenges.

Nonresponse is an even greater problem in nongovernmental surveys. In surveys with varying sponsorship, dealing with varying populations, and using varying definitions of nonresponse, one study found nonresponse ranging from a low of about 5% to a high of about 87% (Panel on Privacy and Confidentiality as Factors in Survey Response, 1979). If the current trend continues, the problem of nonresponse is likely to persist and even to be exacerbated. Without substantial efforts to curb nonresponse, response rates in major national data collection efforts are likely to continue to drop so that survey results will become practically and scientifically useless. Thus the vigorous scientific activity being devoted to developing methods for reducing nonresponse, for adjusting it when it does occur, and for properly analyzing the resulting data are crucial to continued good quality data from surveys.

1. *Reasons for Nonresponse.*   Several reasons for the rise in nonresponse have been suggested, and some have been investigated. Apathy, lack of belief in surveys, and reactions against sales pitches masquerading as surveys might well lead to refusals. Further, distrust of investigators and concern with privacy and confidentiality, perhaps heightened by requests for informed consent (Dalenius, 1979), may well produce both unit and item nonresponse. In an experimental survey by Singer (1978), a promise of confidentiality consistently decreased item nonresponse to sensitive questions. A similar experimental survey conducted under the auspices of the Panel on Privacy and Confidentiality as Factors in Survey Response (1979, p. 116) found steadily decreasing percentages of unit nonresponse (both refusals and total noninterviews) with increasing assurances of confidentiality, but the differences were small. (Perhaps the differences were small because the Census sponsorship of the study produced relatively low nonresponse rates, regardless of promised level of confidentiality.)

Nonresponse in the sense of noncoverage in the frame can be unintentionally introduced in the design stage (Morris, 1979). For example, a design based on imperfectly measured variables or those that are subject to random change will exclude some part of the population. Consider a frame confined to ''low-income'' people; those whose incomes in the critical year were ''accidentally'' higher than their permanent incomes will be excluded. (Of course, those with "accidentally" lower incomes will be mistakenly included.) Similarly, a frame that is constructed to tap large concentrations of a target group will often miss atypical members of that group: Thus, a frame using low-income census tracts to reach low-income people would miss low-income people living in high-income tracts. Of course, telephone surveys miss nontelephone households.

2. *Reducing Nonresponse.*   Certainly the preferred method of dealing with nonresponse is to keep it from happening, though such procedures are often very expensive. Thus a battery of techniques has been developed with the general aim of encouraging the chosen respondents to participate, or of systematically substituting other informants or respondents in the field.

Encouragement to respond takes many forms. In designing field operations, stress is placed on training interviewers to understand the purpose of the study and to establish rapport with respondents. Lead letters are often used and callbacks are routine (though expensive; survey organizations estimate that with a 75% response rate, the first 70% accounts for 50% of the cost, and the last 5% accounts for the other 50%). Especially for surveys under government auspices, enlisting the cooperation of local governmental bodies and professional organizations has proved helpful (Morris, 1979). Incentives to respondents seem to be somewhat useful.

At the same time, extreme efforts to decrease nonresponse may degrade the quality of the data. Some hard-to-locate respondents can be found with extra effort, and the inclusion of their data will increase the response rate and probably the accuracy of the estimates. Those who refuse to participate but are pressured to do so against their will also increase the response rate but perhaps at the expense of the validity of the estimates. For example, in one study the inaccurate reporting of hospitalization by such hard-core nonrespondents caused the overall estimates of hospitalization rates to be worse than if these respondents had never been questioned (U.S. National Health Survey, 1963).

Some nonresponse can be "defined away" by permitting others to answer for an individual, or by substituting for respondents. In household surveys, adults are often permitted to act as informants as to the activities of other family members as well as respondents as to their own activities. Although this approach is primarily a money-saving technique for reducing callbacks, it also reduces nonresponse. In the Charlotte, North Caroline pretest of the National Health Interview Survey, for example, it was found that 50% more callbacks were required when each member of a family had to respond personally than when the rules were relaxed to let related adults respond for those absent (Nisselson & Woolsey, 1959). This sort of proxy reporting has been extended outside the household in network sampling.

But there is mixed evidence about the accuracy of this procedure, which may sometimes substitute response errors for nonresponse. In victimization surveys one study (Biderman et al., 1967) found that many more offenses were reported by respondents as happening to themselves than to other members of their families. Another study (Ennis, 1967) reports accurate results for white household informants but underestimates of crime rates when the method was used for black families.

Many surveys permit substitution, either at random from a similar group or by propinquity, for sample members who refuse or are unavailable. For example, the National Longitudinal Survey of the High School Class of 1972 conducted by the National Center for Educational Statistics used random substitution of schools, whereas the Michigan Survey of Substance Use permitted the substitution of households adjacent to the one designated in the sample. Old-fashioned quota sampling permitted interviewers to choose their own respondents as long as "quotas" for each sex, age group, race, etc. were met. No probability mechanism was used. As it is currently done by professional pollsters (with multistage area probability sampling down to the block level and then controls on such variables as gender, age, and employment status), quota sampling can be thought of as an extension of such substitution rules. There is evidence that this "probability sampling with quotas" (Sudman, 1967) produces usable results: when the National Opinion Research Center split its sample for the 1975 and 1976 General Social Surveys between true probability methods and quotas, it found no differences between the two techniques other than a deficit of one- or two-person households in the quota samples (Stephenson, 1978).

Because assurances of confidentiality tend to increase response rates and anonymity is the ultimate in confidentiality, many surveys routinely arrange for questionnaires to be filled out anonymously. But anonymity cannot be maintained easily in longitudinal studies requiring repeated contacts, and it is seriously compromised in personal interviews. Methods to increase confidentiality in longitudinal studies are discussed under that heading. In telephone interviews, respondents may return calls in order to preserve anonymity, a procedure that also purportedly reduces unit nonresponse. Most special efforts to insure confidentiality in telephone and in-person interviews deal with particularly sensitive questions, however, and are aimed at reducing item nonresponse and inaccuracy. Mailbacks of answers to specific questions have been used and in some cases the randomized response technique reduces item nonresponse (Boruch & Cecil, 1979).

3. *Adjustment for Nonresponse.*   Despite the best efforts of survey designers and field staff, nonresponse, both unit and item, frequently occurs and must be taken into account. What then can be done, after the fact, to adjust for appreciable nonresponse? It is logically impossible to do nothing: Simply to drop the nonresponding units from the sample is to do something, for any estimation procedures that are then implemented tacitly assume that nonresponders are just like responders and that the results of the survey would not have changed had they responded. Doing nothing implies a very specific but simple model: that the forces that prevented some people from responding are unrelated to the variables

of interest, so that the distribution of nonrespondents on these variables is no different from the distribution of respondents. Similarly, more complex techniques for dealing with missing data also require implicit or explicit models of the causes of nonresponse and hence of the distribution of nonrespondents— usually that they are distributed like some subset of the respondents having similar measured characteristics (covariates), but sometimes that they differ from respondents in systematic ways (as would be true if, for example, the probability that people would report their income were proportional to income).

A great number of techniques for dealing with missing data have been developed.[6] Some techniques reweight aggregations of data to take into account missing observations, and others "fill in the blanks," creating pseudo-observations in place of the missing ones. In either case, the analyst must take into account that the data have been adjusted for nonresponse, and that such adjustments affect estimates of the accuracy of quantities derived from the data.

A commonly used means of *weighting for missing data* is ratio estimation. It uses information derived from other studies to improve estimation. Assume the quantity we wish to estimate is $\bar{Y}$ (for example, the average income for the population), and that it will be estimated by the sample mean, $\bar{y}$ (the average income for those in the sample). Assume we also know that Y is related to another variable, X (say number of people per room in living quarters), for which we know both the mean for the respondents in the sample, $\bar{x}$ (mean number of people per room in the sample), and the mean for the total population, $\bar{X}$, from another source such as the Census. If we then make the additional assumption that the ratio of the mean number of people per room in the sample to the mean number of people per room in the population is the same as the corresponding ratio of mean income between the sample and the population ($\bar{x}/\bar{X} = \bar{y}/\bar{Y}$), we can use this relation to adjust $\bar{y}$ to $\bar{y}' = \bar{y}(\bar{X}/\bar{x})$.[7] Recently, investigators (Thornberry & Massey, 1978) found that health characteristics differ between households with and without telephones; they developed a ratio estimator that could be used to adjust estimates of health characteristics for the bias arising from the noncoverage of households without phones, if the survey were redesigned to be done via telephone. The form of the ratio estimator should be valuable for other similar surveys.[8]

---

[6]See, e.g., Bailar, 1978; Brewer & Sarndal, 1979; Kalsbeek, 1980; Little & Rubin, 1979; Morris, 1979.

[7]Deming (1978) presents properties of this estimator and several related ones. Even if the assumptions are only approximately correct, ratio estimation usually improves accuracy; as a bonus, ratio estimation usually reduces sampling error.

[8]Raking ratio estimators, a somewhat different technique (Deming & Stephan, 1940), adjust for strata much finer than the ones for which outside data are available and so must start by estimating the "outside information" for these strata. This estimation uses methods of iterative scaling also used in other sorts of analyses of cross-classified data (e.g., Bishop, Fienberg, & Holland, 1975). The estimated outside information is then used as part of a ratio adjustment for that stratum. Oh and Scheuren (1978) have offered a multivariate version of the raked ratio estimator.

Techniques that fill in missing values individually for item nonresponse are called *imputation techniques*. Such techniques assume that the value of the missing item can be estimated from values of other items for that respondent. One such technique uses the other items as variables in a regression function, either derived from the data at hand or available from outside sources. Such a procedure must assume (or fit) a particular functional form of the model of how the missing item depends on the other variables (covariates).

In the days before high-speed computers, survey analysts often filled in blanks caused by item nonresponse from tables put together from outside sources. Such a table might specify that if the respondent was a married white female between the ages of 30 and 45 who did not answer how many children she had, she should be "assigned" two children. This so-called "cold-deck" procedure, of course, assigned the same number of children to all missing values for women in a specific marital status–race–age group. With the advent of high-speed computers, more flexible procedures became possible.

These "hot-deck" procedures fill in the missing value for the item from the value appearing for another respondent in the same survey who is "similar" to the respondent with missing data. "Similar" is defined by the variables thought to influence the one missing (e.g., for the number of children these might still be marital status, race, and age), and all respondents who are the same on these variables are said to constitute an "adjustment class". Hot-deck procedures make no assumptions about the functional form by which the variables defining the adjustment class determine the missing item, only that they do. There are now a tremendous variety of these hot-deck procedures: The simplest uses the value of the item that occurred in the previous unit processed in the adjustment class. Other variations, made possible by advances in computer science, random access and dynamic creation of the adjustment classes, choose a donor within the adjustment class on criteria of nearness on further important variables or introduce randomness into the process of choice of a donor (G. Sande, 1979).

Care must be exercised when making estimates from data that have been partially imputed because the imputation changes the estimated accuracy of the estimates. Further, the sample size for any item is the number of respondents actually giving data for that item and should not be considered increased by the imputation.

A new idea is a process of multiple imputation (Rubin, 1978, 1979). Here the analyst repeatedly uses an imputation method to fill in missing data. Each time the complete data set is imputed, an estimate is made of the quantity of interest. One can then examine the distribution of these estimates to see if, or how much, they vary with different imputed data sets. If several different assumptions about the "causes" of nonresponse are plausible, a set of multiple imputations might be carried out using each assumption as the model to determine the imputation method, the set of sets of estimates made, and thus the sensitivity of the estimation to the model assumed for nonresponse explored as well. The justification and interpretation of this multiple imputation procedure come from a Bayesian technical stance (Rubin, 1978, 1979).

One can think of multiple imputation as a program for investigating the properties of the various methods of imputation in the context of various models for nonresponse or differential response (cf. Heckman, 1976) using a variety of data sets. Some comparisons of the different methods have already been made (e.g., Bailar & Bailar, 1979; Cox & Folsom, 1978). So far we know that there are differences in both systematic and random error over the techniques, but no consistent pattern is yet visible.

4. *Current Research Prospects.*   Nonresponse, its causes, cures, methods of coping, and their properties represent active lines of research. In 1978 several sessions at the annual meeting of the American Statistical Association discussed nonresponse[9], the Committee on National Statistics established a Panel on Incomplete Data that held a symposium in August, 1979.[10] The Panel reviewed and compared procedures used for incomplete data, summarized theory and methods for field procedures, data processing, and estimation, and made suggestions for reporting surveys so that results of nonresponse can be taken into account. We need more systematic studies of the performance of imputations, perhaps following Dalenius (1979) who asks for a series of simulation experiments. In such experiments complete data would be artificially subjected to nonresponse mechanisms; analysts would attempt to estimate the (known) population characteristics and to describe the nonresponse mechanisms. As it becomes more and more obvious that the most rigorous mathematical treatment of the effects of adjustment for nonresponse is only as good as the model of the process assumed to be causing the nonresponse, it seems likely that treatments of the subject, practices, and comparisons between practices will take on a more Bayesian aspect, either formally or informally.

Total Survey Variability Revisited

Several investigations have examined the accuracy of particular surveys through the synthesizing concept of "total survey error" (or related ideas that examine all possible sources of variability and their impact on estimates made from the data).[11] One major study applied the concept of total survey error to the 1970

---

[9]These are published in Aziz and Scheuren (1978), as well as in the *Proceedings* volumes for that meeting.

[10]A preliminary version of the proceedings has appeared (Panel on Incomplete Data, 1979). The final proceedings volume and the remainder of the reports of the Panel are in press.

[11]Other approaches to the modeling of measurment error than that implied by the concept of total survey error are of course possible and have been suggested. For example, an approach using a set of structural equations to model the relations between a group of questions that all pertain to the same

Center for Health Administration Studies—National Opinion Research Center national health survey, collecting data on health services use and expenditures (Andersen, Kasper, Frankel, & Associates, 1979). Verification data were collected from health-care providers (doctors, hospitals, etc.) to compare with respondents' reports for the measurement of response errors. The effects of nonresponse and of different approaches to imputation of nonresponse were also investigated. One important finding of the study was that conclusions about the differences in health-care experiences between important subgroups of the population (the elderly vs. others; the poor vs. others, etc.) changed very infrequently when adjustment was made for those parts of nonsampling error that could be measured. The magnitude of the differences, however, did change more often. The verification process was a lengthy and expensive one (18 months and accounting for about one-third of the million-dollar cost of the survey), so whether it should be incorporated more regularly into surveys depends on the anticipated changes in estimates that adjustment for error will cause. Probably several more such large-scale efforts in different fields of application will be necessary before such anticipations can be made with any degree of confidence.

"An Error Profile" has been compiled for the measurement of employment by the Current Population Survey (Brooks & Bailar, 1978). Such a profile is related to the concept of total survey error but is constructed by following the operations of a survey, step by step, from the construction of the sampling frame through the publication of results, pointing out possible sources of all kinds of error and presenting evidence of their direction and size when such estimates are available. This effort[12] was intended to serve as a model for such profiles for other major governmental surveys and, as a first attempt, deliberately chose not to consider such matters as conceptual errors; these matters will probably be addressed in future profiles. Another error profile has been compiled for multiple frame surveys by Norman Beller at the Department of Agriculture. It would seem that this sort of project, although also expensive and time consuming, will point to gaps in knowledge about nonsampling errors and stimulate efforts to fill the gaps.

The purpose of these various investigations of total survey error is not to discredit the survey enterprise; surveys have already proved their usefulness in many arenas and will continue to be carried out and relied upon. The aim of error investigations is two-fold. First, a focus on error is useful in trying to improve the results of surveys—there is little payoff in studying that which is already done perfectly. Second, a focus on the components of total survey error permits

---

underlying concept, each measuring it imperfectly but together capturing most of its richness, is now widely used. (See Joreskog & Sorbom, 1979; for a clear exposition of this approach and an enlightening application, see Kohn & Schooler, 1978.)

[12]This is the work of the Subcommittee on Nonsampling Errors of the Federal Committee on Statistical Methodology.

the investigator to evaluate the relative contributions of the components to the total error and thus to concentrate resources—financial and analytical—where they will do the most good in improving accuracy.

Research Triangle Institute is at work on a taxonomy of errors, as an early step towards the institution of a Survey Design Information System. Such a system (Horvitz, 1980) would store information about specific variables as they have been measured in social surveys, including context of the survey, sample design, wording of questions, error components, and costs. This is a concept even broader than that of total survey error and should serve to standardize survey measures, integrate knowledge of survey error components, improve survey design, and provide a broad base for methodological research.

LONGITUDINAL SURVEYS

How many of the American people are poor? The answer depends on what one means by the question. According to the Panel Study of Income Dynamics, in a single year (1975) 9% of the American people were below the official poverty line, 25% were below it in at least 1 of the 9 years before 1976, but only 1% remained in poverty for the entire 9 years (Morgan, 1977). These distinctions can make a difference. For example, strategies for effectively assisting the chronically poor are probably very different from those most effective in aiding the temporarily poor; decisions about the magnitudes of the efforts would probably depend on the relative sizes of the two groups.

For our purposes, the crucial point about these differing figures is that they could have been found out (without unduly trusting people's memories) only by questioning the same people repeatedly—that is, by a longitudinal (or panel) study rather than a cross-sectional one. A cross-sectional study could only have estimated the number of poor in the year of the study, giving no data (except based on fallible memory) on the number of persistently or occasionally poor. The difference is like that between a snapshot of a crowd where we can make some aggregate measure, such as the number of people present, and a motion picture in which we can see the aggregate size of the crowd at each moment and also follow the activities of individuals as they leave or enter the crowd over time. The implementation of such large-scale longitudinal studies gained impetus in the early 1960s (Kalachek, 1979).

Advantages of Longitudinal Studies

The distinctive feature of a longitudinal study is that it permits an investigator to follow people (or other individual units of analysis, e.g., families, organizations) over time; this means that data on individual changes, rather than only aggregated movements, are available for analysis. Thus research can focus on process by asking "how" and "why" and often "for whom" such changes occur. For example, in studying life-cycle processes a panel study might address such a question as "Does early unemployment among teenagers and youth represent a transitory phase that many go through with no particular long-run adverse consequences, or does such a period of unemployment lower future earnings and/or increase the proportion of time in later life that an individual is unemployed?"

Longitudinal surveys are also particularly useful for the collection of cross-sectional data, if the period of time one wishes to consider is not instantaneous. Hence the successive interviews in NCS and in the survey of pesticide use are useful for bounding victimizations within the 6-month reference period and pesticide acquisition/disposal within the 5-month reference period, respectively. Similarly, the longitudinal design for the National Medical Care Utilization and Expenditure Survey permits a full year's worth of data to be accumulated for each family, so that families can be distributed according to utilization of health-care facilities and their costs.

The existence of large-scale longitudinal data sets has inspired both methodological and substantive research and has drawn attention to the need for developing new methodological tools for their analyses. One example of this is in new applications of mathematical models. These include statistical models that treat time as continuous and thus are more likely to coincide with our theoretical understanding of social processes and more likely to represent faithfully actual behavior than are models that treat time as discrete. People do not change jobs, break up marriages, etc. at specific (discrete) times (such as the time they are asked about their status on these variables). Thus any decision about the proper length of the time chunk to consider is necessarily arbitrary. Weekly is probably frequently enough to observe whether job changes occur— but is monthly frequently enough? And analyses that make these arbitrary decisions differently for use in discrete time models can produce substantively different results. Further, continuous time models are often computationally simpler than discrete time models.

In addition, most human behavior is more complicated than the simplest models need to assume. One discrete time model of employment, for example, would define three "states": employed, unemployed, and out of the labor force. It would then need to assume that the chance of a person being in a particular state in the next time period (e.g., month) depends *only* on which state that person is in during this time period. Past history, including amount of time in current state is taken to be irrelevant. (This is called a Markov model.) Clearly the world is more complicated than that. Some people are more likely to stay in the same state from month to month than are others. For example, unemployed members of a particlar ethnic group may be more likely than members of other groups to remain unemployed once they become unemployed. This is the "mover–stayer" model that has inspired a good deal of work in social mobility studies (see Pullman, 1978, for a review).

Or we might think that the chance of changing state depends on how long one is in that state—the longer one has been unemployed, the more likely, perhaps, that one will remain unemployed. Or the chance of moving from one state to another depends not only on the state one is currently in, but on one's prior history—a history of moving continuously into and out of the labor force might suggest that one is more likely to move out of the labor force next month, even though one is currently working, than someone who is currently working but has never been out of the labor force since high school graduation. Various combinations might also apply.

Each of these verbal descriptions of the world implies a mathematical model. The availability of longitudinal data makes it possible to test which model presents the most accurate picture of the world as it is and as policies would have to cope with it. If data are really continuous, constituting a life history for each individual, then both a choice of the proper statistical model and the estimation of its parameters are more easily accomplished than if the data are fragmentary, available only at some points in time (Singer & Spilerman, 1976). It is always important, prior to data collection, to consider what models will be fitted, because data irrelevant for one model can be crucial for others. For example, do we want to measure current state only? Duration in current state? Number of switches in state during the period between interviews?[13]

Research is needed on design for panel studies to facilitate discrimination between models fitted to the same fragmentary data. Such research should address questions of the optimum spacing between interviews to balance problems of reliability of retrospection versus costs and delays of reinterviewing (Singer & Spilerman, 1976).[14]

An application of a continuous time model has come out of the longitudinal data generated by the Income Maintenance Experiments (Tuma, Hannan, & Groeneveld, 1979). Three models (one time independent, one contrasting the first 6 months of the experiment to the succeeding 18 months, and one looking at four successive 6 month periods) were used to investigate the impact of support levels on attrition (or withdrawal) from the experiment and on marital dissolution and remarriage. The findings showed no effect of support level on attrition (cheeringly enough), no systematic effect on remarriage, but a systematic effect of support level on marital dissolution. (Marriages of women receiving income supplements were considerably more likely to break up than marriage of control women, with the effect most noticeable during the first 6 months, but continuing throughout the 2-year period.) Further, the model contrasting the first 6 months

---

[13]Various data collection strategies for longitudinal studies and the analytic techniques appropriate for each are discussed in an excellent review article by Hannan and Tuma (1979).

[14]The research on the relationship between forgetting and telescoping (Sudman & Bradburn, 1973) is relevant here, and there also ought to be consideration of the virtues of irregularly spaced interviews.

with the succeeding 18 closely predicted the percentage of the sample single at each time over the 2-year period, suggesting that the two-period model embodied a process of marital dissolution that is compatible with the data.[15]

Organizing Data Longitudinally

The organization of data collected longitudinally presents many challenges. As researchers meet them we shall see both methodological progress and rich substantive results. Many data sets that are collected longitudinally are stored in computer files as if they were merely cross sectional, so that many of the special benefits of longitudinal data cannot be realized. Moreover, the analytic richness of longitudinal data is unavailable without cross referencing between levels of aggregation. Each of these challenges is discussed in turn.

The first challenge of organizing data from longitudinal surveys arises because different numbers of events happen to different people. One person may be hired and fired many times over the years, generating data on the job description and dates of employment for each job. These data must be stored and catalogued as pertaining to this particular person. Another person may stay in the same job throughout the course of the longitudinal study, generating far less data. It becomes a methodological challenge to arrange a computer file that includes all the data for all respondents.

The simple solution allots each respondent the space necessary to record the data for the respondent with the most job changes. This creates an easily used "rectangular" file but uses a great deal of computer space suboptimally and increases the time necessary to access any piece of data. Another strategy is to use a hierarchical, nonrectangular file structure. This economizes on computer space and access time but creates the need for new computational and statistical methods. Such issues of file organization and their consequences constitute an active research area (e.g., Ramsøy, 1977); nevertheless data files are already beginning to become available in longitudinal form.[16]

Another challenge for file organization for longitudinal data arises from the need to link various levels of analysis. Often a survey is conducted so that locations (for example, housing units) are sampled. Within the housing units are households, made up of individuals. Typically a separate computer file is maintained for locations, for households, and perhaps for individuals. We can easily visualize an investigation where we find that an individual has experienced an

---

[15]Another, less substantive but beautifully explicated application of a continuous time model appears in Singer and Spilerman (1977).

[16]For example, the National Longitudinal Surveys of Labor Force Experience sponsored by the Labor Department (Bielby, Hawley, & Bills, 1977), the American Housing Survey sponsored by HUD (Beveridge & Taylor, 1980), the Panel Study of Income Dynamics (Morgan, 1977), and some parts of the National Crime Survey sponsored by the Law Enforcement Assistance Agency (Reiss, 1980) are now usable longitudinally.

event (say a robbery) and we would then want to ask several levels of questions: Has that person previously been robbed?; has anyone else in the same household been robbed?; was any member of the household that previously lived at this location robbed? These questions are answerable only if efficient cross referencing between the several data files has been provided.

Resources of Longitudinal Data

Longitudinal data today represent an underutilized resource. We are just beginning to explore the richness of the data sets that have been deliberately collected in a longitudinal manner. But, there are other data sets that are only fortuitiously longitudinal that represent an even less exploited resource. NCS, for example, is in part a longitudinal data set (see Fienberg, 1980a; Kalachek, 1979). For reasons of economy in sample selection and control of certain kinds of bias, this survey uses rotating panels, interviewing monthly, with a rotation group being interviewed every 6 months for 3 years. But the survey is designed to give cross-sectional data, that is aggregate victimization each month.

With some effort, however, such a survey could be organized in longitudinal form and used to examine changes experienced by individuals. Some attempts in this direction have indeed been carried out. A longitudinal data file for persons and households present in the NCS from July 1, 1972 to December 31, 1975 has been created (Reiss, 1980). This file has been used to investigate repeated victimization using loglinear models (Fienberg, 1980b). (Note that the analysis of any repeated event is inherently longitudinal.) Because repeated victimization frequently involves crimes of similar type, further investigation might examine the vulnerability or ''proneness'' of groups of households or household locations to certain kinds of crime.

There are both limitations and advantages to using NCS as a longitudinal survey. Its advantage is that it is enormously large—50,000 households report for each 6-month reference period. The breadth of the NCS would permit analysis by subgroups; this is not feasible from the smaller panels.

In other senses, however, the NCS is limited. The length of time any given household location is included is only 3 years. Further, if a family moves out of the sampled household location, that family is not followed but is replaced by the family that moves in (if indeed one does).

Other Aspects of Longitudinal Studies

Besides the challenges of organization of data files, longitudinal studies present design and analytic problems as well. Evidence of what is called ''panel bias'' suggests that people answer questions differently the second time (and perhaps subsequent times) they are asked than they do the first. Perhaps some purchase can be gotten on this problem by ''throwing away'' the first interview with a respondent. The National Crime Survey, for example, uses the first interview for bounding purposes only, not for comparative purposes or as cross-sectional data. Thus the first "real" interview (the second actual interview) is more like subsequent interviews than it is like the first. The severity of panel biases, their effect on measures of change, and the extent to which they continue over time in a panel will be matters for investigation as data become more easily available in longitudinal form.

A second problem is that, when a family takes part in a survey over time, different family members may be interviewed on different occasions. In the discussion of using proxy respondents to decrease nonresponse, we noted that some respondents report differently about themselves than about other family members. Do such differences occur in longitudinal studies, and if so, what effect do they have on data analyzed longitudinally in terms of families?; in terms of individuals?

Still another set of problems with longitudinal surveys involves attrition from the sample. If the housing unit is the sampling unit, but the family is the unit of analysis, what happens when the family moves? What happens when *part* of the family moves, as when a grown child leaves home, or a marriage breaks up? What happens when a person dies? This problem has received little attention from the Census Bureau because for their cross-sectional purposes the household is treated as the unit of analysis. Other large-scale longitudinal studies have answered these questions in various ways. The Health Insurance Study replaced families that moved out of the area and hence became ineligible to participate with those who moved into the vacated dwelling. In cases of divorce and remarriage of both spouses, the Health Insurance Study followed both spouses and the new families they may have formed. The Panel Study of Income Dynamics follows all members of the families originally interviewed in 1968, annually interviewing the head of every family that includes at least one member of the original families. Thus the sample keeps renewing itself with new generations.

Following *individuals* over a long span of years can be particularly difficult, especially if there is a considerable hiatus between interviews, but the success of recent studies suggests it can be accomplished. The secret seems to be telling the respondents that the study is a continuing one, and asking them to give the names of several relatives or friends who would always know how to reach them (Freedman, Thornton, & Camburn, 1980). This seems a good idea for studies dealing with such wholesome activities as family building and career planning; problems of confidentiality might well arise if the issues were more sensitive.

What happens when a heretofore cooperative respondent disappears or refuses to answer some or all questions? The very longitudinal nature of the studies helps in the solution of such problems. Certainly imputation for item nonresponse (unanswered questions) can be more easily accomplished in longitudinal studies where there is prior information about respondents (see Kalton & Lepkowski, 1982). For example, estimating a respondent's income this month is easier if we know last month's income for that respondent. Several investigators have presented models that help deal with attrition from longitudinal surveys. They first model the probability of attrition (or nonresponse or self-selection) based on respondent characteristics that are measured within the context of the survey. For example, a model might suggest that the likelihood of moving, and hence being unavailable for interviewing, increases with the experience of having been the victim of a crime. Then they can attempt to adjust estimates of, for example, current victimization or current unemployment for bias caused by attrition (Griliches, Hall, & Hausman, 1977; Hausman & Wise, 1977; Heckman, 1976, 1979).

This problem of attrition is a special case of the more general problem of "censoring." Someone who leaves the panel can, of course, not have data observed thereafter; such further data are said to be censored. But even with an intact panel of willing respondents, there are some pieces of data not available at any given time for some individuals. To illustrate: at whatever time we stop to make an analysis of amount of time spent in first job, there are some people who have never switched jobs; for them, we can get no measure of how long the first job lasted except to say that it lasted at least from the beginning of the job until the current time. The problem is how to adjust for the censored observations in estimating the average time spent by members of the population in their first job. There has been a recent surge in development of methods for the analysis of such censored data.[17]

Problems of anonymity and confidentiality are especially severe in longitudinal studies because individuals or families must be identified in some manner so that they can be followed over time. Several means of assuring anonymity in longitudinal surveys have, however, been developed (Boruch & Cecil, 1979): Respondents may choose aliases and continue to use them; an agency or broker may act as an intermediary between respondent and investigator, releasing only unidentified data to the investigator; or an insulated "link file" system may be created. In this last case, data in the investigator's files are labeled by arbitrary data-linking numbers, identifications are kept in another file and labeled with another set of arbitrary respondent-identifying numbers, and the only file linking the two sets of arbitrary numbers is held by an incorruptible third party. As successive waves of data arrive, the investigator removes identification and relabels with the respondent-identifying set of arbitrary numbers and ships the data to the third party, who removes the respondent-identifying set of arbitrary numbers and substitutes the data-linking set before returning the data to the investigator—ponderous, but seemingly foolproof, and well-adapted to reducing both unit nonresponse and possibilities of breach of confidentiality in longitudi-

---

[17]A basic reference is Cox, 1972; a recent brief review of the literature is Moses, 1978; and detailed technical expositions are given by Kalbfleisch & Prentice, 1980, and Alandt–Johnson & Johnson, 1980.

nal surveys. Organizations such as the National Opinion Research Center have used link file systems and find that it is crucial and understandably difficult to convince potential respondents of the inviolability of the linkage system.

Resources of longitudinal survey data seem particularly relevant to environmental psychology. Such data would be crucial to monitor long-term effects of environmental changes on physical and psychological well-being on an individual rather than an epidemiological basis. Similarly, any sort of large-scale experimentation to gauge effects of policy changes on people's attitudes towards and use of resources (for example, the experiments investigating the effect of peak load pricing on electricity consumption) generate data very much like longitudinal survey data. The research questions posed here that must be answered before these data can be fully utilized are pressing ones for methdologists and subject matter specialists alike.

ACKNOWLEDGMENTS

This is a revised version of part of a paper commissioned by the Social Science Research Council for the National Science Foundation's second Five-Year Outlook on Science and Technology. Preparation of that version was supported by NSF Contract, No. PRA–8017924. The original version also appeared as a background paper for the report of the Committee on Basic Research in the Behavioral and Social Sciences, Assembly of the Behavioral and Social Sciences, National Research Council. An earlier revised version appeared in *Sociological Methodology 1983/4*. Preparation of this version was supported in part by Grant No. SES – 8119138 from the National Science Foundation to the Research Foundation of the State University of New York. Thanks are due to a great many people for enormous amounts of assistance during the preparation of the original version of this chapter. First of all, the advisory committee who commented inspiringly through interminable iterations of outlines and drafts: William H. Kruskal, Stephen E. Fienberg, Norman M. Bradburn, and Richard A. Berk. Officers and staff at the Social Science Research Council were also unstinting in time devoted to intellectual guidance and moral support: David L. Sills, Peter B. Read, Kenneth Prewitt, and Roberta B. Miller. In trying to describe the cutting edge of research I had to depend in large part on the willingness of investigators to share their work-in-progress and a great many people responded generously, too many to list here, but the blanket nature of such thanks should not be read as a detraction from its warmth. Many friends and colleagues with no official connection with the project gave generously of their time to explain and instruct in their areas of special competence and to make comments on various drafts (several of these people might well be considered honorary members of the advisory committee): Eugene Weinstein, Katherine Wallman, Charles Turner, Wendell Thompson, Edward Tufte, Frank Stafford, Charles Smith, Burton Singer, Merril Shanks, Karl Schuessler, Frederick Scheuren, Gordon Sande, Ingram Olkin, Frederick Mosteller, Susan Miskura, Albert Madansky, Richard Link, Michael Kagay, Edwin Goldfield, Jonathan Cole, Robert Boruch, Albert Biderman, Barbara Bailar. Christine McShane at the editorial offices of the National Academy Press was a paragon of diplomacy and skill. Many of these people also assisted in successive revisions, as did Miron Straf, Thomas M. Murray, Mel Kollander, Herbert Hyman, Joseph S. Carra, Charles Cannell, and R. Clifton Bailey. The errors and infelicities, of course, are my very own. Linda D. Anderson performed miracles of typing, both in speed and in beauty and Karol Pond did the excellent word processing for this version.

REFERENCES

Alandt–Johnson, R. C., & Johnson, N. L. (1980). *Survival models and data analysis*. New York: Wiley.

Andersen, R., Kasper, J., Frankel, M. R., & Associates. (1979). *Total survey error*. San Francisco: Jossey–Bass.

Aziz, F., & Scheuren, F. (1978). *Imputation and editing of faulty or missing survey data*. Washington, DC: U.S. Department of Commerce, Bureau of the Census. (Papers presented at the 1978 meeting of the American Statistical Association and also printed in the Proceedings volumes for the meeting.)

Bailar, B. A. (1976). Some sources of error and their effects on census statistics. *Demography, 13*, 273–286.

Bailar, B. A., & Bailar, J. C. III. (1979). Comparison of the biases of the ''Hot-Deck'' Imputation Procedure with an ''Equal-weights'' Imputation Procedure. In *Panel on Incomplete Data of the Committee on National Statistics/National Research Council* 422–447.

Bailar, B. A., & Miskura, S. (1980). *The 1980 Experimental Program*. Unpublished paper, U.S. Bureau of the Census.

Bailar, J. C. III. (1978). Discussion. In Aziz & Scheuren (Eds.), *Imputation and editing of faulty or missing survey data* 62–64.

Beveriage, A. A., & Taylor, J. B. (1980). *Quarterly Report* (3rd quarter on Grant HUD–5516 RG). A Continuation of the Longitudinal Transformation and Analysis of the Annual Housing Survey.

Biderman, A. D., Johnson, L. A., McIntyre, J., & Weir, A. W. (1967). *Report on a pilot study in the District of Columbia on victimization and attitudes toward law enforcement*. President's Commission on Law Enforcement and Administration of Justice Field Survey (No. 1). Washington, DC: U.S. Government Printing Office.

Bielby, W. T., Hawley, C. C., & Bills, D. (1978). Research uses of the National Longitudinal Surveys. In *A research agenda for the National Longitudinal Surveys of Labor Market Experience: Report on the Social Science Research Council's Conference on the National Longitudinal Surveys, October 1977*. Washington, DC: Social Science Research Council.

Bishop, Y. M. M., Fienberg, S. E., & Holland, P. W. (1975). *Discrete multivariate analysis*. Cambridge, MA: MIT Press.

Boruch, R. F., & Cecil, J. S. (1979). *Assuring the confidentiality of social research data*. Philadelphia: University of Pennsylvania Press.

Bradburn, N. M. (1978). Response effects. In P. H. Rossi & J. D. Wright (Eds.), *The handbook of survey research*. New York: Academic Press.

Bradburn, N. M., Sudman, S., & Associates. (1979). *Improving interview method and questionnaire design: Response effects to threatening questions in survey research*. San Francisco: Jossey–Bass.

Brewer, K. R., & Sarndal, C. E. (1979). Six approaches to enumerative survey sampling. In *Panel on Imcomplete Data of the Committee on National Statistics/National Research Council* 499–597.

Brooks, C. A., & Bailar, B. A. (1978). *An error profile: Employment as measured by the Current Population Survey* (Statistical Policy Working Paper 3). Washington, DC: U.S. Department of Commerce.

Cambridge Reports, Inc. (1982). *The Grand Rapids Test: The impact of television advertising on public perceptions of radiation and nuclear waste* (2 Vols). Prepared for the Committee for Energy Awareness.

Cannell, C. F. (1977). *A summary of studies of interviewing methodology*. Vital and Health Statistics, Series 2, No. 69. Washington, DC: U.S. Government Printing Office.

Cannell, C. F., Miller, P. V., & Oksenberg, L (1981). Research on interviewing techniques. In S. Leinhardt (Ed.), *Sociological methodology 1981*. San Francisco: Jossey–Bass.

Cole, S., & Fiorentine, R. (1983, May). *The formation of public opinion on complex issues: The case of nuclear power*. Paper presented at the annual meeting of The American Association for Public Opinion Research, Buck Hill Falls, PA.

Cox, B. G., & Folsom, R. E. (1978). An empirical investigation of alternative item nonresponse adjustments. In F. Aziz & F. Scheuren (Eds.), *Imputation and editing of faulty or missing survey data* pp. 51–55.

Cox, D. R. (1972). Regression models and life tables. *Journal of the Royal Statistical Society, B, 34*, 187–220.

Csikszentmihalyi, M., Larsen, R., & Prescott, S. (1977). The ecology of adolescent activities and experiences. *Journal of Youth and Adolescence, 6*, 281–294.

Dalenius, T. (1977). Bibliography of nonsampling errors in surveys. *International Statistical Institute Review, 45*, 71–90 (April, A–G) 181–197; (August, H–Q) 303–317; (December, R–Z).

Dalenius, T. (1979). Informed consent or R.S.V.P. In *Panel on Incomplete Data of the Committee on National Statistics-National Research Council* 95–134.

Davis, J. A. (1975). Are surveys any good, and if so, for what? Perspectives on attitude assessment: Surveys and their alternatives. In H. W. Sinaiko & L. A. Broedling (Eds.), *Proceedings of a conference held at Bishop's Lodge, Sante Fe, NM.* (pp. 17–25). Washington, DC: Manpower Research and Advisory Services, Smithsonian Institution.

Deighton, R. E., Poland, J. R., Stubbs, J. R., & Tortora, R. D. (1978). *Glossary of nonsampling error terms*. Prepared for the Executive Office of the President, Office of Management and Budget, Federal Committee on Statistical Methodology, Subcommittee on Nonsampling Errors.

Deming, W. E. (1978). Sample surveys: The field. In W. H. Kruskal & J. M. Tanur (Eds.), *International encyclopedia of statistics*. New York: Free Press.

Deming, W. E., & Stephan, F. F. (1940). On a least squares adjustment of a sampled frequency table when the expected marginal tables are known. *Annals of Mathematical Statistics, 11*, 427–444.

Deutscher, I. (1973). *What we say/what we do*. Glenview, IL: Scott, Foresman.

Dukta, S., & Frankel, L. R. (1980, August 11–14). *Sequential survey design through the use of computer assisted telephone interviewing*. Paper presented at the annual meeting of the American Statistical Association.

Durako, S., & McKenna, T. (1980). *Collecting health interview survey data by telephone: A mailout experiment*. Paper prepared for the annual meeting of the American Statistical Association.

Ennis, P. H. (1967). *Criminal victimization in the United States: A report of a national survey*. Chicago: National Opinion Research Center.

European Scientific Notes. (1983, March 31). *A German wind-shear display*. ONR-London.

Fienberg, S. E. (1980a, July 2–5) *The measurement of crime victimization: Prospects for panel analysis of a panel survey*. Paper presented at "Censuses and Sample Surveys," Institute of Statisticians International Conference, Trinity College, Cambridge, England.

Fienberg, S. E. (1980b). Statistical modelling in the analysis of repeat victimization. In S. E. Fienberg & A. J. Reiss, Jr. (Eds.), *Indicators of crime and criminal justice: Quantitative studies*. Washington, DC: U.S. Government Printing Office.

Freedman, D. S., Thornton, A., & Camburn, D. (1980). Maintaining response rates in longitudinal studies. *Sociological Methods and Research, 9*, 87–98.

Freeman, H. E. (1980). *Research opportunities related to CATI*. Paper prepared for the University of California Conference on Computer Assisted Survey Technology.

Griliches, Z., Hall, B. H., & Hausman, J. A. (1977, August). *Missing data and self-selection in large panels*. INSEE Conference "Economies of Panel Data," Paris.

Groves, R. M., Berry, M., & Mathiowetz, N. (1980, August 11–14). *Some impacts of computer assisted telephone interviewing on survey methods*. Paper prepared for presentation at the annual meeting of the American Statistical Association.

Groves, R. M., & Kahn, R. L. (1979). *Surveys by telephone*. New York: Academic Press.

Groves, R. M., & Magilavy, L. J. (1980, August 11–14). *Effects of interviewer variance in telephone surveys*. Paper prepared for presentation at the annual meeting of the American Statistical Association.

Hannan, M. T., & Tuma, N. B. (1979). Methods for temporal analysis. In A. Inkeles, J. Coleman, & R. Turner (Eds.), *Annual review of sociology* (Vol. 5). Palo Alto, CA: Annual Reviews.

Hausman, J. A., & Wise, D. (1977). Social experimentation, truncated distributions, efficient estimation. *Econometrica, 45*, 919–938.

Heckman, J. D. (1976). The common structure of statistical models of truncation, sample selection and limited dependent variables and a simple estimator for such models. *Annals of Economic and Social Measurement, 5*, 475–492.

Heckman, J. (1979). Sample selection bias as specification error. *Econometrica, 47*, 153–161.

Hill, M. S., & Juster, F. T. (1979). *Constraints and complementarities in time use*. Discussion draft. Survey Research Center, University of Michigan.

Horvitz, D. G. (1980, August 11–14). *On the significance of a survey design information system*. Paper presented at the annual meeting of the American Statistical Association.

Jabine, T., Straf, M., Tanur, J., & Tourangeau, R. (1984). *Cognitive aspects of survey methodology:* Building a bridge between disciplines. Washington, DC: National Academy Press.

Joreskog, K. G., & Sorbom, D. (1979). *Advances in factor analysis and structural equation models*. Edited by Jay Magidson. Cambridge, MA: Abt Books.

Kahn, R. L., & Cannell, C. F. (1978). Interviewing in social research. In W. H. Kruskal & J. M. Tanur (Eds.), *International encyclopedia of statistics*. New York: Free Press.

Kalachek, Edward. (1979). Longitudinal surveys and labor market analysis. In Data collection, processing, and presentation (Vol. II) of Appendix of *Counting the labor force* (Report of the National Commission of Employment and Unemployment Statistics). Washington, DC: U.S. Government Printing Office.

Kalbfleisch, J. D., & Prentice, R. I. (1980). *The statistical analysis of failure time data*. New York: Wiley.

Kalsbeek, W. D. (1980, August 11–14). *A conceptual review of survey error due to nonresponse*. Paper presented at the annual meeting of the American Statistical Association.

Kalton, G., & Lepkowski, J. (1982). *Cross-wave item imputation*. Unpublished manuscript.

Kalton, G., & Schuman, H. (1980, August 11–14). *The effect of the question on survey response*. Paper presented at the annual meeting of the American Statistical Association.

Keyfitz, N. (1957). Estimates of sampling variance where two units are selected from each stratum. *Journal of the American Statistical Association, 52*, 503–510.

Kish, L., & Frankel, M. R. (1974). Inference from complex samples (with discussion). *Journal of the Royal Statistical Society-B, 36*, 1–37.

Kohn, M. L., & Schooler, C. (1978). The reciprocal effects of the substantive complexity of work and intellectual flexibility: A longitudinal assessment. *American Journal of Sociology, 84*, 24–52.

Lebby, D. E. (1980.) *CATI's first decade: The Chilton Experience*. Paper prepared for the University of California Conference on Computer Assisted Survey Technology.

Lessler, J. R. (1979). An expanded survey error model. In *Panel on Incomplete Data of the Committee on National Statistics/National Research Council*. 371–388.

Little, R. J. A., & Rubin, D. B. (1979). Six approaches to enumerate survey sampling. Discussion. In *Panel on Incomplete Data of the Committee on National Statistics/National Research Council* 515–520.

Locander, W., Sudman, S., & Bradburn, N. (1974). An investigation of interview method, threat and response distortion. *Proceedings of the American Statistical Association, Social Statistics Section* (21–27).

McCarthy, P. J. (1966). *Replication, an approach to the analysis of data from complex surveys* (Ser. 2, No. 14). Washington, DC: U.S. Government Printing Office.

McCarthy, P. J. (1969). *Pseudoreplication, further evaluation and application of the balanced half-sample technique* (Ser. 2, No. 31). U.S. Department of Health, Education, and Welfare, National Center for Health Statistics. Washington, DC: U.S. Government Printing Office.

Melber, B., Nealey, S. M., Hammersla, J., & Rankin, W. L. (1977). *Nuclear power and the public: Analysis of collected survey research.* Seattle, WA: Battelle Human Affairs Research Center.

Morgan, J. N. (1977). *Individual behavior, economic analysis, and public policy.* The 1977 Wladmir Woytinsky Lecture.

Morris, C. N. (1979). Nonresponse issues in public policy experiments, with emphasis on the health insurance study. In *Panel on Incomplete Data of the Committee on National Statistics/National Research Council* 448–470.

Moses, L. E. (1978). Statistical analysis, special problems of: Truncation and censorship. In W. H. Kruskal & J. M. Tanur (Eds.), *International encyclopedia of statistics.* New York: Free Press.

Mosteller, F. (1978). Errors: Nonsampling errors. In W. H. Kruskal & J. M. Tanur (Eds.), *International encyclopedia of statistics.* New York: Free Press.

Neter, J., & Waksberg, J. (1964). A study of response errors in expenditures data from household interviews. *Journal of the American Statistical Association, 59,* 18–55.

Neyman, J. (1934). On the two different aspects of the representative method: The method of stratified sampling and the method of purposive selection. *Journal of the Royal Statistical Society* (A), *109,* 558–606.

Nisselson, H., & Woolsey, T. D. (1959). Some problems of the household interview design for the National Health Survey. *Journal of the American Statistical Association, 54,* 69–87.

Oh, H. L., & Scheuren, F. (1978). Multivariate raking ratio estimation in the 1973 exact match study and some unresolved application issues in raking ratio estimation. In Aziz & Scheuren (Eds.), *Imputation and editing of faulty or missing survey data* 120–135.

Paez, A. D., & Dodge, R. N. (1982). *Criminal victimization in the U.S., 1979–80 changes, 1973–80 trends.* Bureau of Justice Statistics (Technical Report, NCJ–80838). Washington, DC: U.S. Department of Justice.

Panel on Aesthetic Attributes in Water Resources Projects, Environmental Studies Board, National Research Council. (1982). *Assessing aesthetic attributes in planning water resource projects.* Washington, DC: U.S. Department of Justice.

Panel on Incomplete Data of the Committee on National Statistics/National Research Council. (1979). *Symposium on Incomplete Data: Preliminary Proceedings.* Washington, DC: U.S. Department of Health, Education, and Welfare, Social Security Administration Office of Policy, Office of Research and Statistics.

Panel on Privacy and Confidentiality as Factors in Survey Response. (1979). *Privacy and confidentiality as factors in survey response.* Washington, DC: National Academy of Sciences.

Pullman, T. (1978). Postscript to social mobility. In W. H. Kruskal & J. M. Tanur (Eds.), *International encyclopedia of statistics.* New York: Free Press.

Ramsøy, N. R., & Clausen, S. (1978). Events as units of analysis in life history studies. In *A research agenda for the National Longitudinal Surveys of Labor Market Experience: Report of the Social Science Research Council on the National Longitudinal Surveys,* October 1977.

Reiss, A. J., Jr. (1980). Victim proneness by type of crime in repeat victimization. In S. E.

Fienberg & A. J. Reiss, Jr. (Eds.), *Indicators of crime and criminal justice: Quantitative studies,* Washington, DC: U.S. Government Printing Office.

Roshwalb, I., Spector, L., & Madansky, A. (1980). New methods of interviewing: A & S/CATI. *Proceedings of the XXXII Esomar Congress, The challenge of the eighties.* Brussels, Belgium, September 2–6, 1979.

Rubin, D. B. (1978). Multiple imputations in sample surveys—A phenomenological Bayesian approach to nonresponse. In Aziz & Scheuren (Eds.), *Imputation and editing of faulty or missing survey data* 1–18. Followed by a discussion and rejoiner.

Rubin, D. B. (1979). *Handling nonresponse in sample surveys by multiple imputations.* Monograph prepared for the Census Bureau.

Sande, G. (1979). Hot-deck discussion-replacement for a ten minute gap. In *Panel on Incomplete Data of the Committee on National Statistics/National Research Council* 431–483.

Schuman, H., & Presser, S. (1981). *Questions and answers in attitude surveys: Experiments on question form, wording, and context.* New York: Academic Press.

Shanks, J. M. (1980). *The development of CATI methodology.* Paper prepared for the University of California Conference on Computer Assisted Survey Technology.

Shimizu, I. M., & Bonham, G. S. (1978). Randomized response techinque in a national survey. *Journal of the American Statistical Association, 73,* 35–39.

Simon, H. A. (1980). The behavioral and social sciences. *Science, 209,* 72–78.

Singer, B., & Spilerman, S. (1976). Some methodological issues in the analysis of longitudinal surveys. *Annals of Ecnomic and Social Measurement, 5,* 447–474.

Singer, B., & Spilerman, S. (1977). Fitting stochastic models to longitudinal survey data—some examples in the social sciences. *Bulletin of the International Statistical Institute, 47,* 283–300.

Singer, E. (1978). Informed consent: Consequences for response rate and response quality in social surveys. *American Sociological Review, 43,* 144–162.

Sirken, M. G. (1975, April). *Alcohol and other drug use and abuse in the state of Michigan.* Office of Substance Abuse Services, Michigan Department of Public Health.

Stafford, F., & Duncan, G. J. (1979). *The use of time and technology by households in the United States.* Working Paper of the Institute for Social Research, University of Michigan.

Stephenson, C. B. (1978). *A comparison of full-probabilty and probability-with-quotas sampling techniques in the General Social Survey* (GSS Technical Report No. 5) National Opinion Research Center, Chicago. (Forthcoming in *Public Opinion Quarterly.*)

Sudman, S. (1967). *Reducing the cost of surveys.* Chicago: Aldine.

Sudman, S., Blair, E., Bradburn, N., & Stocking, C. (1977). Estimates of threatening behavior based on reports of friends. *Public Opinion Quarterly, 41,* 261–264. (Reprinted in N. M. Bradburn & S. Sudman and Associates, 1979).

Sudman, S., & Bradburn, N. M. (1973). Effects of time and memory factors on responses in surveys. *Journal of the American Statistical Association, 68,* 805–815.

Sudman, S., & Bradburn, N. M. (1974). *Response effects in surveys: A review and synthesis.* Chicago: Aldine.

Sudman, S., & Ferber, R. (1971). Experiments in obtaining consumer expenditure by diary methods. *Journal of the American Statistical Association, 66,* 725–735.

Thompson, W. L., Carlson, L. T., Woteki, T. H., & Vagts, K. A. (1980, August 11–14). *Improving the quality of data from monthly gasoline purchase diaries.* Paper presented at the annual meeting of the American Statistical Association.

Thornberry, O. T., Jr., & Massey, J. T. (1978). Correcting for undercoverage bias in random digit dialed national health surveys. In Aziz & Scheuren (Eds.), *Imputation and editing of faulty or missing survey data* 56–61.

Tuma, N. B., Hannan, M. T., & Groeneveld, L. P. (1979). Dynamic analysis of event histories. *American Journal of Sociology, 84,* 820–854.

Turner, C. (1980). Surveys of subjective phenomena: A working paper. Why do surveys disagree?

Preliminary hypothesis and disagreeable examples. To appear in Dennis Johnston, *Measuring subjective phenomena.* Washington, DC: U.S. Government Printing Office.

Turner, C. F., & Krauss, E. (1978). Fallible indicators of the state of the nation. *American Psychologist, 33,* 456–470.

Turner, C. F., & Martin, E. (Eds.). (1981). *Surveys of subjective phenomena: Summary report.* Panel on survey measurement of subjective phenomena, Committee on National Statistics, Assembly of Behavioral and Social Sciences, National Research Council. Washington, DC: National Academy Press.

U.S. Bureau of the Census. (1978). *The current population survey: Design and methodology.* (Technical Paper 40). Washington, DC: U.S. Government Printing Office.

U.S. National Health Survey. (1963). *Comparison of hospitalization reporting in three survey procedures, a study of alternative survey methods for collection of hospitalization data from household respondents.* Washington, DC; U.S. Department of Health, Education, and Welfare, Public Health Service. (By Charles Cannell and Floyd Fowler and republished in *Vital and Health Statistics,* Series 2, Number 8, July, 1965.)

Warner, S. (1965). Randomized response: Survey technique for eliminating evasive answer bias. *Journal of the American Statistical Association, 60,* 63–69.

Woltman, H. R., Turner, A. G., & Bushery, J. M. (1980). A comparison of three mixed-mode interviewing procedures in the National Crime Survey. *Journal of the American Statistical Association, 75,* 534–543.

7

Understanding Environmental Stress: Strategies for Conceptual and Methodological Integration

Andrew Baum
Raymond Fleming
Jerome E. Singer
Uniformed Services University of the Health Sciences

INTRODUCTION

One recent development in the growth of environmental psychology has been the linking of environmental stress to the study of stress and medical outcomes. During the past 5 years, research on topics such as crowding, noise, commuting, and pollution has examined psychological and physiological concomitants of stress (e.g., Baum, Singer, & Baum, 1981; Cohen & Weinstein, 1981; Epstein, 1981; Evans & Jacobs, 1981). Similarities among these stressors have been observed—for example, crowding and noise appear to be associated with comparable aftereffects (Sherrod, 1974)—and these similarities have been explained by the fact that these events affect people in much the same way as do all stressors. In this chapter we consider the implications of the development of an environmental stress perspective and discuss in detail some of the major methodological options presented. Consistent with our belief that stress is a "whole body" phenomenon, we argue that a multimodal strategy of simultaneous assessment of self-report, behavioral, and physiological aspects of stress provides a better view of stress than does reliance on measurement of any one aspect. In order to illustrate this approach, we discuss our recent research at Three Mile Island.

STRESS AND THE ENVIRONMENT

The study of stress is of particular importance to environmental researchers for a number of reasons. First, many of the environmental conditions that are included in this field of study only come to our attention when they are stressful. Crowding, for example, has been primarily portrayed as an aversive experience associated with insufficient space or excessive group sizes. At the nonstressful point on these scales—where the space or number of people is not aversive or troublesome—crowding is ordinarily not recognized or perceived. The same may be said of other environmental circumstances such as noise, temperature, and commuting constraints. Many environmental issues become salient only to the extent that they are stressful. Second, the study of stress is directly relevant to several policy issues including the design of buildings to minimize crowding, effective transportation, planning, and the establishment of noise standards for the protection of areas surrounding airports.

The relationships between basic research and policy are often unclear to both researcher and policy maker; the former typically focuses on research results and does not see why the findings are not immediately relevant to new regulations or standards. Policy makers, on the other hand, are concerned with balancing political and economic factors and, therefore, may see little relevance in the differences typically revealed by basic or applied research. The concepts and theories of stress provide a nexus for these separate domains. Specifically, stress in turn has direct consequences for health, disease, morbidity, and mortality. These outcomes are important public issues in themselves and can be quantified for use in the cost/benefit ratios and cost-effectiveness equations of the policy maker.

Stress

Stress is a process by which environmental events threaten, harm, or challenge an organism's existence or well-being, and by which the organism responds to this threat. The stress reaction is characterized by symptoms such as arousal, fright, and tension that are only part of the stress process. Whereas these symptoms are the most easily recognized and clearly the most familiar, they often represent byproducts of perceiving a threat, coping with it, and adapting to it. This adaptation sequence is to some degree part of our daily routine. Our everyday lives can be characterized as continuous and constant adaptation and adjustment to sudden change or gradual evolution of our surroundings. Thus, stressors need not be major or life threatening. Sometimes these changes are minor and we can adapt to them without even being aware of them, whereas at other times these changes can be severe and clearly threatening.

Selye's (1956) pioneering work on psychological stress revealed a triad of responses that seemed to accompany introduction of almost any alien substance into the body. Injection of any of a seemingly endless number of different extracts into laboratory animals produced this triad over and over again. Each animal showed enlargement of the adrenal cortex, involution of the thymus, and ulceration of gastrointestinal organs. In some ways, this triad was nonspecific;

that is, nearly any noxious agent was capable of producing it. In other ways, it reflected a very specific pattern of response, linked to the adrenal cortex through the pituitary gland.

Response to pathogens and other noxious agents has been systematized in the *general adaptation syndrome* (GAS), based upon the idea that the body can cope with stress but that this coping has costs for subsequent coping (Selye, 1956). Long-term exposure to a stressor or repeated adaptive demand can deplete the body's adaptive reserves and lead to physical dysfunction. When initially exposed to a stressor, the body responds by mobilizing its coping abilities; this *alarm reaction* represents preparation for resistance. After these reserves are made ready, the body enters a state of *resistance,* applying various coping mechanisms and typically achieving suitable adaptation. When these reactions are repeated often, or when coping is not successful, however, adaptive reserves are depleted, and the organism enters a stage of *exhaustion.* At this point resistance declines, physiological breakdown occurs, and the body becomes more susceptible to disease.

Others also have considered stress as a biological phenomenon, but recent developments have emphasized the role of psychological variables in the interpretation of and response to threatening events. Mason (1975a) has provided evidence for psychoendocrine mediation of the stress response and has suggested that cognitive interpretations of stressors are important determinants of physiological response during stress. Several studies, for example, suggest that psychological interpretations of events based on perceived control or valence can influence patterning of corticosteroid secretion by the adrenal cortex (e.g., Mason, 1975b). Psychological variables have been viewed as instrumental in the onset of stress and are associated with the appraisal of environmental events (e.g., Lazarus, 1966; Lazarus & Cohen, 1978). In some instances, psychological variables mediate response to stressors, as is the case with perceived control (e.g., Glass & Singer, 1972; Perlmutter & Monty, 1979).

Appraisal of events can also lead directly to stress. Loss of a job or interpretation of the nature of one's daily work may generate stress just as one's beliefs about high-voltage electric lines and nearby nuclear power plants may affect response (e.g., Baum, Gatchel, Streufert, Baum, Fleming, & Singer, 1980; Frankenhaeuser, 1978; Kasl & Cobb, 1970). Cognitive representations of stressors that are not physically apparent are also important because people respond not only to dangers or threats that have materialized but also are influenced by expectations or symbols of danger experienced previously (Wolf & Goodell, 1968). Anticipation of a stressful experience appears to cause stress itself (Baum & Greenberg, 1975; Spacapan & Cohen, 1982; Street, Baum, & Singer, 1984), and psychosocial variables that evoke stress responses may ultimately be more damaging to the organism than the event itself. This is particularly likely if they precede the physical event, last longer, and continue to evoke stress after the physical event is past.

Evaluation of coping alternatives is also a crucial determinant of response to stress. Lazarus has proposed that these responses can take manipulative or accommodative forms. Though more recent discussions go beyond a dichotomous view of coping appraisal, Lazarus basically proposed that coping may reflect *direct action* responses, when the individual tries to directly manipulate or alter his or her relationship to the stressful situation. Thus, people may change the setting, flee, or otherwise remove the physical presence of the stressor. Alternatively, people may choose a *palliative coping* strategy. Here, the individual accommodates to the stressful situation by altering his or her "internal" environment (e.g., managing emotional response, taking drugs, drinking, learning to relax, using defense mechanisms).

Psychological analyses of stress are not necessarily at odds with more biological descriptions (e.g., Jenkins, 1979). However, psychological and physiological accounts of stress have remained parallel and largely separate endeavors, each giving rise to its own research "tradition." Research in these two traditions focuses on different aspects of the stress process and generally relies on different methodological strategies. By recognizing that these traditions are not necessarily independent of one another, additional understanding of stress-related processes may be obtained. Elsewhere, we have provided a conceptual framework that links these traditions at a theoretical level (Baum et al., 1981). In the sections that follow, we consider the methodological counterpart to such integration.

Measurement of Stress

There are four basic approaches to the measurement of stress. *Self-report measures* provide information about stress-relevant affect, appraisals, and the like. They involve direct questioning of subjects about their feelings, beliefs, and opinions. *Behavioral measures* may reflect either coping or aftereffect assessments. Subjects may be observed in the stressful environment and their behavioral responses recorded and interpreted, or performance measures can be used to assess the effects of stress on motivation or on some ability or skill during or after exposure to a stressor. *Psychophysiological measurements* typically call for assessment of peripheral nervous system response by one or more organ systems (e.g., cardiovascular, respiratory). *Biochemical measures* of stress are the newest addition to the behavioral scientist's tools for measuring stress and providing useful estimates of psychoendocrine response to stressful conditions. These different measurement domains are not necessarily correlated, although there is reason to expect that they might be (e.g., Lang, Rice, & Sternbach, 1972; Mason, 1975b). They tap different aspects of the stress response, follow different time courses, have relatively large variances, and are each influenced by many factors unrelated to stress. Together, however, they begin to provide a more complete picture of the psychological and biological aspects of human response to stress.

Self-report Measures. The easiest way to determine whether people are experiencing stress is to ask them. Economy, ease of administration, and a degree of face validity are all strengths of the interview or questionnaire assessment of stress. Generally, such efforts measure: (1) life events or experiences believed to be stressful, (2) emotional and somatic experience believed to be associated with stress, or (3) ratings of the unpleasantness or aversiveness of the precipitating environmental conditions. The first approach is best represented by research considering stressful life events as determinants of health and well-being. The second approach is primarily concerned with indexing stress by measuring its symptoms. The third approach equates stress with perceived annoyance or displeasure.

Research on life change is concerned with measuring the frequency of experience with various stressors or events that require adjustment or involve disruption of everyday life. The major impetus for this research was Holmes and Rahe's (1967) introduction of the "Schedule of Recent Experience," a checklist designed to measure the number of life events or changes experienced in a given period of time. Initially, respondents simply checked off relevant events. The events ranged from marital difficulties, personal injury, and loss of a job to less disruptive changes in daily routine, thus providing a total number of events experienced. Each event was counted the same, regardless of potential impact (Rahe, 1975). Subsequently, ratings of the magnitude of adjustment required by each event were included. These ratings were used as weights for each event in an attempt to account for differential impact. Events rated as requiring a great deal of adjustment were counted more heavily. However, the utility of obtaining subjective ratings of the impact of life change is unclear; some studies have suggested that it increases the usefulness of life-change measures, whereas others have indicated that such ratings do not prove useful (e.g., Rahe, 1975; Ross & Mirowsky, 1979; Sarason, Johnson, & Siegel, 1978).

Most research employing life-event measures has been retrospective, asking subjects to recall events experienced in the past. Depending on the study, total number of events or a weighted score reflecting total change required during that time period was then compared with health data. These studies generally report evidence of an increase in life change preceding the onset of many illnesses (e.g., Holmes & Masuda, 1974; Jacobs, Spilken, Norman, & Anderson, 1970; Masuda & Holmes, 1978; Rahe, 1969).

The retrospective nature of life-event measures limits the usefulness of this approach to the analysis of stress. Prospective studies have revealed patterns of stress and illness similar to those in retrospective studies (e.g., Rahe, 1969, 1975), but the weights given each event remain insensitive to individual variation in coping assets or vulnerability. Continuous changes in ways of scaling life events have improved this aspect of the method (e.g., Rahe, Ryman, & Ward, 1980). However, the revised measures still do not assess stress as a process involving events and response to them. Instead, stress is inferred from the magnitude of disruption or adjustment believed to be associated with each event.

The ways in which various life events are interpreted are also important and are rarely considered. A divorce is rated as involving 73 life-change units, and remarriage counts an additional 50 units according to one version of the life-events survey. We could assume that an individual who is divorced and remarried within a year or so would have experienced substantial life change. Yet, for many, a quick remarriage may represent less change or disruption (or could reduce the aversiveness of divorce) and might make one's life less stressful. For others, the 123 life-change unit sum might be more reflective of true difficulties. In addition, there appears to be content-related problems that undercut the meaning of stress (life change)–illness links that are identified (Schroeder & Costa, 1984). Though useful, estimates of stress based on life-event inventories alone are imprecise; their major value is assessing the differential stress experienced by experimental and control groups, where those groups have not themselves been selected on a stress-related factor.

Other methods of self-report assessment of stress are less systematic and reflect concern for the many affective and somatic aspects of the stress. Emotional components of stress, such as anxiety, depression, alienation, and fear have been measured in many ways, including use of psychiatric inventories such as the Langner Index (Langner, 1962) or the Symptom Checklist-90 (Derogatis, Rickels, & Rock, 1976). Both of these scales assess psychiatric and/or somatic symptom reporting, including anxiety, depression, concentration problems, and isolation. In fact, it is not uncommon to see various symptom checklists being used to assess psychological or emotional aspects of stress. Studies at TMI and at Mt. St. Helens have considered psychological symptoms as indicators of stress (e.g., Bromet, 1980; Pennebaker & Newtson, 1981), and measurement instruments for general and specific emotional disturbances have been used in other studies.

A third self-report alternative is to measure direct perceptions or beliefs about a given situation. Lazarus and his colleagues (e.g., Lazarus, 1966; Lazarus & Launier, 1978; Lazarus, Speisman, Davison, & Mordkoff, 1964) have demonstrated that the ways in which stressors are interpreted will determine the extent to which an event is experienced as stressful. Thus, questions measuring the degree to which events are viewed as aversive, threatening, or harmful may also be used to assess stress.

Our view of stress as a process rather than as a single event suggests that it is more difficult to measure. Self-report measures tap only a single aspect of this process and are susceptible to intentional and unintentional biases as well. Symptom reporting may reflect any number of things, including actual experience or awareness of experience. When an event has occurred that could have caused physical harm or illness, increased symptom reporting may result not from changes in experience, but rather from changes in the judged importance of specific events. Increased reporting of symptoms can be misinterpreted as changes in somatic experience rather than as changes in awareness or concern for this experience.

A second source of bias occurs whenever some aspect of a stressful situation is controversial. When people believe that they will benefit from a given type of response, intentional biases are more likely. Problems of unintentional bias and recall also limit the meaningfulness of self-report measures when used alone. They are useful, however, in measuring awareness of stressful conditions or related problems. Unfortunately, time, logistics, and expense often limit studies of stress to this one form of measurement.

Studies at TMI are no exception—all have relied solely on self-report for their data. Although these studies have provided useful findings, we felt it best to go beyond this one mode. However, we did collect some self-reports. Our research at TMI tapped two types of self-report measures. First, participants were asked to report their feelings and concerns about TMI. Included were ratings of threat, feelings about the damaged reactor, and attitudes toward nuclear power. Second, subjects completed the SCL–90, providing a measure of somatic, psychological, and emotional symptom reporting.

Behavioral Measures. Performance measures of stress are generally less susceptible to biases noted previously, but may be affected by other influences. These assessments are based on the idea that arousal or distress can reduce abilities that determine quality of performance on tasks attempted during and after exposure to stress. Arousal has been related to both improvements and decrements in performance depending on the nature of the task (e.g., Evans, 1978; Zajonc, 1965).

Aftereffects refer to changes in performance that occur after exposure to a stressor rather than during exposure. These consequences are among the more fully researched performance aspects of stress (see Cohen, 1980, for a review of these studies). The most difficult aspect of this measurement approach is to choose a task that reliably differentiates between stressed and nonstressed subjects. One such measure has been provided by Glass and Singer's (1972) research on noise and urban stress.

In a number of studies, Glass and Singer found that subjects who had been exposed to stressful conditions performed more poorly on a proofreading task that required a great deal of concentration than did subjects exposed to less aversive conditions. They also found aftereffects of stress using a tolerance for frustration task, which required subjects to try to solve an unsolvable puzzle. Then differential performances occurred after exposure to the stress had been terminated and seemed to reflect a cost of coping with it. Glass and Singer's findings have been replicated a number of times, underscoring the usefulness of this measure (Cohen, 1980).

Observational measures of behavior under stressful conditions can also provide useful information. The use of behavioral mapping in various settings (e.g., Ittelson, Rivlin, & Proshansky, 1976) can provide a wealth of information about how people cope in a given situation. Similarly, observation of behavior in dormitories, such as walking and socializing patterns, leaving doors open, and frequency of social behaviors, has proven useful in substantiating the presence of crowding stress in these environments (Baum, Mapp, & Davis, 1978). However, the meaning of these kinds of behaviors is often difficult to determine and interpretational biases on the part of the investigator are possible.

Our studies of stress at TMI considered two performance measures as well as self-reports. Subjects were given the proofreading task used by Glass and Singer (1972) because it reliably shows effects of stress. A second task, an embedded figures task, was used to tap motivation and persistence. These figures were very difficult and often frustrating.

Psychophysiological Measures.   Psychophysiological measurement of stress must often assess arousal associated with the sympathetic nervous system (SNS). This focus dates back to the work of Cannon (1936) and others who originally linked arousal to stress. Lang et al. (1972) consider the startle response to be a prototype for this activation with its increases in heart rate, respiration, blood pressure, and cardiac stroke volume.

Measurements of peripheral nervous system arousal have been used to indicate stress in a number of different research settings. Blood pressure has been used to index responses to chronic exposure to aircraft noise, loss of employment, imprisonment, crowding, and a variety of other stressors (e.g., Cohen, Evans, Krantz, & Stokols, 1980; D'Atri, 1975; Kasl & Cobb, 1970; Paulus, McCain, & Cox, 1978). Heart rate, GSR, respiration rate, pulse wave velocity, and other measures have been used to assess stress associated with crowding, induced anger or fear, cold pressor pain, and viewing gruesome films (e.g., Aiello, Epstein, & Karlin, 1975; Ax, 1953; Lazarus, Speisman, Mordkoff, & Davison, 1962; Saegert, 1974; Schachter, 1957). These studies are important in understanding a number of aspects of stress and emotional response. However, individual differences in mode and magnitude of psychophysiological response have been reported (e.g., Engel, 1960; Lacey, Bateman, & Van Lehn, 1953; Lacey & Lacey, 1958; Malmo & Shagass, 1949), and this specificity of response style can make such data more difficult to interpret.

Although measurements of cardiovascular or other physiological functions are extremely useful for examining stress, there are other limitations on their use. First, the instrumentation required for measuring psychophysiological responses is expensive, bulky, and problematic when working in the field. Measurement of most aspects of physiological arousal requires sensitive instruments that are difficult to transport and subject to decalibration with movement. In addition, subjects must remain still during measurement, and the necessary electrodes are obtrusive. Difficulties in making psychophysiological measurements are not insurmountable and in some instances may be irrelevant or minor. The relative ease of transporting and using instruments to take blood pressure assessments make it the most frequently used of these measures in field research, but assessment of psychophysiological responses also requires a relatively large amount of time for each subject, making it more difficult to monitor large samples. These problems are primarily obstacles to the use of psychophysiological measurement in field investigations of stress.

In addition to the problems of making psychophysiological measurements in the field, care must be taken even in the laboratory when stress is being assessed. Subjects' initial contact with a psychological laboratory itself may result in physiological changes and thereby confound measurements of stress (e.g., Sabshin, Hamburg, Grinker, Persky, Basowitz, Korchin, & Chevalier, 1957). Baseline measurements must be taken, and the effects of movement (or the necessary lack thereof) must be considered.

Biochemical Measures.   Biochemical measures of stress are usually based on changes in levels of various hormones in blood or urine samples taken from subjects exposed to stress. Research has clearly established that endocrine function is a part of the stress response (e.g., Frankenhaeuser, 1975; Mason, 1975; Selye, 1976). Secretion of corticosteroids by the adrenal cortex and catecholamines by the adrenal medulla have been related to a variety of psychosocial stimuli associated with stress. Other substances have also been considered but, for the most part, research has considered either adrenal cortical or adrenal medullary responses. A minority of studies has simultaneously measured both adrenal responses to stress (e.g., Mason, 1975). Corticosteroids, secreted by the adrenal cortex, serve many important functions, including regulation of body electrolytes and water, metabolism of energy stores, protein and fat metabolism, and inflammation of body tissue. Psychological influences on the hypothalamic–pituitary–adrenal cortex axis, which regulates corticosteroid secretion, are among the most extensively studied of any endocrine system, and substantial evidence of psychosocial determination of adrenal cortical activity has been reported. Even before Selye's work with biologic stress, some research suggested that excitement or emotional state affected secretion of adrenal corticosteroids (e.g., Uno, 1922); but it was Selye who provided the major impetus for research on these hormones.

Selye's work demonstrated that animals exposed to physical stressors showed adrenal cortical enlargement and had higher levels of circulating corticosteroids (e.g., cortisol). Since this research program began, several others have reported increased adrenal cortical activity among experimental animals following exposure to stressors such as noise, restraint, or shock (e.g., Elmadjian & Pincus, 1945; Herrington & Nelbach, 1942; Selye, 1936). Studies of animals subjected to naturalistic stressors such as high population density have also provided evidence of stress-linked adrenal cortical activity (Christian, 1955, 1963). Further, Selye (1956) has demonstrated that the typical response shown by these animals to stressors can be prevented by removing the adrenal glands. Studies with human subjects also have linked increased adrenal cortical activity to stress associated with crowding, athletic competition, changes in surroundings, loss of control, emergency duty in hospitals, and airplane flights (e.g., Davis, Morrill, Fawcett, Upton, Bondy, & Spiro, 1962; Frost, Dryer, & Kohlstaedt, 1951; Heshka & Polypuk, 1975; Mason, 1975; Pincus & Hoagland, 1943; Thorn, Jenkins, & Laidlaw, 1953). The 17-hydroxycorticosteroids (17–OHCS), primarily cortisol, have been well established as indicators of stress (e.g., Bliss, Migeon, Branch, & Samuels, 1956), and assays of both blood and urinary 17–OHCS have been perfected for the study of this relationship.

Measurement of 17–OHCS is useful in the study of stress. Assays for these hormones are now easily available and can be performed at moderate expense. However, interpretation of these assays is difficult. As with other measures of stress, a number of problems are posed. Some stressors apparently evoke increases in 17–OHCS, whereas others do not, and large individual differences in adrenal cortical response (especially when stress is chronic rather than acute) further obscure the meaning of these changes (Mason, 1975). For example, different coping styles appear to alter 17–OHCS responses to similar stressors (e.g., Mason, 1975; Rose, Poe, & Mason, 1968; Wolff, Friedman, Hofer, & Mason, 1964). In one study, examining 17–OHCS levels of combat and medic units in Vietnam, some subjects (those considered to be chronic low 17–OHCS secretors) showed decreases rather than increases in 17–OHCS levels during and after exposure to stress (Bourne, Rose, & Mason, 1967).

Catecholamines also have proven to be a useful biochemical measure of stress (e.g., Frankenhaeuser, 1975). Secreted by the adrenal medulla rather than by the adrenal cortex, catecholamines reflect activation of a different system than does elevation of corticosteroid levels. The adrenal medulla is innervated by the sympathetic nervous system (SNS) and is an important element in sympathetic arousal. Thus, one would expect SNS arousal and related increases in catecholamines to accompany episodes of stress. Research has confirmed this expectation, linking increased secretion of epinephrine and norepinephrine to such conditions as pain, anoxia, commuting stress, and extreme temperatures as well as to psychosocial stimuli involving failure, threat, and uncertainty (e.g., Euler, 1966; Frankenhaeuser, 1973; Frankenhaeuser, Nordheden, Myrsten, & Post, 1971; Frankenhaeuser & Rissler, 1970; Levi, 1972; Lundberg & Frankenhaeuser, 1978).

Catecholamine levels also vary as a function of many factors that are independent of stress. Exercise tends to increase catecholamine levels and a number of dietary and pharmacological substances also affect them (e.g., Frankenhaeuser, Myrsten, Post, & Johansson, 1971; Johansson & Post, 1972; Levi, 1967). In one study, Elmadjian, Hope, and Lamson (1967) compared catecholamine levels of hockey players who participated in a game with those of players who only watched. Active participation was associated with higher levels of norepinephrine and epinephrine than was inactive observation. This was prticularly true for norepinephrine, which appears to be more sensitive to activity and exertion.

Increases in catecholamine levels, then, are not necessarily related to stress. In addition to activity effects on catecholamine secretion, increases in these levels are associated with ingestion of coffee, tobacco, or alcohol. These effects must be considered in interpreting data collected from subjects who are allowed to engage in normal activities. In many cases, however, changes in catecholamine levels are related to psychosocial stressors such as uncertainty, loss of control, crowding, and overload. Frankenhaeuser and Rissler (1970), for example, found that having control over aversive events reduced catecholamine response to these events. Research also indicates that perceived control over noise is associated with lower levels of catecholamines than not having such perceptions (e.g., Lundberg & Frankenhaeuser, 1976, 1978), and that perceptions of control are related to catecholamine response to crowding on commuter trains (Singer, Lundberg, & Frankenhaeuser, 1978).

Typically, catecholamine levels are estimated directly from measurement of blood plasma or urine levels. The situations in which these different sources should be used vary along several dimensions. In cases of chronic stress, assay of plasma samples is more problematic than the use of urine samples because fluctuations in plasma catecholamine levels are rapid and extremely sensitive to movement. The half-life of catecholamines in blood is less than a minute, and it may therefore be difficult to obtain appropriate blood samples to assess the effects of stress. In addition, taking blood is an invasive and potentially reactive process, and stress may be induced by this procedure. There is evidence, for example, that simple venipuncture is a stressor (Davis et al., 1962).

Studies of chronic stress typically have relied on examination of urinary catecholamine levels. These samples show a slower rate of change and can be used to detect long-term (e.g., 24 hours) estimates of stress. The collection of urine samples is relatively easy and not very invasive. Physician supervision is not required for urine sampling, and long-term samples can be collected without pain or fear. For these reasons, estimations of epinephrine and norepinephrine in the urine are particularly well suited to studies of relatively prolonged stress.

It should be noted that the catecholamines in urine reflect only a small fraction of free amines in the body (Frankenhaeuser, 1973). Therefore, direction of changes or relative levels are meaningful, but absolute numbers have limited value. Epinephrine found in urine can be considered to be a reliable estimate of adrenal-medullary activity because the adrenal medulla is the sole source of epinephrine (e.g., Frankenhaeuser, 1973, 1975). Norepinephrine is somewhat more complex because it is secreted by sympathetic nerve fibers as well as by the adrenal medulla. In addition, a substantial portion of norepinephrine is absorbed by nerve endings and thus is not reflected in urine levels. Despite these complexities, it appears that estimates of catecholamines derived from these assays provide useful indices of SNS arousal.

As with other measures, biochemical markers of stress should not be used alone. They also tap only some aspects of stress, and the fact that catecholamine levels are sensitive to many things besides stress is reason enough to collect additional data in order to evaluate it. As we have already noted, activity can affect levels of epinephrine and norepinephrine. Drinking coffee, smoking cigarettes, and drinking alcoholic beverages are also associated with changing cate-cholamine levels. Gender, age, body weight, and other personal characteristics may also affect catecholamine production. It is, therefore, crucial to gather information about personal habits, daily activities, and so on, in the assessment of stress.

Multimodal Assessment.   An implicit assumption underlying our discussion of stress measurement has been that no single measure is adequate to measure the complexities of stress. Rather, simultaneous measurement of several channels of response should be used. Most conceptual formulations of stress consider it to be not a simple stimulus–response situation, but rather a process involving a stressor impinging on an individual, appraisals by the individual, and response to the stress as experienced. In studies of stress, psychologists have understandably relied most heavily on paper and pencil psychometric devices. In recent years, some investigations have used behavioral and performance measures, psycho-physiological indicants, and neuroendocrine markers. We have pointed out the complementarity of these classes of measures and have briefly discussed the strengths and shortcomings of each, with particular reference to the biochemical indices—those most likely to be unfamiliar to psychologists.

Stress at Three Mile Island

The usefulness of a multimodal assessment strategy can be illustrated by consid-ering research on stress experienced by people living near the Three Mile Island (TMI) nuclear power station. The accident there, in March 1979, has been shown to have been stressful by several studies (Bromet, 1980; Houts & Goldhaber, 1981). Concern over possible exposure to radiation, mistrust of responsible officials and the information they released during the accident, and other sources of stress have been mentioned as being responsible for difficulties experienced by area residents. Measures of stress, including symptom reporting and indices of psychological difficulty, have consistently indicated that the accident and emergency period following it were stressful for these residents (Flynn, 1979; Houts & Goldhaber, 1981).

Research on longer-term consequences of the TMI accident is less clear. At least one study suggests that problems for TMI area residents had disappeared 3 to 4 months after the accident (Dohrenwend, Dohrenwend, Kasl, & Warheit, 1979), and several studies have suggested that the level of stress experienced by TMI area residents decreased considerably during the 9 months following the accident (Bromet, 1980; Houts, Miller, Tokuhata, & Ham, 1980). However, these studies also suggest that TMI area residents continued to exhibit more symptoms of stress than did presumably unaffected control samples despite the drop in the intensity of their distress. Apparently many area residents experi-enced chronic stress as a result of living near the TMI plant up to a year after the accident.

The studies that form the basis for these conclusions relied solely on self-report assessments of stress. The exclusive use of self-report measures has led to some reluctance to accept the general finding that problems persisted well beyond the accident and emergency period. All of these studies, for example, used symptom reporting as a way of measuring stress-related problems. We have already noted a number of evaluation problems with such an approach.

Even assuming that people are accurate judges of bodily sensations, several other problems remain. An increase in symptom reporting at TMI, or a greater reporting rate at TMI, could reflect an increase in disturbing somatic sensations. Alternatively, such data could reflect heightened concern for the meaning of these sensations. A local physician noted several months after the accident that TMI area residents were reporting more symptoms to their doctors after the accident than they had before the accident (Leaser in *Behavioral Medicine*, 1979). Complaints that normally might not warrant a visit or sensations that normally might have been ignored now brought patients to their physicians' offices. Because of the uncertainty and general lack of knowledge about the effects of radiation, these complaints could be seen as people "checking" to see if a pain or sensation could be a danger signal related to radiation from the TMI accident. This raises the possibility that higher levels of symptom reporting reflect interpretive rather than sensation processes.

Other possible explanations for such findings can also be argued. Do people who report higher levels of symptom distress have any expectations about what their report will mean in policy formulation? Might not people who would like to see TMI closed forever believe that if they report a great deal of distress they could further this goal? Conversely, it is possible that residents who would like to see TMI cleaned up and reopened could report very little symptom distress to further this goal. Without belaboring the point further, it is possible to put forth several alternatives to the conclusion that TMI residents are stressed if we base such a conclusion on symptom reporting alone.

Our research program at TMI used several types of complementary measures of stress. Specifically, we have collected self-report measures of psychological health and emotional disturbance (including symptom reporting), behavioral measures reflecting task performance, and biochemical estimates of sympathomedullary activity and arousal. These measures were collected simultaneously and, together, provided a more complete picture of the "whole body" stress response. This also allowed us to avoid some of the interpretive problems created by more restricted assessment and to make more confident conclusions regarding the conditions manifested by TMI area residents.

In our discussion of the research at TMI, comparisons were made between a group of people living within 5 miles of the damaged reactor and control subjects living 80 or more miles from TMI. TMI and control groups were demographically comparable. More detailed descriptions of this research may be found in Baum, Fleming, and Singer (1982) and Baum, Gatchel, and Schaeffer (1983).

Self-report Measures.   As we have noted, the easiest and most economical method of examining stress is to ask direct questions, and much of the work at TMI has relied on telephone or face-to-face interviews. Indeed, it may have been sufficient to go to the TMI area and hand out standard psychological inventories dealing with anxiety or stress. It is possible that one could demonstrate stress at TMI by asking residents there whether or not they were experiencing stress. The problems with such an approach can be illustrated quite simply. Among the questions that we asked our subjects was an item requesting them to rate their agreement with the statement, "I am concerned about emissions from Three Mile Island." Hypothetically, response to this item should provide an estimate of the degree to which emissions from TMI were seen as threatening. However, as can be seen in Table 7.1, there were no differences between groups in response to this question. Both TMI and control subjects indicated concern, suggesting that interest in or misgivings about TMI extend beyond its local area. But, going back to the central question, any inferences about stress based on these data are problematic. Although the ratings for both groups suggest agreement with the statement of concern, these scales yield little information about absolute values. Their primary function is to provide relative information based on comparisons among groups. From the data summarized in Table 7.1, we might have falsely concluded that TMI area residents were not experiencing stress because they reported no greater concern than did control subjects.

The issues raised in the preceding example are not necessarily due to self-report methodologies per se. Questions can be worded well or they can be worded poorly. Some questions discriminate between groups whereas others do not. We were able to observe differences between TMI and control subjects on other self-report items that were more directly focused on threat perception. As can be seen in Table 7.2, TMI area residents reported significantly greater perceived threat to their health and well-being than did control subjects. These data were obtained in response to the question, "To what extent is Three Mile Island a threat to the health and well-being of yourself and your family?" Two problems are immediately evident, however, pointing out additional limitations of relying on self-report measures.

The problems alluded to previously are related to the meaning of the differences between groups on this item. In making the question more direct we

TABLE 7.1
Mean Ratings of Concern About TMI Emissions

	Pre-Vent	Vent	Post-Vent I	Post-Vent II
TMI residents	4.9	4.8	4.8	4.5
Frederick residents	4.0	4.4	4.5	4.0

TABLE 7.2
Mean Ratings of Perceived Threat Due to TMI (7 = Threatening)

	Threat to Self				Threat to Family			
	Pre-Vent	Vent	Post-Vent I	Post-Vent II	Pre-Vent	Vent	Post-Vent I	Post-Vent II
TMI residents	5.0	4.9	4.8	4.6	5.4	5.3	5.2	5.0
Frederick residents	3.6	3.4	2.8	2.9	3.4	3.2	3.0	3.2

may have also increased its demand characteristics and potential subject reactivity. TMI and control subjects generally opposed to the use of nuclear power and/or to the TMI plant itself might be prone to rate TMI as a greater threat to maintain consistency or to cast an unofficial "vote." The average correlation between perceived threat and degree of opposition to the general use of nuclear power was .58 and the average correlation between threat and opposition to the TMI plant was .64. Apparently, people opposed to nuclear power in varying degrees were also people rating greater perceived threat. Of course, the direction of causality cannot be specified and the possibility remains that these data reflect actual differences in perceived threat.

The second problem is somewhat more difficult to overcome. In essence, we were asking people living 80–100 miles from TMI to rate the threat posed to them by the plant. Because they live so far from the plant, one would expect their ratings to be relatively low, or lower at least than those of a group living only 5 miles away. It is very possible that ratings of perceived threat would follow this pattern regardless of whether an accident had occurred. TMI area residents may have perceived greater threats than our control subjects *before* the accident simply because they lived nearby and the control subjects did not. We did ask subjects to rate their concern with TMI before the accident and, not surprisingly, TMI area residents also rated greater concern beforehand. This item introduces additional demand and potential reactivity, and the issue of how meaningful differences in rated threat were afterwards remains unsettled. Had we relied solely on these types of measures in our study at TMI, we would have had problems making strong conclusions.

Behavioral and Biochemical Measures. As we have noted, response to stress includes changes in behavior and physiological functioning. These changes are often inaccessible through self-report but reflect important aspects of stress. Based on the logic presented earlier, we included direct measures of these changes in our study design. Specifically, subjects were asked to work on two tasks that have been shown to vary with stress, and urine samples were collected and assayed for levels of epinephrine and norepinephrine.

One of our behavioral measures was performance on a proofreading task drawn from Glass and Singer's (1972) studies of noise. Deficits on this task most likely reflect motivational or concentration difficulties, and our self-report data suggested that TMI area residents were experiencing both types of problems. If performance on the proofreading task paralleled these self-report findings, our interpretation of both measures would be strengthened. Performance on this task did correspond to self-reported problems; TMI residents found fewer of the inserted errors than did control subjects. Further, performance on the proofreading task was correlated with both self-reported concentration difficulties ($r = -.25$) and motivational problems ($r = -.30$).

Because proofreading performance was unrelated to demographic variables (e.g., education level), it may have provided an indication of stress-related problems among TMI residents. If used alone, it would not have been much more meaningful than the self-report measures alone. Together, they provide a clearer picture of stress responding. Part of our interpretation of each measure was provided by the other.

Although we found agreement between our major self-report and behavioral measures, does this agreement necessarily suggest that we have tapped a chronic stress response in the TMI area residents? We have the evidence provided by our self-report measurements and have shown direct behavioral verification of effects suggested by these self-reports. Our use of a measure of sympathetic arousal (urinary levels of catecholamines) provided direct testing of suggested somatic consequences. Again, correspondence among the various measurements should provide additional confidence in drawing conclusions.

Our findings for urinary catecholamines corresponded with self-report data and behavioral findings as well. TMI area residents exhibited higher levels of both epinephrine and norepinephrine, suggesting heightened sympathetic arousal. Because this arousal is a basic component of the stress response, these findings suggested that TMI area residents were experiencing stress. Once again, however, the meaning of one measure was strengthened by its convergence with other modes of assessment. Biochemical estimates of arousal are not necessarily more rigorous measures of stress than are self-report or behavioral markers. They are susceptible to a number of biases as well, and finding that TMI area residents were more aroused than were controls does not necessarily mean anything by itself. When considered with other types of measures, their interpretation was facilitated.

Multimodal Assessment of Environmental Stress. Our data suggest that TMI area residents experienced chronic environmental stress more than a year after the accident there. They reported greater threats associated with TMI and greater symptom distress than did control subjects and showed task performance difficulties associated with stress. They also exhibited higher levels of physiological arousal, and self-report, behavioral, and biochemical measures were moderately correlated with one another. Taken together, these data provide a picture of stress effects on psychological, behavioral, and physiological levels.

Campbell and Fiske (1959) suggest that convergent validation is obtainable through a multitrait–multimethod matrix. They suggest that if one wishes to demonstrate the response, one should measure several ''traits'' correspondent to the response in question. In our example at TMI this amounts to measuring not only self-reported symptoms of somatic complaints (or affective stress respond-ing) but also measuring behavioral and physiological responses to TMI as well. Although there may be several implications of convergence among these mea-sures, one thing is fairly clear. The fact that ''traits'' or symptoms of stress appear in three different, partially independent response modes makes one more confident in concluding that stress is present than if these effects had been measured in only one.

The value of any set of measures can ultimately be determined by how well it predicts subsequent outcomes. One would expect measures of chronic stress to predict long-term consequences of stress, and we are presently in the process of collecting such data. Preliminary analyses of one such outcome, blood pressure, suggest that a composite of self-report, behavioral, and biochemical measures is a better predictor of blood pressure changes among TMI area residents than are any of the measures by themselves. Regardless of the final outcome of these analyses, it should by now be apparent that a measurement strategy that uses several different means of assessing stress has much to recommend it. One of the things that makes environmental research so challenging is that behavior must be considered in the environmental context in which it occurs. The study of environ-mental stress emphasizes two different contexts that must be respected. Behavior occurs in the context of the external environment and the internal environment. A multimodal assessment considers response to environmental stressors in its bodily context as well as its situational context.

ACKNOWLEDGMENTS

The authors would like to thank Daniel Collins, Laura Davidson, Neil Grunberg, Steph-anie Nespor, and Marc Schaeffer for their help with earlier drafts of this chapter. The research reported in this chapter was partially supported by research grants from USUHS (C07205 and C07216).

REFERENCES

Aiello, J. R., Epstein, Y., & Karlin, R. (1975). Effects of crowding on electrodermal activity. *Sociological Symposium, 14,* 42–57.

Ax, A. F. (1953). The physiological differentiation between fear and anger in humans. *Psychoso-matic Medicine, 15,* 433–442.

Baum, A., Fleming, R., & Singer, J. E. (1982). Stress at Three Mile Island: Applying psychological impact analysis. In L. Bickman (Ed.), *Applied social psychology annual*. Beverly Hills, CA: Sage.

Baum, A., Gatchel, R. J., & Schaeffer, M. A. (1983). Emotional, behavioral and physiological effects of chronic stress at Three Mile Island. *Journal of Consulting and Clinical Psychology, 51*, 565–572.

Baum, A., Gatchel, R. J., Streufert, S., Baum, C. S., Fleming, R., & Singer, J. E. (1980). *Psychological stress for alternatives of decontamination of TMI-2 reactor building atmosphere*. Washington, DC: Nuclear Regulatory Commission (NUREG/CR–1584).

Baum, A., & Greenberg, C. I. (1975). Waiting for a crowd: The behavioral and perceptual effects of anticipated crowding. *Journal of Personality and Social Psychology, 32*, 671–679.

Baum, A., Mapp, K., & Davis, G. E. (1978). Determinants of residential group development and social control. *Environmental Psychology and Nonverbal Behavior, 2*, 145–160.

Baum, A., Singer, J. E., & Baum, C. S. (1981). Stress and the environment. *Journal of Social Issues, 37*, 4–35.

Behavioral Medicine Special Report. (1979, May). Stress and nuclear crisis. *Behavioral Medicine*.

Bliss, E. L., Migeon, C. J., Branch, C. H., & Samuels, L. T. (1956). Reaction of the adrenal cortex to emotional stress. *Psychosomatic Medicine, 18*, 56.

Bourne, P. G., Rose, R. M., & Mason, J. W. (1967). Urinary 17–OHCS levels: Data on seven helicopter ambulance medics in combat. *Archives of General Psychiatry, 17*, 104.

Bromet, E. (1980). *Three Mile Island: Mental health findings*. Pittsburgh: Western Psychiatric Institute and Clinic and the University of Pittsburgh.

Campbell, D. T., & Fiske, D. W. (1959). Convergent and discriminant validation by the multitrait–multimethod matrix. *Psychological Bulletin, 56*, 81–105.

Cannon, W. B. (1936). *Bodily changes in pain, hunger, fear, and rage* (2nd ed.). New York: Appleton–Century–Crofts.

Christian, J. J. (1955). Effect of population size on the adrenal glands and reproductive organs of male mice in populations of fixed size. *American Journal of Physiology, 182*, 292.

Christian, J. J. (1963). The pathology of overpopulation. *Military Medicine, 128*, 571–603.

Cohen, S. (1980). Aftereffects of stress on human performance and social behavior: A review of research and theory. *Psychological Bulletin, 88*, 82–108.

Cohen, S., Evans, G. W., Krantz, D. S., & Stokols, D. (1980). Physiological, motivational, and cognitive effects of aircraft noise on children: Moving from the laboratory to the field. *American Psychologist, 35*, 231–243.

Cohen, S., & Weinstein, N. (1981). Nonauditory effects of noise on behavior and health. *Journal of Social Issues, 37*, 36–70.

D'Atri, D. (1975). Psychophysiological responses to crowding. *Environment and Behavior, 7*, 237–252.

Davis, J., Morrill, R., Fawcett, J., Upton, U., Bondy, D. K., & Spiro, H. M. (1962). Apprehension and elevated serum cortisol levels. *Journal of Psychosomatic Research, 6*, 83.

Derogatis, L., Rickels, K., & Rock, A. (1976). The SCL-90 and the MMPI: A step in validation of a new self-report scale. *British Journal of Psychiatry, 128*, 280–289.

Dohrenwend, B. P., Dohrenwend, B. S., Kasl, S. V., & Warheit, G. J. (1979, October). *Report of the task group on behavioral effects to the President's Commission on the accident at Three Mile Island*. Washington, DC.

Elmadjian, F., Hope, J. M., & Lamson, E. T. (1967). Excretion of epinephrine and norepinephrine in various emotional states. *Metabolism*, 608–620.

Elmadjian, F., & Pincus, G. (1945). The adrenal cortex and the lymphocytopenia of stress. *Endocrinology, 37*, 47.

Engel, B. T. (1960). Stimulus–response and individual-response specificity. *Archives of General Psychiatry, 2*, 305–313.

Epstein, Y. M. (1981). Crowding stress and human behavior. *Journal of Social Issues, 37*, 126–144.

Euler, U. S. von. (1966). Twenty years of noradrenaline. *Pharmacological Review, 18*, 29.

Evans, G. W. (1978). Human spatial behavior: The arousal model. In A. Baum & Y. M. Epstein (Eds.), *Human response to crowding*. Hillsdale, NJ: Lawrence Erlbaum Associates.

Evans, G. W., & Jacobs, S. V. (1981). Air pollution and human behavior. *Journal of Social Issues, 37*, 95–125.

Flynn, C. B. (1979). *Three Mile Island telephone survey*. Washington, DC: Nuclear Regulatory Commission (NUREG/CR–1093).

Frankenhaeuser, M. (1973). *Experimental approaches to the study of catecholamines and emotion*. Stockholm: Reports from the Psychological Laboratories, University of Stockholm.

Frankenhaeuser, M. (1975). Experimental approaches to the study of catecholamines and emotion. In L. Levi (Ed.), *Emotions: Their parameters and measurement*. New York: Raven Press.

Frankenhaeuser, M. (1978). *Coping with job stress: A psychobiological approach*. Stockholm: Reports from the Department of Psychology, University of Stockholm.

Frankenhaeuser, M., Myrsten, A. L., Post, B., & Johansson, G. (1971). Behavioral and physiological effects of cigarette smoking in a monotonous situation. *Psychopharmacologica, 22*, 1–7.

Frankenhaeuser, M., Nordheden, B., Myrsten, A. L., & Post, B. (1971). Psychophysiological reactions to understimulation and overstimulation. *Acta Psychologica, 35*, 298–308.

Frankenhaeuser, M., & Rissler, A. (1970). Effects of punishment on catecholamine release and efficiency of performance. *Psychopharmacologia, 17*, 378–390.

Frost, J. W., Dryer, R. L., & Kohlstaedt, K. G. (1951). Stress studies on auto race drivers. *Journal of Laboratory and Clinical Medicine, 38*, 523.

Glass, D. C., & Singer, J. E. (1972). *Urban stress*. New York: Academic Press.

Herrington, L. P., & Nelbach, J. H. (1942). Relation of gland weights to growth and aging processes in rats exposed to certain environmental conditions. *Endocrinology, 30*, 375.

Heshka, S., & Polypuk, A. (1975, June). *Human crowding and adrenocortical activity*. Paper presented at the meeting of the Canadian Psychological Association, Quebec.

Holmes, T. H., & Masuda, M. (1974). Life change and illness susceptibility. In B. S. Dohrenwend & B. P. Dohrenwend (Eds.), *Stressful life events*. New York: Wiley.

Holmes, T. H., & Rahe, R. H. (1967). The social adjustment rating scale. *Journal of Psychosomatic Research, 11*, 213–218.

Houts, P., & Goldhaber, M. (1981). In S. Majundar (Ed.), *Energy, environment and the economy*. Harrisburg, PA: Pennsylvania Academy of Sciences.

Houts, P., Miller, R. W., Tokuhata, G. K., & Ham, K. S. (1980, April). *Health-related behavioral impact of the Three Mile Island nuclear accident*. Report submitted to the TMI Advisory Panel on health-related studies of the Pennsylvania Department of Health, Hershey, PA.

Ittelson, W. H., Rivlin, L. G., & Proshansky, H. M. (1976). The use of behavioral maps in environmental psychology. In H. M. Proshansky, W. H. Ittelson, & L. G. Rivlin (Eds.), *Environmental psychology: People and their settings*. New York: Holt, Rinehart, & Winston.

Jacobs, M. A., Spilken, A. Z., Norman, M. M., & Anderson, L. S. (1970). Life stress and respiratory illness. *Psychosomatic Medicine, 32*, 233.

Jenkins, D. C. (1979). Psychosocial modifiers of response to stress. *Journal of Human Stress, 5*, 3–5.

Johansson, G., & Post, B. (1972). *Catecholamine output of males and females over a one-year period*. Stockholm: Reports from the Psychological Laboratories, University of Stockholm (379).

Kasl, S. V., & Cobb, S. (1970). Blood pressure changes in men undergoing job loss: A preliminary report. *Psychosomatic Medicine, 32*, 19–38.

Lacey, J. I., Batemen, D. E., & Van Lehn, R. (1953). Autonomic response specificity: An experimental study. *Psychosomatic Medicine, 15*, 8–21.

Lacey, J. I., & Lacey, B. C. (1958). Verification and extension of the principle of autonomic response stereotypy. *American Journal of Psychology, 71*, 50–73.

Lang, P. J., Rice, D. G., & Sternbach, R. A. (1972). The psychophysiology of emotion. In N. S. Greenfield & R. A. Sternbach (Eds.), *Handbook of psychophysiology*. New York: Holt, Rinehart, & Winston.

Langner, T. S. (1962). A twenty-two item screening scale of psychiatric symptoms indicating impairment. *Journal of Health and Human Behavior, 3*, 269–276.

Lazarus, R. S. (1966). *Psychological stress and the coping process*. New York: McGraw–Hill.

Lazarus, R. S., & Cohen, J. B. (1978). Environmental stress. In I. Altman & J. F. Wohlwill (Eds.), *Human behavior and the environment: Current theory and research* (Vol. 2). New York: Plenum.

Lazarus, R. S., & Launier, R. (1978). Stress-related transactions between person and environment. In L. A. Pervin & M. Lewis (Eds.), *Internal and external determinants of behavior*. New York: Plenum.

Lazarus, R. S., Speisman, J. C., Davison, L. A., & Mordkoff, A. M. (1964). Experimental analysis of a film used as a threatening stimulus. *Journal of Consulting Psychology, 28*, 23–33.

Lazarus, R. S., Speisman, J., Mordkoff, A., & Davison, L. (1962). A laboratory study of psychological stress produced by a motion picture film. *Psychological Monographs, 76*.

Levi, L. (1967). The effect of coffee on the function of the sympathoadrenomedullary system in man. *Acta Medica Scandinavia, 181*, 431–438.

Levi, L. (1972). Stress and distress in response to psychological stimuli. Laboratory and real life studies on sympathoadrenomedullary and related reactions. *Acta Medica Scandinavia* (Supp.), 528.

Lundberg, U., & Frankenhaeuser, M. (1976). *Adjustment to noise stress*. Stockholm: Reports from the Department of Psychology, University of Stockholm.

Lundberg, U., & Frankenhaeuser, M. (1978). Psychophysiological reactions to noise as modified by personal control over stimulus intensity. *Biological Psychology, 6*, 51–59.

Malmo, R. B., & Shagass, C. (1949). Physiologic study of symptom mechanisms in psychiatric patients under stress. *Psychosomatic Medicine, 11*, 25–29.

Mason, J. W. (1975a). A historical view of the stress field. *Journal of Human Stress, 1*, 22–36.

Mason, J. W. (1975b). Emotion as reflected in patterns of endocrine integration. In L. Levi (Ed.), *Emotions: Their parameters and measurement*. New York: Raven Press.

Masuda, M., & Holmes, T. H. (1978). Life events: Perceptions and frequencies. *Psychosomatic Medicine, 40*, 236–261.

Paulus, P., McCain, G., & Cox, V. (1978). Death rates, psychiatric commitments, blood pressure, and perceived crowding as a function of institutional crowding. *Environmental Psychology and Nonverbal Behavior, 3*, 107–116.

Pennebaker, J., & Newtson, D. (1981). *The psychological impact of Mt. St. Helens*. Unpublished manuscript, University of Virginia.

Perlmutter, L. C., & Monty, R. A. (1979). *Choice and perceived control*. Hillsdale, NJ: Lawrence Erlbaum Associates.

Pincus, G., & Hoagland, H. (1943). Steroid excretion and the stress of flying. *Journal of Aviation Medicine, 14*, 173.

Rahe, R. H. (1969). Multicultural correlations of life change scaling: America, Japan, Denmark, and Sweden. *Journal of Psychosomatic Research, 13*, 191–195.

Rahe, R. H. (1975). Life changes and near future illness reports. In L. Levi (Ed.), *Emotions: Their parameters and measurements*. New York: Raven Press.

Rahe, R. H., Ryman, D. H., & Ward, H. W. (1980). Simplified scaling for life change events. *Journal of Human Stress, 6*, 22–27.

Rose, R. M., Poe, R. O., & Mason, J. W. (1968). Psychological state and body size as determinants of 17-OHCS excretion. *Archives of Internal Medicine, 121*, 406–413.

Ross, C., & Mirowsky, J. (1979). A comparison of life-event-weighting schemes: Change, undesirability, and effect proportional indices. *Journal of Health and Social Behavior, 20,* 166–177.

Sabshin, M., Hamburg, D. A., Grinker, R. R., Persky, H., Basowitz, H., Korchin, S. J., & Chevalier, J. A. (1957). Significance of preexperimental studies in the psychosomatic laboratory. *Archives of Neurological Psychiatry, 78,* 207.

Saegert, S. (1974). *Effects of spatial and social density on arousal, mood, and social orientation.* Unpublished doctoral dissertation, University of Michigan.

Sarason, I. G., Johnson, J. J., & Siegel, J. M. (1978). Assessing the impact of life changes: Development of the Life Experiences Survey. *Journal of Consulting and Clinical Psychology, 46,* 932–946.

Schachter, S. (1957). Pain, fear, and anger in hypertensives and normotensives: A psychophysiologic study. *Psychosomatic Medicine, 19,* 17–29.

Schroeder, D. H., & Costa, P. T. (1984). Influence of life event stress on physical illness: Substantive effects or methodological flaws? *Journal of Personality and Social Psychology, 46,* 853–863.

Selye, H. (1936). A syndrome produced by diverse nocuous agents. *Nature, 138.*

Selye, H. (1956). *The stress of life.* New York: McGraw–Hill.

Selye, H. (1976). *The stress of life.* New York: McGraw–Hill.

Sherrod, D. R. (1974). Crowding, perceived control, and behavioral aftereffects. *Journal of Applied Social Psychology, 4,* 171–186.

Singer, J., Lundberg, U., & Frankenhaeuser, M. (1978). Stress on the train: A study of urban commuting. In A. Baum, J. E. Singer, & S. Valins (Eds.), *Advances in environmental psychology.* Hillsdale, NJ: Lawrence Erlbaum Associates.

Spacapan, S., & Cohen, S. (1982). *The effects and aftereffects of anticipating stressor exposure.* Unpublished manuscript.

Street, S. W., Baum, A., & Singer, J. E. (1984, April 12–15). *Is anticipation worse than the actual experience?* Presented at the annual meeting of the Eastern Psychological Association, Baltimore, MD.

Thorn, G. W., Jenkins, D., & Laidlaw, J. C. (1953). The adrenal response to stress in man. *Recent Program Hormone Research, 8,* 171.

Uno, J. (1922). Effect of general excitement and of fighting on some ductless glands of male albino rats. *American Journal of Physiology, 61,* 203.

Wolf, S., & Goodell, H. (Eds.). (1968). *Stress and disease* (2nd ed.). Springfield, IL: Thomas.

Wolff, C. T., Friedman, S. B., Hofer, M. A., & Mason J. W. (1964). Relationship between psychological defenses and mean urinary 17-OHCS excretion rates: A predictive study of parents of fatally ill children. *Psychosomatic Medicine, 26,* 576.

Zajonc, R. (1965). Social facilitation. *Science, 149,* 269–274.

Author Index

Italics denote pages with bibliographic information.

Subject Index